BLUE MOON
OVER CUBA

OSPREY
PUBLISHING

In memory of
Capt William B. Ecker, USN (ret.)

Dedicated to
Mrs. William B. (Kit) Ecker
and
The Officers and Enlisted Men of Light Photographic Squadron 62 (VFP-62)

BLUE MOON
OVER CUBA

AERIAL RECONNAISSANCE DURING
THE CUBAN MISSILE CRISIS

Capt William B. Ecker, USN (ret.) & Kenneth V. Jack

Foreword by Michael Dobbs

First published in Great Britain in 2012 by Osprey Publishing
Midland House, West Way, Botley, Oxford, OX2 0PH
44-02 23rd Street, Suite 219, Long Island City, NY, 11101, USA

E-mail: info@ospreypublishing.com

Osprey Publishing is part of the Osprey Group

A CIP catalogue record for this book is available from the British Library

ISBN: 978 1 78096 071 5

Edited by Tony Holmes
Cover artwork by Gareth Hector © Kenneth Jack
Profile artwork by Tom Tullis
Scale drawings by Mark Styling
Cartography by Mapping Specialists Ltd
Page layout by Myriam Bell Design, UK
Index by Alan Thatcher

Back cover image supplied from Capt William B. Ecker collection.

Excerpts from *Fidel: A Critical Portrait* by Tad Szulc: copyright © 1986 by Tad
Szulc. Reprinted with permission of HarperCollins Publishers.

Printed in China through Worldprint Ltd.

12 13 14 15 16 17 10 9 8 7 6 5 4 3 2 1

Osprey Publishing is supporting the Woodland Trust, the UK's leading
woodland conservation charity, by funding the dedication of trees.

www.ospreypublishing.com

CONTENTS

Acknowledgments   7

Foreword   11

Author's Notes   16

CHAPTER 1
The Making of a Fighter Pilot   23

CHAPTER 2
"Eyes of the Fleet"   33

CHAPTER 3
The Military Build-Up in Cuba – July to October 15, 1962   51

CHAPTER 4
The Cuban Crisis Begins – October 16–22, 1962   63

CHAPTER 5
Executing the Mission – October 23, 1962   87

CHAPTER 6
Pentagon Briefing – October 23, 1962   107

CHAPTER 7
The USAF Gets Its Chance – October 24, 1962   115

CHAPTER 8
Showdown at the United Nations – October 25, 1962   123

CHAPTER 9
The Marines Join *Blue Moon* Missions – October 25, 1962   133

CHAPTER 10
   The Crisis Mounts – October 25-29, 1962   139

CHAPTER 11
   Unarmed, Unescorted, & Unafraid   169

Chapter 12
   Night Photo Missions Over Gitmo – November 5, 1962   183

CHAPTER 13
   Verifying the Removal of Missiles – November 1962   189

CHAPTER 14
   Medals and Commendations   203

CHAPTER 15
   Thirteen Days – the Movie   213

CHAPTER 16
   "Hooligans in the Sky"   221

Endnotes   244

Appendices
   Scale drawings of the RF-8A   258
   Map: The Nuclear Umbrella Facing President Kennedy   260
   Map: Cuba, October 1962   261
   Map: The Cuban Military Build-Up   262
   Address by President John F. Kennedy, October 22, 1962   263
   President Kennedy's Remarks in Key West upon Presenting
      Unit Citations at the Boca Chica Naval Air Station on
      November 26, 1962   270
   VFP-62 Recipients of the Navy Unit Commendation   272

Index   281

ACKNOWLEDGMENTS

As a first-time author, I've learned that writing is a demanding process – a jealous mistress if you will. I have been fortunate to receive the guidance, support, encouragement, and contributions from many who have believed in this project as I have. I would first recognize Capt Ecker's memoir, which forms the backbone of this book. His consultation and trust during the first months of the writing effort gave me the motivation to go forward. Sadly, he did not live to see his memoir come to life in this book. Fortunately, David Ecker saw the promise in his father's writing, transformed it into digital format and put his faith in me to perpetuate his father's legacy. To both, I'm humbly grateful.

I'm fortunate to have had a diverse group of reviewers who critiqued the various drafts of the manuscript. Foremost in that group is Cdr Peter Mersky USNR (ret.), the author of *Osprey Combat Aircraft 12 - RF-8 Crusader Units Over Cuba and Vietnam*, among many other books and articles. Peter's instruction, critiques, and patient nudging forced me to reach for a higher standard of excellence that helped me to understand the mechanics and high demands of writing a serious book. His review resulted in an extensive rewrite of the original manuscript. Peter followed that up with providing a second review, connections to the publishing world, and sources of additional research and photographs. I will always be indebted to him for his mentoring, leadership, and friendship.

Peter recommended reviewer, naval analyst, and author Norman Polmar, whose expertise on all things military provided a critical assessment and put me on a path of researching and adding more historical information to support my premises and technical information.

Additionally, Peter's friend and colleague during his naval career, Capt Louis R. Mortimer USNR (ret.), provided technical insights into photo interpretation, as well as needed encouragement.

Of the pilots that provided personal memories, I'm most indebted to Lt Cdr Tad Riley USN (ret.). Tad was on the first day's missions over Cuba, and made many after that. His input is detailed, insightful, and provides us with a rare look into a fighter pilot's experience over Cuba. He also reviewed and provided improvements to the first draft.

Another pilot contributor, Capt Jerry Coffee USN (ret.), flew one of the first Cuban missions and provides interesting details on how he captured evidence on the existence of tactical nuclear weapons in Cuba. A true national hero, he was a prisoner of war for seven years in North Vietnam after his RA-5C Vigilante was shot down in 1967. Jerry is a fine writer himself and has a knack for making a story live.

Other pilot contributors were Capt Ed Feeks USN (ret.), Cdr Newby Kelt USN (ret.), Lt Col Dick Conway USMC (ret.), Capt Len Johnson USN (ret.), and Col Edgar Love USMC (ret.). Capt Phillip J Smith USN (ret.) provided his never-been-told story of clandestine missions over Cuba before the crisis. He also reviewed the book and encouraged me to go forward. Thanks are also due to Capt Ron Knott USN (ret.), who was an F-8 fighter pilot who gave me permission to include a story of US Navy fighter escorts from his book *Supersonic Cowboys*. All these aviators provided important details on their missions.

Capt Jim Curry USN (ret.) provided the information on the night photographic missions over Cuba. In 2008, Jim signed the canopy rail of the restored RF-8A that he flew over Cuba which is now an exhibit at Battleship Park in Mobile, Alabama.

An important contributor and reviewer was Col Wayne Whitten USMC (ret.), who provided information for the chapter on VMCJ-2's augmentation detachment to VFP-62. "Flash" (his call sign) helped me see discrepancies in the as-written timeline of the original draft. He also provided connections to Marine aviators who flew missions over Cuba. He is an excellent author of a number of articles on Marine aviation. Most of all, I appreciate his hearty endorsement of this project. Along with Col Whitten, LCpl Jack Hayden provided the humorous details of Marine pranksters at Naval Air Station (NAS) Boca Chica, in Key West.

I am very grateful to the prolific author and former *Washington Post* reporter Michael Dobbs for his permission to use many passages from his superbly detailed book *One Minute to Midnight* – an important scholarly resource for any researcher of the Cuban crisis. His volume sets the standard for excellence and his writing skills make history read like a suspense novel. Michael also provided one of the final reviews and graciously agreed to write the Foreword to this book.

Another author and reviewer is the former high official at the CIA's National Photographic Interpretation Center (NPIC) during the crisis, Dino A. Brugioni. Dino's excellent book *Eyeball to Eyeball: The Inside Story of the Cuban Missile Crisis* provided many excerpts and supporting material, which I gratefully appreciate. Dino also provided one of the excellent low-level photographs included in this book. He knew Capt Ecker and had a high regard for his leadership. He told me how Capt Ecker would train his pilots to pick out an intersection of a road and place it in the center of a photograph.

VFP-62 squadron members Capt Adam Miklovis USN (ret.), who was the photo intelligence officer on my USS *Forrestal* (CVA-59) detachment during the crisis, Pete Wallace, former VFP-62 aviation mechanic and co-sponsor for our website, www.vfp62.com, and his wife Betty read the manuscript carefully and provided important suggestions for improvement. Former VFP-62 enlisted men Vinnie Zabicki and Richard Flake provided details of the all-important VFP-62 groundcrew at NAS Key West. Vinnie also provided the rare photograph of the VFP-62 detachment at Key West.

Pilots get the glory but they know their lives are in the hands of young men with the huge responsibility for keeping the aircraft ready to fly. Only one mission was aborted because of mechanical failure.

My gratitude is also due to former VFP-62 personnelman George Montgomery and aviation electrician's mate Frank Schrader for their written input on the evacuation of dependents from Guantanamo Naval Base (Gitmo) and the secret photo mission during the Bay of Pigs invasion. I also owe a debt of gratitude to Bill Newby PHCS USN (ret.) for his assistance in providing the technical information on aerial cameras.

And, I need to acknowledge the information obtained from William T. Hocutt PHCS, USN (ret.) by way of his unpublished document on the Cuban Missile Crisis. Chief Hocutt's document provided many insights into photo interpretation and accounts of the handling of U-2 photography. Along with that information came a wonderfully detailed description of mission planning at VFP-62 by Lt Cdr Bernard W. Kortge.

I owe much gratitude to the good people at Osprey Publishing for first putting their faith in this book, and for their professional contributions to the many details that resulted in its production. One in particular, my editor Tony Holmes, read the proposed manuscript way before it was truly ready, saw the potential in it and recommended it to Osprey for commissioning. Tony has a huge reputation in the publishing world, and his gentle nudging encouraged me to expand the book to reach its potential. His insightful edits demonstrated his expansive expertise in military history of all eras. And, my kudos and gratitude go to Charly Ford, development editor at Osprey, who provided a friendly, helpful interface to the publishing hurdles that almost overwhelmed me, but produced our great maps, photos, and cover. Gareth Hector's artistic talent is obvious when one looks at our cover. He accurately captured the majesty of the RF-8A Crusader climbing out after a Cuban photo mission.

Finally, I owe everything to my loving wife, Darlene, for her support, skill as a critical reviewer, and willingness to share three years of her life with my obsession for this project.

FOREWORD

BY MICHAEL DOBBS

Shortly after noon on October 23, 1962, a US Navy commander named William B. Ecker took off from NAS Key West and headed south toward the island of Cuba. He was accompanied by his wingman, Lt Christopher Bruce Wilhelmy, in an identical RF-8A Crusader. Their mission was to take high-quality, low-level photographs that could be used to prove to the world that the Soviet Union had deployed medium- and intermediate-range nuclear weapons in Cuba, in violation of promises made to President John F. Kennedy by Soviet leader Nikita Khrushchev.

The photographs that Ecker shot that day – showing Soviet soldiers working frantically on a nuclear bunker, and missile equipment lined up in neat rows – provided dramatic evidence of Soviet duplicity. Over the next few days Ecker's Light Photographic Squadron (VFP) 62 brought back some of the most important intelligence collected by the United States during the Cuban Missile Crisis. Ecker was summoned to Washington, D.C. to brief the Joint Chiefs of Staff (JCS), but was not permitted to grant press interviews. He and other US Navy reconnaissance pilots remained largely unsung heroes. Their role in resolving the most dangerous crisis of the Cold War only became known decades later following the declassification of top secret government documents.

Ecker returned to Cuba in October 2002 with an American delegation led by former defense secretary Robert McNamara. In Havana, they met with Cuban leader Fidel Castro and retired Soviet generals, reminiscing about the Thirteen Days when the world came closer than ever before – or since – to nuclear destruction. When the conference was over, the participants were taken to see what was left of the San Cristobal nuclear missile site that Ecker had photographed four decades before. A journalist asked Ecker – then 78, and living in retirement in Florida – what it was like to be back.

"I don't know," he replied in his usual gruff, no-nonsense manner. "I was only here for about two or three seconds the last time."

William Boyce Ecker passed away in November 2009 at the age of 85, but he has left behind a book (co-authored by Kenneth Jack) that will serve as a living memorial to the exploits of a remarkable band of brothers. In an age when intelligence is routinely scooped up by satellites and unmanned drones, it is easy to forget the vital contribution of a handful of brave pilots in gathering the intelligence that gave America the edge in the longest war in its history.

As the name implies, the Cold War was largely an intelligence war. Spies and code-crackers played a role but the most useful, actionable intelligence, particularly during the Cuban Missile Crisis, was usually that gathered by reconnaissance pilots like Ecker. Operating long before the invention of automated GPS systems, the pilots had to rely on primitive (at least by today's standards) navigation techniques, using maps and compasses as their primary guides. Flying over the treetops at near-sonic speed, they used visual aids like bridges, railroads, and rivers to reach their targets. They had to operate a battery of cumbersome cameras while keeping an eye out for "suspicious activity," such as construction sites, military vehicles, or other unusual goings on. In order to take useful pictures, they had to keep their platforms steady and level for the all-important few seconds when they were actually over the target. They had little time to worry about the risk of mechanical failure or getting shot down, which was more or less continuous from the moment they arrived over enemy territory.

This book tells the story of the Cuban Missile Crisis from the vantage point of the pilots who risked their lives to bring back the intelligence required by Kennedy for each stage of his high-stakes poker game with Khrushchev. Ken Jack has succeeded in weaving the dramatic accounts of Ecker and the other VFP-62 pilots into a much larger narrative. He has shown how the photographs helped shape the president's actions and decisions during the crisis, in addition to winning the propaganda war with Khrushchev.

JFK had first learned about the deployment of Soviet missiles on Cuba from high-level imagery shot by US Air Force U-2 pilots, but he came to depend on the lower-level photographs to keep abreast of day-to-day developments. The photographs taken by VFP-62 revealed just how close the Soviets were to completing work on the missile sites. They also exposed overnight exercises of the missile equipment. Although there were no nighttime reconnaissance flights over the missile sites, intelligence analysts were able to identify nighttime activity from tracks left in the rain-soaked mud the following morning. Armed with this intelligence, the president was able to figure out how much time he had left before ordering the destruction of the missile sites and/or an invasion of the island.

VFP-62 pilot Lt Gerald Coffee veered off course to take the first photographs of nuclear-capable short-range FROG missiles in Cuba on October 25. This was a particularly ominous development, as it demonstrated that the Soviets might be preparing to use nuclear weapons to destroy American beachheads in the event of a US invasion of Cuba. Once it was known that the Soviets had probably deployed tactical nuclear weapons in Cuba, in addition to the medium- and intermediate-range missiles capable of reaching American cities, US generals began demanding similar weapons of their own. The consequences of a US invasion are alarming to contemplate – a limited nuclear exchange on the island of Cuba could have escalated very quickly to an all-out nuclear war.

The photographs taken by Ecker and his men were pored over by analysts from the Central Intelligence Agency (CIA), and formed part of the president's daily intelligence brief throughout the crisis. When the crisis was over, thousands of cans of raw intelligence film ended up on dusty shelves, and were eventually transferred to a National Archives facility in Kansas. There they remained, for more than a decade, until a former CIA analyst named Dino Brugioni alerted me to their existence while I was doing research for my book, *One Minute to Midnight: Kennedy, Khrushchev, and Castro on the Brink of Nuclear War.*

I was stunned to discover that I was the first researcher to actually request the cans, which provided a unique day-by-day record of military activities in Cuba during the missile crisis. There was only one hitch — most of the finding aids to the cans remain "classified." I could detect little rhyme or reason to the numbering of the cans, making the research process roughly equivalent to looking for needles in haystacks. The Archives airfreighted the cans from Kansas to Washington, D.C. for my inspection, in batches of 20.

Reeling through hundreds of cans of intelligence film, I was able to vicariously immerse myself in the experiences of the US Navy pilots who flew over Cuba during the missile crisis. The series of black-and-white negatives captured the cameras being checked at NAS Key West, the Crusaders flying low over the Florida Straits as surf splashed up against the fuselages, crossing the beaches of Cuba and heading over the mountainous spine of the island. There were intimate photographs of peaceful plazas and baseball diamonds, alongside images of missile sites and military airfields. It was as if I was suddenly peering down into the island through a miraculous time machine, long before the invention of Google Earth. The most jarring images of all were a series of shots of a landscape going suddenly haywire as the pilot detected antiaircraft fire in his rear view mirror, and banked his airplane sharply. Reeling through the five-by-five-inch negatives, I felt as if I was in the cockpit alongside the pilot, holding my breath as he escaped back over the mountains to the open sea.

Examining these images four-and-a-half decades later, I was able to resolve mysteries about the Soviet military deployment that had flummoxed the CIA. The agency was unable to respond to the president's repeated queries about the location of Soviet nuclear warheads. This was a crucial piece of information since the missiles could not be fired until they were "mated" with the warheads. In the end, the CIA concluded that the warheads were probably stored somewhere near the port of

Mariel. This turned out to be wrong. By analyzing the raw intelligence film shot by low-level American reconnaissance airplanes, and interviewing former Soviet military officers, I showed that the warheads were actually stored near a town called Bejucal, a few miles south of Havana airport. Successive Blue Moon missions photographed the Bejucal nuclear storage bunker – complete with specially configured vans waiting to transport the warheads to the missile sites – without knowing what they were photographing.

It is sobering to consider what might have happened had the CIA interpreted the intelligence correctly. There are various possibilities. If JFK had known where the warheads were stored, he might have been tempted to order a pre-emptive strike to destroy them. The mission could have been a success, strengthening Kennedy's hand against Khrushchev. Or it could have gone badly wrong, resulting in firefights between Americans and Soviets guarding a nuclear weapons site. We will never know. What we do know is that the CIA misinterpreted the evidence collected by the reconnaissance pilots about the Bejucal bunker, leaving Kennedy in the dark. Armed with only partial intelligence on what the Soviets were doing, the president ended up displaying great restraint. That, too, is part of the Blue Moon story, told so expertly here by Kenneth Jack and the late Bill Ecker.

AUTHOR'S NOTES

Even in the aftermath of the September 11, 2001 terrorist attacks and the looming threat of more harm to come from al Qaeda, I don't sense the same national paranoia that my generation experienced during the Cold War. The lingering horrible images of the total destruction of two Japanese cities by two relatively primitive atomic bombs were still imprinted on the American psyche, and the arms race that produced ever more powerful thermonuclear weapons made the Cold War years fraught with danger – both real and imagined. That, combined with the Korean War stalemate, the Soviet's ruthless blockade of West Berlin and their tyranny in Eastern Europe, as well as the startling debut of a beeping Sputnik in outer space, made us anxious and fearful that the communists were powerful, evil, and wanted to dominate the world and destroy us.

Our generation lived with a fatalistic expectation that the entire world could come to an end by an exchange of megaton-thermonuclear hydrogen bombs hundreds of times more powerful than the Hiroshima and Nagasaki fission atomic bombs.

A constant reminder of this impending Armageddon was the relentless above-ground testing of those horrible weapons of mass destruction undertaken by both superpowers. And it reached into our everyday personal lives with civilian defense drills, initiated by a weekly air raid siren test, commanding teachers to close windows and blinds and students to seek shelter under desks. Many families built their own bomb shelters, stocked with beds, food, water, and emergency supplies. In truth, governmental officials held a dismal view of the fallout-shelter program but pursued it to put the public at ease. Civil defense against such weapons was useless, except for the purpose of boosting the morale of the general public.

This was the national climate on Sunday morning, October 14, 1962, when a U-2 spyplane, flown by USAF Maj Richard Heyser, crossed over western Cuba to begin a routine photo mission. Flying at 70,000ft (more than 13 miles high), its powerful camera lenses revealed that Soviet Premier Nikita S. Khrushchev had deceived us and was secretly installing medium-range ballistic missiles (MRBMs), with a range of up to 1,300 miles (capable of reaching Washington, D.C. and New York City), on Cuba. Our eyes in the sky revealed the construction of missile installations, which would soon be operational with nuclear-tipped missiles aimed at American cities. The ensuing struggle between the world's two nuclear superpowers for their removal would trigger the most dangerous conflict of the Cold War – the Cuban Missile Crisis.

The Cuban Missile Crisis is commonly condensed to the thirteen days (October 16-28) when the world did not know if the confrontation would end in thermonuclear war. There is, however, an interesting historical intersection of earlier events – often not linked together – that predestined the crisis. The shoot-down of the CIA-owned U-2 over the Soviet Union in May 1960, the failed Bay of Pigs invasion in April 1961 and the Soviet-backed military build-up in Cuba between July and September 1962 would all compound the misjudgments, adventurism and ideological struggles shared by Dwight D. Eisenhower, John F. Kennedy, Nikita S. Khrushchev, and Cuban President Fidel Castro.

This book looks at the motivating circumstances and the political imperatives that confined these leaders to the paths they chose, and the international consequences that ensued. President John F. Kennedy's demand for the removal of these offensive weapons of mass destruction would cause the world to teeter on the brink of the nuclear war we all feared.

The concept for this book arose from the 25-year-old memoir written by Captain William B. Ecker, commanding officer of VFP-62, colloquially known as "Fightin' Photo." It documented VFP-62's selection, preparation, missions over Cuba, and the commendations and awards lavished upon it for the hard intelligence that guided President Kennedy to a peaceful resolution. Capt Ecker's memoir, which provided exceptional details of his first mission over Cuba, was used as a primary reference source for a number of television documentaries, in addition to the motion picture *Thirteen Days*. Beyond that, it languished, unpublished, until it was rescued by his son, David, who went on a search for a co-author to expand the manuscript – a wonderful story of a son's devotion to perpetuating his father's historical legacy.

There is a saying that death is like a library burning, where a wealth of knowledge is lost, sometimes forever. The pilots and young enlisted sailors who were on the frontline of history in October 1962 are now reaching advanced age, and a number are no longer with us. We are fortunate that Capt Ecker was able to consult on the book's expansion up until his death in November 2009. This volume hasn't been written too soon.

Our objective is to tell the important story of the Cuban Missile Crisis, both to those who may know something about it as well as to those who don't, in a fresh approach that highlights the important role that aerial photographic intelligence played in the resolution of the crisis. It was Capt Ecker's passion to tell the full inside story of how this US Navy commanding officer and his squadron flew unarmed supersonic RF-8A Crusaders in support of the secret low-level photographic operation codenamed *Blue Moon*. It also draws a comparison to the other military assets gathering photo intelligence for President Kennedy – the USAF's U-2 high-altitude spyplane and RF-101C Voodoo low-level photo-reconnaissance aircraft that flew missions in conjunction with VFP-62.

Often books, documentaries, and articles on the Cuban Missile Crisis quickly mention the U-2's discovery of the missiles – giving the impression that the Lockheed-built spyplane did it all – and then ignore the interesting, largely unknown, story of the full intelligence gathering capabilities that were deployed against the threat in Cuba, and the impact they made in the peaceful outcome of the crisis.

There are many excellent books that analyze and document the presidential-level decision-making during the high-stakes nuclear "chess game" that made this conflict so interesting and important. The best of them give insight into the dilemmas of governing, the travails of the presidency, and the inner workings of the secret world of our intelligence agencies.

Our aim is to provide a fresh approach to the sequence of events that made up the Cuban Missile Crisis from the perspective of those who execute presidential commands – the so-called "tip of the spear," whose courage and competence, or lack of it, hold the security of the United States in their hands. The reader will experience the excitement and dangers of the crisis as seen from the cockpit of an operational, low-altitude, photo-reconnaissance jet. The story is told by Capt Ecker and the RF-8 pilots (and the enlisted men that kept their jets flying) of VFP-62 and Marine Corps Composite Squadron VMCJ-2.

Declassified archival information from the Kennedy White House, JCS, State Department, and CIA provide the historical context and timeline for events. New information obtained for this book reveals how centrally important photographic intelligence was to the military, intelligence community, and the Executive Committee of the National Security Council (ExComm). That photography was obtained at great risk to the pilots, and one, USAF U-2 pilot Maj Rudolph Anderson, lost his life.

For its performance, VFP-62 would receive the respect of a grateful president. In a letter to Cdr Ecker, President Kennedy wrote:

> As I said in our meeting at Boca Chica, the reconnaissance flights, which enabled us to determine with precision the offensive build-up in Cuba, contributed directly to the security of the United States in the most important and significant way.

Twelve VFP-62 and four VMCJ-2 pilots would be awarded the Distinguished Flying Cross, and President Kennedy personally presented the Navy Unit Commendation to the entire squadrons.

It is our hope that, as we approach the 50th anniversary of the Cuban Missile Crisis, a new generation of readers will learn the vital lesson that emerged from this Cold War stand-off – sometimes nations act irrationally in their national interest, and the resulting unintended consequences can thrust nuclear-armed countries into a death spiral that could impact all of human civilization. This is the story of how men at all levels helped to prevent that fate.

Ken Jack
Photographer's mate second class, VFP-62, 1960–63

"Any man who may be asked in this century what he did to make his life worthwhile, can respond with a good deal of pride and satisfaction, 'I served in the United States Navy.'"

—President John F. Kennedy
Annapolis, Maryland, 1963

CHAPTER 1

THE MAKING OF A FIGHTER PILOT

William B. Ecker's entrance into Naval Aviation was typical of many who answered the nation's call to duty in World War II. The US Navy gave him the opportunity and leadership to succeed and serve. It is a story that continues to this day. In a newspaper interview with the *Jacksonville Journal*'s Staff Writer Jack Williams after the Cuban Missile Crisis, Capt Ecker explained:

> I guess I first got interested in flying when I was in the fifth grade. I remember writing away to the US Navy, the Army Air Corps, the Coast Guard, and civil aviation authorities to find out all I could about becoming a pilot. I don't really know why I ended up picking the US Navy, maybe it was just the old story of people from the Midwest being attracted to the chance of seeing salt water.

Capt Ecker tells how his Naval Aviation career began:

> On December 7, 1941 I was a senior in high school in Omaha, Nebraska. The following morning, Monday, December 8, all of the seniors were called to an assembly in the school auditorium, where we listened to the President ask Congress for a Declaration of War against the Japanese Empire. Immediately upon completion of the speech, a large number of my classmates rushed up the aisle, left school, and headed for various

recruiting offices. However, I had decided early on that I wanted to fly for the US Navy and be a carrier pilot.

I delayed enlisting until June, and upon graduation, with my diploma in one hand and my track letter in the other, I went to the US Navy recruiting office. Prior to the war, the US Navy stipulated that an applicant must have completed two years of college prior to applying for flight training. This requirement was waived soon after Pearl Harbor.

In an interview for the *Jacksonville Journal* 20 years later, Capt Ecker elaborated on his circumstances:

Since I had just turned 18 my mother had to sign my enlistment papers before I could join. She wanted me to wait, so we made a deal that I would wait three months and then she would sign.

At the local US Navy recruiting office in downtown Omaha I was given only a very cursory physical examination, followed by a basic mental examination as well. After passing both, they issued me a TR (Transportation Requisition or ticket) and written orders to take the train from Omaha to Kansas City, Missouri the following day. It was late afternoon when the train arrived at Kansas City, and I (with about a dozen other candidates whom I had met on the train) checked into a small hotel that was within walking distance of the Navy examination center.

At 0700 hrs the next day we began a battery of tests and examinations – everything from the "spinning chair" (test for vertigo), to depth perception, the most detailed comprehensive physical, flight physiology, and even a psychiatric evaluation. As the day progressed, I began to notice that from time to time the person who had been in front of me or behind me would disappear, having been disqualified! Finally, at about 1700 hrs, the doctors declared I was fully qualified and the ordeal was over.

Only two of the other candidates I had met on the train had made it as well. We three celebrated with a big steak dinner (only part of which was covered by our US Navy per diem), and after one more night in our Kansas City hotel we returned to our homes. I never saw either of the successful candidates again.

For the next three months I waited anxiously, day-by-day, for my orders to flight training. During this period I learned that naval investigators had been contacting neighbors, teachers, ministers, and the police, checking on my behavior, my reputation, and general overall personality and lifestyle. Finally, I received orders to report to Central Missouri State Teachers' College in Warrensburg, Missouri – about 40 miles southeast of Kansas City – and for the next three months I flew light aircraft (Cubs and Porterfields) for half of each day and had academics (mathematics, recognition, code, Civil Air Regulations, navigation, and principles of flight) for the other half. It was here, after seven hours of dual instruction, on a morning with light snow on the ground, I soloed!

For the young aviation cadet, Ecker's training continued with athletics, various academics, and accumulating 125 hours of flight time in an old open-cockpit Naval Aircraft Factory N3N biplane trainer better known as a "Yellow Peril." He continues:

I went on to NAS Corpus Christi, in Texas, where I flew North American SNV and SNJ training aircraft. This was the first time that I had flown all-metal airplanes with radios, flaps, variable-pitch propellers, retractable landing gear, guns, bombs, and closed canopies. Training involved advanced formation, aerobatics, instruments, gunnery, bombing, and some dogfighting.

I received my wings and commission as an ensign in the US Naval Reserve on May 20, 1944 and went directly to Operational Flight Training flying Grumman F6F Hellcat fighters at NAS Vero Beach, in Florida. This was the last training I would receive before being assigned to a fleet squadron, and the syllabus included FCLP (Field Carrier Landing Practice) as the final phase. After leaving NAS Vero Beach, I made my first carrier landing. It is a little known fact that almost all carrier pilots in the 1943–44 timeframe made their first eight landings on a side-paddle-wheel carrier in Lake Michigan. My carrier was USS *Wolverine* (IX-64) and there was a second called USS *Sable* (IX-81). These ships had been overnight steamers that ran from Chicago to St Joseph, Michigan. When the war required training carriers that were safe from enemy submarines, the US Navy acquired these ships and mounted flight decks on them.

Lake Michigan would become the graveyard for many US Navy aircraft due to accidents, and decades later it became an historical reservoir for their retrieval, restoration, and exhibition in aviation museums.

COMBAT DUTY IN THE PACIFIC

While Ens Ecker was making his way to his new fighter squadron (VF-10), which was bound for the Pacific theater, another future VC-62/VFP-62 pilot, then Lt(jg) Howard Skidmore, was in his Grumman TBF Avenger on November 25, 1944 aboard the carrier USS *Cabot* (CVL-28). His aircraft was last in line to be launched from the starboard catapult. *Cabot* had been on patrol off Luzon, in the Philippines, conducting strikes in support of operations ashore and repelling kamikaze attacks. *Cabot*'s gunners had fought off several kamikazes when one, already flaming from hits, crashed into the flightdeck on the port side, destroying the 20mm gun platform and disabling the 40mm mounts and gun director. Another crashed alongside the carrier, spewing shrapnel and flames across the flightdeck. Skidmore ordered his crewman to abandon the aircraft and ran for cover. His hair was scorched and he had burns on his hands. *Cabot* lost 62 men killed and wounded.

In 1953, Lt Cdr Skidmore reported to VC-62 (VFP-62's predecessor squadron) as its executive officer. Nearly a decade later he would be in a Pentagon intelligence group deeply involved with receiving VFP-62's low-level photography during the Cuban Missile Crisis (see Chapter 6).

US Navy Fighter Squadron 10, known as the "Grim Reapers," originated on June 3, 1942 as VF-10 at NAS San Diego, California, flying Grumman F4F Wildcats. It deployed on the legendary USS *Enterprise* (CV-6) to the southern Pacific in 1942, where the unit fought in the battle of Guadalcanal. During its second combat tour aboard the *Enterprise* in 1944, VF-10 participated in operations in the Marshall

Islands, Jaluit, Emirau, the Western Caroline Islands, and the battle of the Philippine Sea (including the famous "Marianas Turkey Shoot"). Capt Ecker continues his story:

In September 1944 I reported to Fighter Squadron 10 (VF-10) and began flying the Vought F4U-1D Corsair. We deployed to the Pacific as part of Carrier Air Group (CAG) 10 in February 1945 aboard USS *Intrepid* (CV-11). I had two combat tours, each of which ended early. The first combat tour ended because of a kamikaze strike on the carrier, and the second because the war ended.

I flew my first combat mission on March 18, 1945. The target was the airfield near the town of Usa, on the northern-most shore of Kyushu, Japan. That same day *Intrepid* was attacked by a kamikaze but the ship's gunners blew him up about 50ft before he hit, so the ship received only superficial damage to the forward, starboard hangar deck blast curtain. Routine combat missions were flown almost every day in support of the Okinawa campaign, both before and after the landings of April 1, 1945.

Then, on April 16 (this was to be a day to remember by all, the ship, the air group, and me), I started the day with a predawn launch for a Combat Air Patrol (CAP). The four-hour CAP was uneventful, with no bogies or targets sighted. Just as I was landing back aboard, the division (four aircraft) that relieved us called a "Tally ho" on a whole bunch of enemy aircraft – all kamikazes! In the ensuing fight they splashed 20. If there were any remaining in the bunch, they were either shot down by other fighters or ships' gunners, as none got through to the carriers. This was a day of heavy fighting, and we remained at GQ (general quarters) battle stations continuously.

At 1100 hrs I went into Condition 10 – that is, strapped in the cockpit of my airplane on the catapult and with a warm engine. We remained like this for one hour at a time. At 1158 hrs my relief appeared in the catwalk and climbed onto the flightdeck. Just as I began to unstrap, the air officer in PriFly (Primary Flight Control) announced excitedly, "Launch the Condition 10." My relief, Ens Morrie Dubinsky, tossed me a salute and quipped, "You got it." Within a minute or so, I was airborne.

While he mentions a kamikaze attack on the carrier later, Capt Ecker fails to mention that sometime after he was catapulted from *Intrepid*, a Japanese aircraft dived into the carrier's flightdeck causing a fire, killing eight men and wounding 21. This was the second time *Intrepid* avoided being sunk, for on February 17, 1944 an aerial torpedo had struck the vessel's starboard quarter, flooding several compartments and damaging the rudder. In that incident, the ship limped back to Pearl Harbor for repairs. Capt Ecker continues his story:

Of the four of us that launched, only three went on the mission – Lt(jg)s Wes Hays and Holly Hollister and myself. The fourth pilot, Ens Russ Carlisi, had to turn back with a rough-running engine. As soon as we checked in with the fighter controller, we were vectored to the Inland Sea area between Kyushu, Shikoku, and the southernmost tip of Honshu. Here, one of our "Dumbos" (a Martin PBM Mariner seaplane named after Walt Disney's flying elephant) was trying to land and pick up a downed pilot, but two Zeros were attacking him.

We went after the Zeros but they had seen us and high-tailed it for the nearest land. We gave chase, and soon saw that they were trying to suck us right over their base, where their antiaircraft artillery [AAA] gunners could have a shot at us – trying to even the three-to-two odds. About this time, the "Dumbo" started hollering for us to come back ASAP. He had landed and picked up the downed pilot, but couldn't get back into the air because of glassy water and no wind. He was helpless – a sitting duck. We resumed our cover over him while he rigged JATO (Jet Assisted Take Off) rockets. On the next try, he blew himself into the air.

We started for home with a long way to go. The PBM was so much slower than we were that we had to either weave back and forth over him or try to slow to his speed. We throttled back, put our props into full high pitch, and flew at near-stall speed. You could almost count the blades as they went by. Time went by peacefully, and as our fuel reached the point indicating it was time to head back to the carrier, we announced to the "Dumbo" that we had to leave him.

Within a couple of minutes of having set our course for *Intrepid*, a voice came up on the radio with our call sign and ordered, "Stay with the 'Dumbo'!" We countered that we did not have enough fuel to see him to his base and still get back to our carrier. Again the voice repeated, "Stay with the 'Dumbo'!", and this time it authenicated with the proper sign for that day so that we knew that it was not a Jap trying to con us. We escorted the "Dumbo" to his base on Kerama Retto – an island just southwest of Okinawa – and just after he landed, we heard him call for assistance. He had run out of fuel while taxiing in. He had been airborne for about 14 hours.

By now it was almost dark, and as we flew up the west side of Okinawa the whole invasion fleet, of about 400 craft, was blinking for a recognition sign from us. Because we had had no intention of coming near the invasion fleet, we did not know the recognition signal for that day. So, we slowed up, flew at an even 1,000ft, and turned on all the exterior lights on our airplanes. Thank God for our inverted gull bent wings and just enough daylight. If just one trigger-happy young seaman gunner had fired just one round that would be all she wrote.

We landed on a Marsten-matted (perforated steel plates) strip called Yonton Field on Okinawa just as the first of the night raids came in and attacked the base. I just pulled back the mixture control (to kill the engine) and let the airplane coast to a stop at the end of the strip, whereupon I jumped out and headed for the nearest fox-hole or slit-trench.

After the raid, some ground troops gave us a five-pound can of Spam, some crackers, and a big can of grapefruit juice. This was the first of many "dining experiences" that would come along in the next couple of weeks. We spent about half the night in a tent, perforated with many bullet holes, on a cot with bare springs, and the other half in a slit-trench. After three or four needless trips to the shelter, we said the hell with it and stayed put. I did, however, on the advice of the ground troops, sleep with my knife in my hand because my gun was back hanging on the ready-room wall – nobody ever gets launched from a Condition 10!

I spent a part of the next day informing various naval authorities of our situation, and asked that the squadron be informed of where we were.

It was at this point that we learned that the ship had been severely damaged in a kamikaze attack. With dead and wounded, the vessel had left the battle zone the previous afternoon. Had we returned to the rendezvous position, there would have been no carrier to land on – a carrier pilot's most dreaded situation.

Late in the afternoon, we were given 233 gallons of gasoline for our main tank, but none for our external belly-tanks. Earlier, a Curtiss SB2C Helldivier dive-bomber had landed on Yonton Field, and from him we got the authenticator code and the "YE-YG" navigation Hayrake wheel for the day. Hayrake got its nickname from the shape of the antenna used as a navigation homer to return to the carrier. The wheel was a circle, cut into 12 segments, each with an identifying letter. This lettering was changed every day. Thus by picking up the letter by radio, the pilot simply flew toward the center of the wheel. Also, each carrier had its own code and homer frequency. The SB2C was from "Wonder Base." We were ordered to fly out to it, now!

As we approached "Wonder Base" I could see that it was the USS *Essex* (CV-9). Although it was late in the afternoon when we took off, the vessel was only 40 to 50 miles off Okinawa. Since we were the last airplanes of the day, we were taken aboard immediately and the ship then left the battle area to be in a position for replenishment operations the next day.

As we were climbing out of our airplanes, we were told that the Rear Adm Fred Sherman wanted to see us up on the bridge. He asked us what ship and squadron we were from, and then offered us the option of either staying with him and joining one of his squadrons or of returning to our own unit, VBF-10 – just before we left California VF-10 had been split into VF-10 and VBF-10, the latter ostensibly being a fighter-bomber unit. We elected to return to our own outfit and he said okay, but that he was keeping our aircraft! This was not at all unusual as it saved him the effort of having to ferry out replacement fighters to cover his losses. We were given written orders back to *Intrepid* and VBF-10, along with a pair of grey pants and a grey shirt, plus a parachute bag for our gear. Somewhere along the way I later acquired a tooth brush and a razor, as well as a towel and a bar of soap.

During the replenishment evolution (replenishment of everything – fuel for both the ship and the 80 to 100 aircraft, food stores, ammunition and bombs, mail, candy, medical supplies, spare parts, and sometimes even people), which took place the next day, we were highlined – riding in a big canvas sack across a wire or cable – over to the tanker USS *Escalante* (AO-70).

Ecker's odyssey found him once more being highlined to a destroyer and once again to a jeep carrier. Finally, he departed Guam on a Marine Corps Curtiss R-5C Commando aircraft bound for the Ulithi fleet anchorage, in the western Pacific, where *Intrepid* was undergoing a temporary face-lifting repair job before returning to the Naval Shipyard at Hunters Point, California. Ecker had been gone for exactly two weeks.

Intrepid and Carrier Air Group 10 returned to the war in late July. The conflict ended on September 2, 1945. Capt Ecker concludes:

After the holidays, I was ordered to another F4U squadron, VF-74, at NAS Oceana, Virginia. While attached to this unit I applied for a regular US Navy commission, and in the spring of 1947 I was assigned to the regular Navy, now as a lieutenant, junior grade, USN. Almost immediately after becoming regular Navy, I was ordered to Stanford University, California, where I studied until late 1949. The US Navy figured it was easier to educate a two-tour combat pilot than it was to provide a college graduate with flight training and combat. The tour at Stanford was intended to bring my educational level up to that of my peers from the Naval Academy.

While attending Stanford, I married my wife of more than 60 years, Kit, an American Airlines stewardess.

In June 1954, (then) Lt Cdr Ecker underwent training in jet fighter photographic reconnaissance at NAS Pensacola, Florida – training he would not use until eight years later as the commanding officer of VFP-62 during the Cuban Missile Crisis.

CHAPTER 2

"EYES OF THE FLEET"

As previously noted, the US Navy's VFP-62 was also known colloquially as "Fightin' Photo." In the 1950s the squadron had had a contest for a squadron motto, and the winning entry was "Fleet Eyes." Later, that got changed to "Eyes of the Fleet," and both VFP-62 and VFP-63 (the West Coast photo-reconnaissance squadron) shared it. The unit's mission was to provide carrier task force commanders with an integral intelligence gathering capability for pre-strike planning intelligence and battle damage assessment (BDA).

The US Navy had learned the importance of aerial reconnaissance during World War II, when attempting to land troops off invasion beaches in unknown depths of water often meant needless deaths. Photographic reconnaissance was often no more sophisticated than a photographer hanging out the open hatch of an aircraft, with a heavy camera strapped to his body. As naval aerial photography progressed, cameras became an integral part of the aircraft, allowing the pilot to both fly the airplane and operate the camera equipment.

In the years following World War II, the US Navy had a small number of combat-experienced photo pilots attached to carrier air groups, but there was no standard syllabus or specialized training for replacement Naval Aviators. Late in 1948, Fleet Aircraft Service Squadron (FASRON) 3 at NAS Norfolk, Virginia, formed a photographic detachment. On January 8, 1949, 13 officers and 88 men attached to this photographic unit mustered to watch the birth of a unit – Composite Squadron (VC)

62, predecessor to VFP-62. Similarly VC-61 was formed on the West Coast. VC-62's mission was to train and maintain the readiness of units tasked with carrier-based photographic reconnaissance of designated targets in the area of naval operations.

The first aircraft complement of the new squadron consisted of ten Grumman F8F-2P Bearcats and four F4U-5P and two F4U-4P Corsairs. Usually, a single camera was mounted in the fuselage aft of the wings in these aircraft. Since photographic reconnaissance was only a small part of the mission being performed by Naval Aviators assigned to VC-62, the unit's training syllabus then provided for proficiency flights in aerial gunnery, rocketry, and bombing. Navigation and instrument training were also emphasized, for getting home was of great importance to the photo-pilot because his mission was not completed until the finished prints were delivered.

In 1950 the squadron was moved to NAS Jacksonville (referred to colloquially as JAX), Florida. VC-62 had transitioned to the McDonnell F2H-2P Banshee by mid-1951, this machine being the answer to a photo-pilot's prayer. Powered by a Westinghouse J34 turbojet engine, the Banshee had tremendous versatility thanks to its 600mph+ top speed and service ceiling in excess of 40,000ft. The F2H-2P was fitted with three cameras, all of which could be rotated from the cockpit. The aircraft's photo-viewfinder gave the pilot a complete view of everything beneath his aircraft, as well as the ability to center his pictures exactly. The quality and quantity of photographs increased accordingly.

By October 1953 the first examples of the Grumman F9F-6P Cougar had been added to VC-62's stable of Banshees, giving the squadron a higher performance jet configured with a multitude of cameras – the unit also operated a handful of Lockheed TV-2 jet trainers and piston-engined Beech SNB-5Ps photo/liaison aircraft.

By the early 1950s it had become clear that faster airplanes required faster cameras, as existing cameras did not recycle fast enough at low altitudes.

On August 9, 1955 VC-62 made the first jet flights into a hurricane, taking aerial photographs of Hurricane "Connie." Photographs from on top, and then into the eye of the hurricane, were published around the world.

VC-62 was redesignated VFP-62 on July 2, 1956.

In many ways the Bearcats and Corsairs had been unsuited for their mission, but as long as the photo-pilot flew a piston-engined airplane, he could shoot back. Not so with the unarmed jets that replaced them. Speed, maneuverability, and superior head work were the photo-pilot's only defense in combat areas from 1951.

In early 1958 the squadron's F9F-6Ps and -8Ps and F2H-2Ps were replaced by the sleek F8U-1P (redesignated RF-8A in 1962), the photo-variant of the Vought F8U (fighter) Crusader. The US Navy's first supersonic jet, the Crusader could attain speeds of over 1,000mph. The unarmed F8U-1P variant had four camera stations – three aft of the pilot and a forward-pointing bay beneath the air intake. The cameras were controlled by state-of-the-art electronics that received altitude and speed data (which was either manually input by the pilot or calculated automatically by an optical device called a scanner) to take sharp images from very low altitude up to 50,000ft.

At the speeds that the Crusader flew, the image would have been blurred on the light-sensitive photographic film had it remained stationary during exposure, even at shutter speeds (the time it takes light to pass through the lens) of one one-thousandth of a second. To obtain these high-resolution, focused pictures required an enormous amount of optical, mechanical, and electronic equipment that implemented a technique called image motion compensation (IMC).

In the RF-8A, a cockpit-mounted "black box" called the Master Control coordinated the aircraft's altitude and speed with other electronic components to move the light-sensitive film in the camera at the appropriate speed and in the *opposite* direction of flight precisely at the moment that the shutter opened. The whole objective of IMC was to keep the movement of any point on the ground (relative to the aircraft passing over it) "fixed" on a precise point on the film as its reflected light came through the lens at the time of exposure. The exact sequence was as follows – a vacuum sucked the film flat against a device called a shuttle; the shuttle moved the film in the *opposite* direction of flight; the shutter opened and exposed the film; the vacuum released the film to advance to a new frame; the vacuum was re-applied and the process repeated. The movement of the film "followed" the points on the ground, avoiding blurring, during the exposure. When everything worked just right, the photographs obtained showed incredible detail.

In addition to IMC, the camera system electronics controlled the recycle rate of exposures to conform to the desired overlap of the ground images. This concept is explained later in this volume.

VFP-62 moved to NAS Cecil Field (the East Coast master jet base), near Jacksonville, Florida, in 1958. It was an unusually large squadron, made up of 55 officers, 500 enlisted, and 35 aircraft. Its primary mission was to provide a jet photographic reconnaissance detachment to each carrier air group of the Atlantic Fleet. A large number of the squadron's detachments (each of which usually consisted of three aircraft and 35 men) were deployed at any given time. VFP-62 was still a large squadron based at Cecil Field when 38-year-old Cdr Ecker joined it in January 1962, having been a fighter pilot for the previous eighteen years. He recalled:

In the early 1960s, fighter pilots had a tendency to look down their noses at other pilots. A common saying was, "If you ain't a fighter pilot, you ain't shit." Truthfully, however, the job of a fighter pilot can be somewhat boring in peacetime because the only day-to-day interesting part (besides the pure joy of just flying a fighter airplane) consists usually of about two or three weeks of aerial gunnery per year and the firing (maybe) of one missile, if you're lucky.

After getting into the photographic reconnaissance squadron, I realized that every day a product was brought back where you could evaluate your performance. It was a constant challenge and a much more rewarding type of job. Looking back, my divergence from the role of a straight fighter pilot into that of jet photo-recon was a true blessing.

In January 1962 I reported to VFP-62 as PCO (prospective commanding officer), with temporary duty as executive officer. Then in September, I took command of the squadron. Because of my predecessor, Cdr George Winslow (throughout, I will use the rank held by an individual at that particular time), the squadron was in an outstanding condition and operationally ready in all respects. This condition of the unit, coupled with the "can–do" professional attitude of all hands, was the prime reason for our outstanding success.

The headquarters of the squadron was situated permanently ashore at NAS Cecil Field, and those who usually remained at home were called the "Palace Guard" by those who deployed.

The RF-8A was unique in its design, being one of a kind! It had a variable incidence wing – that is, the wing was hinged at the rear where it met the fuselage, and could be rotated upward to an angle of 7½ degrees. This was required because the Crusader had a very long fuselage and sat low to the ground. Without the 7½ degrees angle-of-attack provided by this wing, the rear end of the jet would scrape badly on every takeoff and landing. The Crusader's variable incidence wing was a marvel of its day, enhancing takeoff and landing performance and slow–flight maneuvering.

The RF-8A was delivered to the US Navy with Fairchild CAX-12 70mm (2¼-inch square) format (picture size) cameras with focal lengths of 1.5, 3, 6, and 12 inches – focal length is the distance from the center of the lens to the surface of the film. Smaller focal lengths give wider–angle of coverage. The original configuration consisted of three trimetrogen cameras (one oblique camera on each side and one vertical) giving horizon-to-horizon coverage in camera bay 2, aft of the cockpit. Further back, camera bays 3 (port side) and 4 (starboard side) held one camera each, both providing vertical and oblique coverage. The pilot could select the degree of obliquity from the cockpit, while using an optical "reticle" device attached to the lower canopy for aligning the target and camera correctly. Also, much older 9-inch format cameras could be installed in bays 3 and 4, but they were mostly used for color and air-to-air US Navy PR photos of aircraft and ships.

The as-delivered camera in bay 1 (the so-called "gun camera" under the jet's nose) was inferior and was seldom used prior to 1962. A movie camera was also fitted into bay 1. The jet's forward-firing capability was not fully appreciated until VFP-62's chief photo officer Cdr Robert Koch and chief photographer's mate Frank Wolle collaborated to fit new 5-inch format (commonly referred as such, but it actually had a 4.5-inch square negative) Chicago Aerial Industries Inc. KA-45 or KA-46 cameras into the tight camera bay 1 compartment. The KA-46 had a between-the-lens shutter (metal blades) and the KA-45 a focal-plane shutter (metallic curtain capable of shutter speeds of one three-thousandth of a second) but otherwise were similar. The larger negative size and higher resolution of these forward-firing cameras gave VFP-62 the technological edge over all other photo-reconnaissance units at the beginning of the Cuban Missile Crisis.

SPYING ON THE COMMUNISTS

The Cold War was characterized by the pursuit of intelligence. However, the closed society of the Soviet Union made human intelligence (HUMINT) extremely difficult to obtain. When Gen Dwight D. Eisenhower assumed the presidency in 1953, he quickly became aware of US intelligence deficiencies and set out to improve its collection capabilities. It was at the same time that Arthur C. Lundahl joined the CIA and received the president's mandate to organize "a first-class photographic intelligence center." Thus, with the president's blessings, the CIA developed the NPIC and Lundahl became its Director.[1]

Late in 1954, the CIA sponsored the super-secret development of the Lockheed U-2 high-altitude spyplane. The aircraft's state-of-the-art photographic capabilities boosted US understanding of the USSR's military and industrial capacities, thus providing a first line of defense against a surprise attack – a nuclear Pearl Harbor. Aerial reconnaissance had reached a new level of excellence and capability.

Flying at more than 70,000ft, the U-2 evaded Soviet fighters, incapable of reaching such altitudes, from 1956 to 1960. The Kremlin knew the U-2s were flying over the USSR but did not call public attention to the incursions because it did not want its citizens to know that the Soviet military was incapable of shooting the aircraft down. The Soviet government protested privately to the United States about these flights, however.

Prior to the advent of the U-2, the US military carried out a variety of reconnaissance missions (including air sampling to detect Soviet atmospheric nuclear tests) utilizing a variety of aircraft both around and directly over the USSR. During this period many reconnaissance aircraft and crewmen were lost to Soviet ground and air defenses.

With the introduction of the U-2 into service in 1956, aerial photography became the primary asset for providing much of what the CIA knew about key Soviet military, industrial, and missile complexes. The Americans would duly use this information to calculate the extent of the so-called "missile gap" (a gap that favored the United States) between the two nuclear superpowers. Additionally, the intelligence helped the Pentagon refine target folders in case of a nuclear war.

That intelligence ceased with the shoot-down of a CIA U-2, piloted by Francis Gary Powers, on May 1, 1960 (May Day), just months before John F. Kennedy's election. Thought to be invulnerable, the U-2 was brought down by the powerful SA-2 "Guideline" (designated the S-75 Dvina in Soviet service) surface-to-air missile (SAM). The SA-2 was first deployed in 1957, and had a solid-fuel booster engine, an altitude reach of more than 60,000ft, a fragmentation warhead, and a top speed of Mach 3.5 (three-and-a-half times the speed of sound). The SA-2 site used early-warning "Spoon Rest" searching radar, with a 70-mile range, and "Fan Song" guidance radar that could direct three SA-2s against a single target. In a future war the SA-2 would be the nemesis of US pilots over North Vietnamese skies.

The unexpected incident embarrassed the US government when the Eisenhower administration initially tried to hide the spyplane's mission. The president felt confident that an effective cover-up could be made because he had been assured by the CIA that the flimsily built long-winged jet, as well as the pilot, would not survive under any circumstances. Indeed, a contingency to ensure the aircraft would not survive such a mishap had been developed. The pilot was instructed to throw a switch before ejecting, thus arming a timed explosive device behind the cockpit. The pilot was also provided with a suicide pen if capture was inevitable, although he was not ordered to use it.

In the wake of the shoot-down Powers claimed that he was unable to blow the U-2 up and chose not to use the pen. Miraculously, much of the airplane survived the crash and was put on display in Moscow, giving the communist propaganda machine its "Exhibit A," exposing the imperialists' spying activities. Powers also survived ("alive and kicking" as Chairman Nikita Khrushchev boasted), became a prisoner, and was put on trial. Over the years the circumstances of the shoot-down have been debated. Some believe that the U-2 was a victim of an indirect hit, or that Powers had brought the aircraft to a lower altitude to restart a flamed-out engine. Some conspiracy theories even stated that Powers was a double agent. Certainly with vested interests at stake, CIA Director (DCI) Allen Dulles believed that the U-2 was never shot down.[2]

Embarrassingly, the incident occurred at a time when Soviet–American relations were improving. Khrushchev had made a successful widely publicized tour of the United States (including talks with the president at Camp David), and in return Eisenhower was invited to visit the Soviet Union. For a brief period the world was upbeat and looked forward, with high expectations, to a scheduled four-party summit in Paris that was only weeks away. The United States, Great Britain, France, and the Soviet Union were to discuss disputes over Berlin and limiting the arms race. Hopes for world peace and reduced Cold War tensions were running high, but they were all dashed by the U-2 disaster.

At the summit, Khrushchev, striving for maximum propaganda value, demanded President Eisenhower apologize for violating Russian airspace, and when Eisenhower refused, he dramatically withdrew from the summit before it began. The summit collapsed and the U-2 incident stained the last months of the Eisenhower presidency – a low moment for the old general, who was criticized for poor judgment in authorizing the surveillance flight at such a delicate time in foreign relations. To confidants, a chastened Eisenhower even mused about resigning.[3] With worldwide criticism mounting against the United States, the president promised that American airplanes would not penetrate Soviet airspace again, ending years of successful intelligence gathering. Two years later, the

U-2 disaster would negatively impact the authorization of surveillance flights over a small island nation in the Caribbean, arming itself with Soviet nuclear weapons against the United States.

On January 1, 1959 Fidel Castro's revolutionary forces achieved victory over Cuban President Fulgencio Batista's regime, and shortly thereafter Castro was named premier. A number of his key revolutionaries, including his brother Raul and Che Guevara, were communists. Somewhat slowly, Fidel declared he was also a communist, and structured his new government around a Marxist-Leninist ideology. Cuba established diplomatic relations with the Soviet Union in May 1960. By the end of that same year the specter and fear of communism spreading to the Western Hemisphere evolved into US covert (disguising American government involvement) actions against Cuba including the CIA placing a hit on Castro through Mafia connections. There is little doubt that President Eisenhower surreptitiously approved the plan, while maintaining plausible deniability. For his and the next presidency, assassination plots against foreign leaders would become a component of American foreign policy.

As everyone watched the hopeful possibilities of the Cuban revolution being rapidly abandoned, the Eisenhower administration severed diplomatic relations and pursued a policy of isolation and hostility towards Cuba. Eisenhower stopped petroleum shipments to Cuba and imports of Cuban sugar (80 percent of Cuba's exports went to the US) in retaliation for Castro's nationalization of petroleum plants and private property owned by American companies – Castro did not compensate the private or corporate owners.

These first attempts to destabilize Castro's regime largely failed to loosen his grip on power. The Soviets quickly replaced the petroleum and purchased the sugar that had been destined for the United States, thus starting an alliance with the Cubans. The fear of the exportation of communism to Latin America would soon dominate the waning days of the Eisenhower administration and set into motion policies that would lead to the Cuban Missile Crisis.

THE BAY OF PIGS INVASION

The foreign policies of the Eisenhower and Kennedy administrations reflected the sentiments and anti-communist hysteria in the country. Both administrations feared that a successful Cuban socialist state would expand the spread of communism to the Western Hemisphere, particularly in Latin American countries where leftist groups were actively emerging. Both presidents planned and pursued covert operations to undermine the Castro regime, but the Kennedy administration inherited a daring plan to invade Cuba, approved by President Eisenhower in March 1960. One of many poorly conceived CIA-managed and -funded operations, the scheme to invade Cuba using Cuban exiles and dissidents, trained and equipped by the CIA, would become a "baptism by fire" for the 35th president less than 90 days after his inauguration. That operation was to be known as the Bay of Pigs invasion.

During his 1960 campaign John F. Kennedy advocated a strong anti-Castro stance and denigrated the Eisenhower administration, particularly his opponent Vice President Richard M. Nixon, for being too weak against Cuba. This played well to the electorate. Many scholars and historians credit Kennedy's anti-Cuban strategy and his exaggeration of a missile gap between the United States and the USSR as central factors in his win in the tight election of 1960. As president, the shrewd political maneuver that helped him win the election now worked against him, pressuring him to accept the plan, or face charges of hypocrisy if word ever got out about the operation. With CIA and Pentagon assurances, he approved the Bay of Pigs plan. However, he did moderate the size of the operation to protect the covert nature of the invasion, weakening it to the point that it was destined to fail.

With US support, approximately 1,400 Cuban anti-Castro émigrés (known as the Cuban Expeditionary Force, or CEF) attempted a counter-revolution on April 17, 1961, invading Cuba by night in boats and establishing beachheads. The bold beach-storming invasion plan was to be preceded by CEF B-26 Invader air strikes against Castro's air force. The air component was operating under the supervision of the CIA's Richard Bissell, who had superbly managed the development and deployment of the U-2 spyplane under President Eisenhower. Bissell was an extremely intelligent, adventurous heir-apparent to Kennedy's CIA Director, Allen Dulles, who had been retained from the previous administration. Bissell and Dulles had both assured President Eisenhower in 1960 that the U-2 would never be shot down.

As D-Day approached, the operation was doomed from the start due in part to the president's reducing by half the number of B-26s attacking Cuban airfields prior to D-Day, and then canceling another critical air attack on D-Day itself. This upset the original plan and allowed Castro to mount air attacks on the invaders, which in turn meant that communist forces could quickly move against the weakly defended beachheads. By reducing the level of B-26 participation, Kennedy intended to further enhance the ruse that the Bay of Pigs invasion was a homegrown insurgency, thus concealing US involvement. Although the majority of the CEF were not professional soldiers, they fought bravely and destroyed a number of Cuban tanks and trucks, as well as inflicting casualties on approaching forces.

By April 18, and without assistance from the US Navy, the tragic end of the operation became apparent to a frantic CEF, Pentagon, White House, and CIA. The JCS were briefed at 0730 hrs on communications received from the pleading commander of the CEF: "Have you quit? Aren't you going to support me anymore?" He stated that he couldn't hold out without help, but later radioed, "Regardless of whether you help or not, I will fight on regardless."[4] President Kennedy remained adamant that no US forces would become involved in the combat. The CEF felt abandoned and bitter towards the CIA, the US military, and the president, who talked a good game, but carried a short stick.

Pre-invasion photo intelligence was provided by U-2s. Photographs of the waters off Playa Giron, designated *Blue Beach* by the CIA, showed shadows under the water. Analysts thought they were caused by seaweed, but when the invasion took place it was discovered that they were in fact submerged coral, which slowed the invasion and destroyed some landing craft – the first hint of disaster to come. VFP-62's Detachment 41 was aboard the attack carrier USS *Independence* (CVA-62), which was in the area at the time, and it got the chance to fly secret surveillance missions over the invasion beaches. The story of these overflights is told by aviation electrician's mate second class Frank Schrader:

The crew was led to believe that they were going to pick up President Kennedy for an airshow. We left Norfolk aboard *Independence*, heading south, and we thought we were going to pick the president up at Jacksonville. The crew was given new flightdeck jerseys – everyone thought they were issued so as to make a good impression on the president.

It kept getting warmer and warmer as we went south – Jacksonville isn't that warm in April – so we didn't know what was going on, except that we were a lot farther south than Jacksonville.

It was also curious that we weren't doing any flight operations. We assumed this was done so all aircraft needed for the airshow would be "up and ready." Later, we were told that the airshow had been canceled, but we didn't head north. I remember reading in the daily bulletin Plan of the Day that we shouldn't speculate on where we were in our letters home – sort of a strange note! I also noticed that our carrier task force was much larger than usual as we headed south. It wasn't just us and our plane guard destroyers.

One day the officer in charge of our detachment, Lt Cdr John Barrow, told the crew that the Det's three RF-8As were going to be repainted, with all identification markings painted over. We didn't understand why since they looked pretty good (we had just painted them on our recent Mediterranean cruise). Then we found out how we were going to paint them – we needed to paint out all English language markings, and we were going to have help in performing this task. Detachment personnel were instructed to mask off static ports and other such areas that shouldn't be painted. I remember one RF-8A got painted that night on the flightdeck in a very short time. We had help in this task from other squadrons and even some of the ship's company. The other two jets were repainted the next day.

To keep track of the airplanes, Roman numerals I, II, and III were painted in the wheel wells. When one of the photo aircraft had to be moved, an announcement came over the flightdeck speaker referring to them as "Gray Ghost One," "Two," or "Three."

Frank also recalled that when the air group (CVG-7) commenced flight operations, half of the aircraft on the flightdeck were loaded with conventional bombs (not "nukes") but remained chained to the deck. The aircraft carrier's attack jets were ready to support the CEF if the president gave the order. It never came. Frank continues with the story:

> One day, the detachment was ordered to plan a mission, and our pilots removed their name tags from their flightsuits and carried extra ammunition for their 0.38cal pistols. They looked like Pancho Villa with two belts of ammo crisscrossed over their chests.
>
> When the RF-8As returned, the film was quickly removed from the cameras, even as they were still taxiing forward to be parked. I was helping the plane captain for one of the aircraft and caught a glimpse of a map on the pilot's kneeboard as he handed his equipment down from the cockpit – it showed Cuba, with a red line going from east to west.

Shortly thereafter Frank learned about the Bay of Pigs invasion. The crew of both CVA-62 and CVG-7 were awarded the Armed Forces Expeditionary Medal for "clandestine operations in the Caribbean."

Rear Adm Bobby Lee (the only VFP-62 officer to reach flag rank, and a lieutenant pilot with Detachment 41, the VFP-62 detachment) concurs, "I was there and the story is true. We flew over the bay the day after the invasion's D-Day (April 18) and found nothing except a beached small boat and the signs of the skirmish. They spray-painted our airplanes almost as they were being taxied to the catapults. We carried nothing identifying us as American."

The VFP-62 reconnaissance flights would confirm what both the Pentagon and the White House already knew – the invasion had failed and the CEF would soon be overwhelmed by Castro's forces. But, the Crusaders' overflight of the combat area was also intended to give a morale boost to the beleaguered anti-Castro brigade men, and perhaps convince Castro's air forces not to attack them. President Kennedy's determination to hide American involvement in the invasion included the order to not use US armed forces to support the brigade, which was nearly out of ammunition and pinned down by Castro's army and militia. The failure to provide adequate air support and destroy Castro's air force condemned the venture to failure from the beginning.

On the second day of the invasion, the brigade desperately requested naval air support. The president was also under siege by his military and CIA advisors pleading the cause of the brigade. A meeting at the White House ended in stalemate at 1326 hrs. Nobody knew what to do, including the CIA, which was running the operation. The president remained adamant that no US Navy aircraft would be permitted to support the CEF. Considering the total lack of information on the evolving situation, the president recognized that good intelligence was desperately needed, and he authorized US Navy reconnaissance (VFP-62) jets to fly over the invasion area.[5]

Immediately, with this presidential authority, Maj Gen David W. Gray, chief of the Joint Subsidiary Activities Division, acting as a liaison between the CIA and the Pentagon, issued a telegram to Adm Robert Dennison, Commander-in-Chief of the Atlantic Fleet (CINCLANTFLT). "With unmarked naval aircraft fly photo and eyeball reconnaissance ASAP to detect situation on the beach."[6] Jim Rasenberger, in his recent book *Brilliant Disaster*, writes a vivid account of the reaction of the completely surrounded counter-revolutionaries to the US Navy overflights:

Finally [at 1530 hrs on April 18], the American jets arrived over Playa Giron. There were two, possibly three of them, unmarked, silver with swept-back wings. They flew in tight formation, coming from the sea and soaring over the beach, blazing toward the interior. The men saw them first at Giron, then seconds later up the road at San Blas, where they dipped their wings but did not slow. All along the front the fighting stopped as men looked up at the gleaming metal roaring across the clear blue sky. The brigade men whooped with joy, leaping from the foxholes and waving guns in the air.[7]

While victorious, Castro's forces suffered relatively large casualties to the inferior counter-revolutionary brigades. Nevertheless, he became consumed with a fear that the United States would continue its efforts to overthrow his government, including an invasion of its own. Some historians believe that by not canceling the invasion, and more importantly losing the fight, Kennedy created the environment that would make the Cuban Missile Crisis inevitable eighteen months later. Certainly, with the U-2 disaster the year before and now this fiasco, the CIA's reputation plummeted and the credibility of the United States was diminished in the eyes of the international community, including some allies who voiced comments such as "Kennedy has lost his magic," and "It will take years before we can accept the leadership of the Kennedy administration."[8]

In his transition meeting with President Eisenhower, the president-elect was warned that no easy problems come to the president. After the Cuban Missile Crisis, a seasoned President Kennedy wistfully mused to a reporter, "I would say that the problems are more difficult than I had imagined. There are greater limitations upon our ability to bring about a favorable result than I had imagined them to be. It is much easier to make the speeches than it is to finally make the judgments."[9]

The dramatic failure of the invasion would have a profound impact on the young president, and the humiliation would transform his leadership and relationship with the JCS and the CIA when the Cuban Missile Crisis presented a greater challenge in the coming months. When asked about the failed Bay of Pigs operation, a chastened president said:

> I looked at those four stars and that wide gold braid and those other three braids next to the wide one. I figured the selection process that they had to go through in the military – you know, having been in the military myself – I just figured these fellows have got to know what they're doing when it comes to bringing in the diplomatic and political side of the house. They're trained to fight, and it was my job to know that. I abdicated my responsibility when I left the decision up to them as what we should do.[10]

That advice also came from the best and brightest minds in CIA covert operations, but planners ineptly disguised the American involvement in the operation. As with the Gary Powers' U-2 incident, it would be exposed, thus diminishing the credibility of the president and America worldwide. For the CIA planners, as well as the president, to assume an invasion of Cuba would not be identified with the United States was absurd.

Fidel took approximately 1,200 prisoners while 161 of his forces died in combat. A total of 107 CEF fighters were killed.

President Kennedy, a man unaccustomed to failure, was devastated. Like Eisenhower before, who had to face the aftermath of the May Day U-2 disaster, Kennedy doubted himself, and confided, "If they think they're going to get me to run for this job again, they're out of their minds."[11] Author Ralph G. Martin writes in his book, *A Hero for Our Times*:

> Kennedy told Dave Powers, "I must have been out of my goddamn mind to listen to those people [CIA and JCS]." And later he told his adviser Ted Sorensen, "How could I have been so far off base? All my life, I've known better than to depend on experts. How could I have been so stupid to let them go ahead?"
>
> Defense Secretary Robert McNamara afterwards told him that the responsibility should be shared. "We could have recommended against it and we didn't."
>
> "Absolutely not," Kennedy insisted. "I'm the President. I could have decided otherwise. It's my responsibility."[12]

Taking responsibility for the failure was not viewed as strength of leadership by Nikita Khrushchev, who was emblematic of the Soviet style of government where leaders never admitted failure and cast blame on scapegoats. Some who have studied this era have concluded that this perceived sign of weakness gave Khrushchev the encouragement to introduce missiles into Cuba.

In a press conference on April 21, John F. Kennedy faced his critics with a memorable and oft-repeated remark. "There's an old saying that victory has a hundred fathers and defeat is an orphan." Surprisingly, the

American public rallied around the president, and in early May a Gallup poll showed that Kennedy had an astonishing 82 percent approval rating. With his famous Irish wit, the president said, "It's just like Eisenhower. The worse I do, the more popular I get."

EARLY CUBAN VFP-62 MISSIONS

After the Bay of Pigs fiasco VFP-62 was tasked to keep an eye on Castro's Cuba. There is very little official information on these missions, but they happened, as told by VFP-62 pilot, Capt (then Lt) Phillip "P.J." Smith:

Sometime in April 1962, Skipper George Winslow alerted me that we would be flying that weekend. I had no clue as to where we might be going. He briefed that if either [of us] went down the flight was to return to Cecil Field. As we continued out, just south of the Bahamas, I recognized that we were headed for Cuba. The skipper said that we would make some photo-runs, and they would be done on mike clicks – no voice commands.

We flew east, just north of Cuba, and on radar it would have seemed that we were a flight of two headed for Gitmo [the Marine Corps name for Guantanamo Naval Base]. We descended rapidly and turned onto a westerly heading and made a pass that took us within sight of Havana. Cdr Winslow never shared with me what our targets were, but after reading *One Minute to Midnight*, I now believe that we were looking for missile storage sites and new construction that was needed to support the missile build-up.

We did this two weekends in a row, having simulated an approach to Key West and then proceeded low-level west-to-east over Cuba. We launched from Cecil but recovered at Homestead AFB, Florida, where our film was off-loaded by people I never saw again.

I never really thought much about those flights until the VFW (Veterans of Foreign Wars) found the Navy Expeditionary Medal (Cuba) award in my service jacket and informed me. Skipper Winslow never told me that he had written that up, either – it was news to me.

A humbled, but angry, president and his brother Robert, the attorney general, were more determined than ever to destroy Castro and his communist regime. At a meeting with key administration officials in the White House on November 3, 1961, the president approved top secret plan Operation *Mongoose* by forming the so-called "Special Group (Augmented)" – a slightly expanded group of the National Security Council that oversaw covert operations. It was supervised by Robert Kennedy, who would provide an informal link between the group and the president. The group's objective was to undermine the Castro government by "stirring things up" on the island with "espionage, sabotage and general disorder."[13]

The CIA developed an operational force of approximately 400 people at its headquarters and at its Miami Station, and they had primary responsibility for the implementation of *Mongoose* operations. A major component of the operation was to have "the people themselves overthrow the Castro regime, rather than US engineered efforts from outside."[14]

"We were hysterical about Castro at the time of the Bay of Pigs and thereafter," noted Secretary of Defense Robert McNamara.

Now the stage was set. As a result of the May Day U-2 incident and the failed Bay of Pigs invasion, Khrushchev and Castro were emboldened to assess President Kennedy as weakened and indecisive and America as a paper tiger. This combined miscalculation and adventurism on the part of the United States, Cuba, and the Soviet Union would bring the world to the edge of World War III in the coming months.

CHAPTER 3

THE MILITARY BUILD-UP IN CUBA
JULY TO OCTOBER 15, 1962

After the failed Bay of Pigs invasion, Soviet Premier Nikita S. Khrushchev, Chairman of the Council of Ministers, seized the opportunity to expand communism to the Western Hemisphere and sealed a relationship with Cuba by offering to supply oil shipments (which the Americans had cut off), buy Cuban sugar and provide military assistance in the form of weapons and training. The latter was particularly valuable to Castro as his revolutionaries had never used heavy weapons such as tanks or antiaircraft guns. Early in 1962 Khrushchev offered Cuba aging medium-range Ilyushin Il-28 "Beagle" jet bombers (capable of delivering nuclear weapons), SAM installations, modern supersonic MiG-21 "Fishbed" fighters, tanks, and antiaircraft guns.

For decades historians have tried to determine who was the motivation behind the delivery of nuclear weapons to the island as part of the deal. In various interviews and written accounts, Khrushchev and Castro have taken credit or, alternatively, implicated the other in the decision. It is most likely that Khrushchev did, as he had the most to gain – but it hardly matters – because it is clear a Soviet nuclear presence off the coast of the United States served the purposes of both. For his part, Fidel saw it as a defensive shield against an inevitable American invasion. Author Tad Szulc gives us insight into his decision. "Castro's calculation was that, in effect, the threat of nuclear conflict would save him from a non-nuclear attack by the USA."[1]

In an extended interview with Szulc 24 years after the crisis, Castro demonstrated he had no regrets about the introduction of missiles to his island:

> We preferred the risks, whatever they were, of great tension, a great crisis," he said, "to the crisis of the impotence of having to wait, impotently, for a US invasion of Cuba. At least they gave us a nuclear umbrella, and we felt much more satisfied with the response we were giving to the policy of hostility and aggression toward our country. From a strictly moral as well as strictly legal viewpoint, as a sovereign country we had the right to make use of the type of arms we considered gave us a guarantee. And in the same way that the United States has bases in all parts of the world around the Soviet Union, we, as a sovereign nation, considered we had the absolutely legal right to make use of such measures in our own country."[2]

For Khrushchev, the consummate risk taker and survivor of the great purges and mass-murders instigated by Joseph Stalin, who had ordered the execution of tens of thousands of high-ranking party officials and military officers in the 1930s, he saw the installation of nuclear missiles so close to the United States as a means to quiet his Kremlin adversaries. The latter had been critical of his reduction of the Soviet armed forces (for economic reasons) and his courting good relations with America prior to the U-2 shoot-down. He also saw it as a means to narrow the missile gap with the USA.

What is difficult to understand, however, is how Khrushchev expected to get away with the complex operation of getting the missiles operational before the United States became aware of the threat? In hindsight, it seems he underestimated American reconnaissance capabilities – all the more strange since he was in charge of the Kremlin when Gary Powers' U-2 was shot down. Whatever he was thinking, he certainly miscalculated the likely American response. And, he believed he had the *right* to introduce these weapons to the Cubans, as he justified in his memoirs:

We hadn't given the Cubans anything more than the Americans were giving their Allies [referring to the Jupiter nuclear missiles placed in Italy and Turkey]. We had the same rights and opportunities as the Americans. Our conduct in the international arena was governed by the same rules and limits as the Americans.[3]

The arms deal was consummated in July 1962.

THE SOVIET AIR FORCE'S MOVE TO CUBA

In his book *Pages of History of the 32nd Guards - Air Fighter Regiment Awarded with Lenin and Kutuzov Orders*, Sergey Isaev writes a descriptive memoir of how Soviet Air Force commanders were informed of their deployment to Cuba. "We have decided to send you [on] a business trip to a hot, humid country. Any questions?" Maj Victor Sharkov describes the process of deploying the MiG-21s to Cuba:

> It took us more than a month to disassemble and load our airplanes – combat-capable MiG-21F-13s and two-seat MiG-15UTI trainers – detaching fuselages, preserving engines, draining fuel tanks, placing fuselages on dummy chassis, disconnecting tail plumage, etc., and then placing all that stuff into special containers.[4]

Lt Col Nikolay Pakhomov, Major Deputy Chief of Staff of the Soviet Regiment in Cuba, provides a colorful account of how the Russian pilots tried to disguise themselves to listening American electronic surveillance while on training missions in Cuba:

> We tried to communicate in Spanish [to the Cuban Air Controllers]. On one flight, the control gear failed to operate and the Russian pilot tried to explain in Spanish what was wrong, only to hear the Cuban flight controller curse, "What are you muttering there? Speak Russian. You're over a crocodile nursery. If one drops down there then in no time you will be gobbled up!"[5]

We now know from declassified CIA documents that cargo coming into Cuba by sea was being watched by US intelligence agencies during the summer months of 1962. Analysts followed crate-carrying vessels from European ports to Cuban destinations. Detailed shipping manifests and photographs of deck cargo provided evidence of a huge Soviet military build-up taking place. It became common for US Navy patrol squadrons, flying piston-engined Lockheed P-2 Neptune antisubmarine warfare aircraft, to make low-level reconnaissance passes over Cuba-bound Russian freighters. Chief photo petty officer William T. Hocutt, a photo interpreter for the Atlantic Intelligence Agency (AIC), detailed in an unpublished memoir how analysts utilized this photography:

> Many of the Soviet ships that carried freight to Cuba had deck cargo in addition to what was carried below decks. Sometimes the deck cargo gave a clue to what was below decks. Over the years, the intelligence community had developed books that contained photographs and drawings of vehicles which were associated with specific systems. By identifying the vehicles on the deck of a ship, we could sometimes figure out what equipment was in the hold. For example, we might see a truck with a box body on the deck of a ship. The Soviets had many variations of box body trucks. The location of windows and doors on the trucks were often unique. A box body truck on the deck could identify a specific radar system in the hold.[6]

Additionally, there were many reports of missiles in Cuba coming from Cuban refugees, but they often read like reports where the refugee was telling the interviewer what he thought the interviewer wanted to hear – most were not considered credible as a result. We will later see that the CIA was criticized for not taking these reports more seriously. One report that was not so easily dismissed occurred on August 31, when Senator Kenneth Keating, a New York Republican, delivered a charge from the Senate floor that offensive missiles were being installed in Cuba. The sources of his information have never been revealed, but at the time the CIA thought it was based on rumors or pre-election posturing. They dismissed it too.

Nevertheless, in September HUMINT sources (perhaps CIA agents) within Cuba reported seeing trucks transporting 8ft wide, 65–70ft long crates. And on September 9 Fidel Castro's personal pilot, Claudio Morinas, boasted, "We have 40-mile-range guided missiles, both surface-to-surface and surface-to-air, and we have a radar system which covers, sector by sector, all of the Cuban airspace and (beyond) as far as Florida."[7]

Fortunately, before September, the CIA was conducting U-2 flights each month over Cuba. This normally consisted of two passes – one pass usually penetrated the north coast and the other the south coast. In addition, US Navy ships and Marine Corps aircraft collected electronic intelligence (ELINT) on Cuban radar signatures and other communications.

A declassified CIA memorandum discussed the difficulty of getting approval for U-2 missions to check out these reports:

> In planning for any U-2 operations over well-defended, denied territory we were always aware of criticism that attended the U-2 incident over the USSR in May of 1960 [Gary Powers' shoot-down]. Also not helpful were two other incidents that served to sharpen the already existing apprehensions regarding U-2 missions – one involved the straying of a U-2 over Sakhalin [in the Soviet Union] on August 30th [1962], and the other resulted in a Chinese Nationalist U-2 being shot down over the China mainland on September 8th [1962].[8]

Tim Weiner described in his Pulitzer Prize winning book *Legacy of Ashes* how the detrimental ramifications of the spyplane's missions were viewed with "universal repugnance, or, at the very least, extreme uneasiness" at the State Department and the Pentagon. McGeorge Bundy, the president's national security advisor, railed, "Is there anyone involved in the planning of these missions [who] wants to start a war?"[9] Bundy was emblematic of President Kennedy's trusted "New Frontiersmen" – a slogan for the administration's fearless energy. He was highly intelligent and full of self-confidence, having been a Harvard junior fellow at the age of just 22 and dean of the Harvard Arts and Sciences faculty at 34.

During this prelude to the crisis, "these serious reservations regarding the use of the U-2 included expressions of extreme concern from some public leaders over the increase in tension that might result from overflights, and others voiced the opinion that such flights were illegal or immoral."[10] International law left doubt about the legalities, but some feared that intrusions of sovereign airspace could be considered an act of war. Despite these concerns, it was recognized that surveillance was necessary for US national security, and two U-2 missions were flown, covering a large swath east to west, on August 5 and 29.

On August 25, CIA Director John McCone urged Lt Gen Marshall Carter, CIA deputy director, to propose low-level reconnaissance flights over certain Soviet-Cuban installations in order to obtain detailed technical information.[11] McCone had been a successful California industrialist and Atomic Energy Commission official during the Eisenhower administration. After the Bay of Pigs, President Kennedy replaced Allen Dulles with McCone to gain control over the CIA. Secretary of Defense Robert S. McNamara was not receptive to the low-level missions. McNamara was president of the Ford Motor Company when President Kennedy recruited him to join his administration. At Ford, he and other brilliant managers were nicknamed the "Whiz Kids" for their analytical approach to solving problems.

Gen Carter recognized that the U-2 was vulnerable to SAMs, while cloud cover over the target areas often meant large gaps in photographic coverage. Missions were scheduled for days when there was less than 25 percent overcast (75 percent of the target area was cloud free). All this was made more difficult by the fact that it was hurricane season in the Caribbean.

Despite McNamara's reticence at this stage of the crisis, the intelligence community anticipated the need and eventual approval for higher-resolution low-level photography and started to prepare for it. CIA documents reveal that on August 27, Gen Carter asked Gen Lyman Lemnitzer, Chairman of the JCS (he held this position until October 1, 1962), about the possibility of low-level photography using (USAF) RF-101 and (US Navy) F8U-1P (RF-8A) aircraft. At the

Special Group Meeting of the United States Intelligence Board (USIB) on August 30, Gen Lemnitzer raised the issue and said that the use of RF-101 or F8U-1P aircraft flown by US pilots would be feasible from a military point of view.

Gen Carter pressed the point by indicating that other types of photography did not give sufficient detail and precise identification of certain types of equipment. After some discussion, the Special Group agreed to take cognizance of this matter and requested it be reopened at an appropriate time when specific targets and information needs could be identified.[12] With support from the JCS and the USIB's consideration, senior-level planners at the Pentagon started to prepare for the eventual approval of low-level (tactical) surveillance.

Meanwhile, the photography from the August 29 U-2 mission showed eight SAM sites being set up (some could be operational within a week or two) in the western third of the island. ELINT had detected radar signals compatible with these types of missiles, but now it was visually confirmed too. Analysts projected that as many as 24 SAM sites might be set up – the entire island would soon be protected by the sophisticated Soviet missiles that had brought down Gary Powers' U-2.[13] Fearing political implications for the upcoming midterm elections, President Kennedy directed Gen Carter (in McCone's absence, the acting director of the CIA) to sequester the SAM report. The president ordered, "Put it in the box and nail it shut."[14]

Soviet Ambassador Anatoly Dobrynin met with Robert Kennedy on September 4 and delivered a message from Chairman Khrushchev to President Kennedy. "There would be no surface-to-surface missiles or offensive weapons placed in Cuba." In response to Dobrynin (and Senator Keating), President Kennedy released a statement revealing some of the newly obtained intelligence:

> That SAMs and substantially more military personnel than previously estimated have been detected in Cuba – there is no evidence of the presence of offensive ground-to-ground missiles, or of other significant offensive capability. Were it otherwise, the gravest issues would arise.[15]

On September 5, a U-2 mission was flown covering a similar path as the August 29 flight, but heavy cloud cover was encountered. Nevertheless, some interesting intelligence was obtained from the cloud-free areas, as noted by photo interpreter William Hocutt:

> At AIC, we identified a new installation following the September 5 U-2 mission. It appeared to be an anti-ship missile system east of Havana, near Banes. We had no reference material for a similar Soviet system. We sent a message to the Defense Intelligence Agency (DIA) with a report about this new installation. We received a reply with directions that we make a list of everyone who had knowledge of this site. We were not to speculate or discuss the installation. A few days later we received a message from DIA releasing us from these restrictions. The message also identified the site as a cruise missile launch site.[16]

In the abovementioned DIA security concern noted by Hocutt, it is clear that President Kennedy's clampdown on security-related Cuban intelligence was taking effect. A strict "need to know" protocol and the rigid control of documents were intended to protect against security leaks. Many have guessed that Senator Keating's information was leaked by the Defense Department.

Meanwhile, on September 8, the Kremlin high command sent the following list of weapons and instructions to its commander in Cuba. The communiqué noted that tactical nuclear weapons were being shipped to Cuba, and their launch authority had been delegated to local-level commanders in the event of an American invasion:

- Squadron of Il-28 bombers and 6 [tactical] nuclear bombs
- Three battalions of Luna [tactical surface-to-surface cruise missile, known also as the "FROG"] missiles, with 6 launchers, 12 missiles, 12 special warheads [nuclear] and 24 conventional missiles
- In the event of an enemy landing on the island of Cuba and of the concentration of enemy ships with amphibious forces off the coast of Cuba in its territorial waters, when the destruction of the enemy is

delaying [responding to further actions] and there is no possibility of receiving instructions from the USSR Ministry of Defense, you are permitted to make your own decision, and to use the nuclear means of the Luna, Il-28 or FKR-2 [cruise missile] as instruments of local warfare for the destruction of the invaders on the Cuban territory and to defend the Republic of Cuba.[17]

This bone-chilling memorandum giving officers authority to launch nuclear weapons was signed by R. Malinovsky, USSR Minister of Defense, and M. Zakharov, Chief of the General Staff, and was not rescinded until October 27 – the next-to-last day of the crisis. We will see later that the presence of tactical nuclear "Lunas" in Cuba was not discovered until VFP-62 photographed them on October 25.

The frustration over bad weather caused Gen Carter, on September 10, to address a memorandum to McNamara requesting tactical-type reconnaissance against Banes (in central Cuba), where cruise missiles were suspected but remained unidentified. McNamara delayed a decision "until the results of CIA high-level reconnaissance became available."[18] His repeated refusal to allow low-level reconnaissance flights to take place was most likely based on the belief that U-2 flights were undetected. The same would not be the case for low-level flights. He did not want to reveal American knowledge of Soviet secrets until the time was right.

With the accumulating evidence, John McCone started to connect the dots and began asking the question what were the SAMs protecting? He voiced a concern that the SAM sites were there to protect Cuba from overflights that would discover the future introduction of offensive weapons, including medium-range ballistic missiles (MRBMs). He was the only one who thought so. On September 16, a National Intelligence Estimate (NIE) stated that the introduction of offensive weapons was unlikely because the Soviets would not introduce offensive weapons and risk a US intervention. Furthermore, the NIE concluded it would be contrary to Soviet foreign policy and high-level statements. All too soon, · McCone would be proved correct.

Bad weather delayed the next U-2 flight until September 17, and this mission produced no useable photography because of cloud cover over the target. Weather continued to bedevil mission planners until the September 26 and 29 overflights – three more SAM sites were discovered. All of these delays caused a 21-day gap in photography at a critical time in the military build-up.

Even so, the increased frequency of U-2 flights caused Secretary of State Dean Rusk to voice concern with the international implications if an airplane were to be shot down. He managed to get agreement that U-2s should try to gather photo intelligence by flying off the coast of the island. It was believed that the slant-range of the SAMs was 25 miles, so the U-2s flew that far off the coast. The photography obtained from these peripheral flights was not very good for interpretation, but the October 5 mission revealed one additional SAM site, and a sortie 48 hours later discovered four more.[19]

On October 11, worrisome signs appeared in the photos – an island-wide SA-2 defense was being constructed. The Director of Central Intelligence showed the president photographs of the crates that presumably were carrying Il-28 medium-range bombers and were deck loaded on a ship which had arrived in Havana a few days before.[20] The president was briefed on the accumulating intelligence and he made the remark, "We'll have to do something drastic about Cuba."[21]

On October 12 operational control of U-2 overflights of Cuba was transferred from the CIA to the USAF's Strategic Air Command (SAC). This was a controversial reversal of President Eisenhower's mandate, which had required non-military pilots to fly U-2s because aircraft flown by USAF pilots intruding on foreign airspace was technically an act of war.

With the August and September U-2 photos showing a rapid increase in SAM sites, old invasion and strike plans were ordered to be updated. At the time the crisis erupted, there were three contingency operational plans (OPLANS) for action against Cuba. OPLAN 312-62 was an air strike plan for the rapid response of US air power, involving 500 aircraft, against Cuban SAM sites, airfields, and military locations. OPLAN

314-62 was a joint military operation by combined US Navy/Marine Corps, USAF, and US Army forces that called for a simultaneous amphibious and airborne assault in the Havana area by a joint task force within eighteen days after receipt of the order to execute. In response to the evolving Cuban situation, OPLAN 316-62 was developed as a short-reaction version of OPLAN 314 (operations to commence five days after ordered).[22] Tactical photographic reconnaissance was a key component of those plans.

Adm Robert L. Dennison alerted Cdr Ecker to prepare for low-level reconnaissance. The secret operation was codenamed Operation *Blue Moon*. Capt Ecker recalls getting the squadron ready:

> I had the command for only about five weeks before the outbreak of what came to be known as the Cuban Missile Crisis. The first inkling that I had of the initial alert came on Saturday, October 13, 1962. Cdr Bob Koch and I were fishing in Doctor's Inlet just south of Jacksonville, Florida. Bob was my senior photographic officer. We were out in the middle of the lake at about 1000 hrs when suddenly a small boat came charging out from the shore and a person aboard informed us that we had an urgent telephone call from Washington.
>
> We immediately went ashore, took the call, and found that the person calling was a naval officer in the Pentagon. This officer, Cdr Bud Edmisten, was a friend of ours who was stationed in what is called the National Reconnaissance Office, or the NRO. Bud had previously alerted the JCS to the squadron's new forward-firing photographic capability, and he wanted to confirm that the pictures Bob had sent him, shortly before, were for real, and that we could do the job as depicted. We were asked, "Can you really take pictures this good?" Bob confirmed and affirmed, "Not only yes, but HELL YES!"

When it became obvious that intelligence requirements were not being met, it was decided to discontinue off-the-coast (peripheral) U-2 missions. With clear skies over Cuba, SAC successfully flew a short south-to-north flight on October 14, covering the suspect area west of

Havana (near San Cristobal), where mission planners thought the SAM site was most likely to be operational. The flight, flown by USAF Maj Richard Heyser, was the first to discover the construction of MRBM sites.[23] Khrushchev's gamble to get the MRBMs operational before the Americans detected them had failed.

Following CIA procedures, the processed photographic film of the October 14 six-minute flight over Cuba was delivered the following day to the NPIC under armed guard. As NPIC photo interpreters (PIs) rolled the 928 images across their light tables, their special optical devices revealed long covered objects that would confirm the CIA's worst fears – three Soviet MRBM sites were being constructed near San Cristobal. The PIs counted eight large MRBM transporters and four erector launchers in tentative firing position. Key officials at the CIA and White House were alerted and they decided to brief the president in the morning.[24]

Months later it would be learned that on October 14 there was no more than a ten-day supply of photographic film on hand in the entire country to meet the impending stepped-up demand for U-2 aerial reconnaissance.[25]

The USA, Soviet Union, Cuba, and the world were only a day away from the start of the Cuban Missile Crisis.

CHAPTER 4

THE CUBAN CRISIS BEGINS
OCTOBER 16–22, 1962

Presidential National Security Advisor McGeorge Bundy briefed President Kennedy in his bedroom at 0845 hrs on Tuesday, October 16. "Mr President, there is now hard photographic evidence that the Russians have offensive missiles in Cuba." While the previous months' intelligence hinted of this possibility, the doomsday scenario had become a reality. The nation was only weeks away from the midterm Congressional elections and the president had been fending off Congressional pressure to "get tougher with Cuba." As he was digesting the emerging threat, in the back of his mind he was concerned that if the news got out and became part of the election, his freedom of action would become limited. At 1145 hrs he convened an emergency meeting of what would be called the Executive Committee of the National Security Council (ExComm) to consider strategies for dealing with the new national security threat in Cuba. The first day of the Cuban Missile Crisis had begun.

The National Security Act of 1947 created the National Security Council (NSC) to unify the military departments and to create a central organization to provide presidents with the information and advice needed to confront national security issues. Kennedy, after the Bay of Pigs, recognized that foreign policy had to be centralized in the White House, not the State Department. He installed a "Situation Room" in the White House where all cables coming in from intelligence sources could be retrieved.

Unlike Eisenhower, he favored small working groups of trusted advisors, representative of the various governmental departments. Thus, ExComm would become central to the crisis management in the days ahead.

The first ExComm meeting started with a briefing by NPIC Director Arthur Lundahl, who disclosed the photographic details of the October 14 mission to the shocked group of advisors:

> Photo interpreters discovered two areas in the Sierra del Rosario Mountains, about 50 nautical miles [1 nm is 1.2 statute miles] west southwest of Havana, which appear to contain Soviet MRBMs in the early stage of deployment. The site includes 14 large tents, 15 smaller tents, and 75 vehicles of different types. The most significant vehicles at this site are six canvas-covered trailers of 80ft in overall length, which are of the general size and configuration of those used to transport the Soviet SS-3 and SS-4 (ballistic missiles). A second site 5 nm east of the first site contains four specially configured vehicles or pieces of equipment, which could be used for missile erection in a field environment.[1]

Arthur M. Schlesinger in his highly documented book *Robert Kennedy and His Times* mentioned that it was at around this time that two new metaphors made their debut into the popular lexicon – "hawks" and "doves." Among the latter were Robert Kennedy (after his initial shock and anger at the news of the MRBMs dissipated), Robert McNamara, Roswell Gilpatric (the deputy secretary of defense), George Ball (the undersecretary of state), Ambassador Llewellyn Thompson, Theodore Sorensen (presidential advisor and speech writer), Adlai Stevenson (UN ambassador and former presidential candidate), and Robert Lovett (the former secretary of defense during the Korean War).

Heading the hawks were former secretary of state in the Truman administration, Dean Acheson, Gen Maxwell D. Taylor (chairman of the JCS, CJCS), the JCS (with the exception of Gen David Shoup, the commandant of the Marine Corps), John McCloy (former viceroy in Germany), Assistant Secretary of Defense Paul Nitze, and, initially, Treasury Secretary Douglas Dillon and John McCone.

The hawks favored air strikes against the missile sites and the MiG airfields. The doves cautioned that such an action would carry the "Pearl Harbor" effect, and the United States would be blamed for attacking a small country. Hundreds, perhaps thousands, of Russians and Cubans would be killed, and the likelihood of a Soviet response was great.

Kennedy, aware of the tendency to suppress or tailor opinions – even by powerful men – in the presence of the president, included advisors with known philosophies different from his own. Gen Taylor, a former Army chief of staff, was highly regarded by the president and was brought back from his retirement to serve as his special military advisor and CJCS. Dean Acheson was a sharp-tongued no-nonsense type who held a low opinion of the Kennedys and their style of decision-making. John J. McCloy, Kennedy's reliable troubleshooter and diplomat, was President Franklin D. Roosevelt's assistant secretary of war and president of the World Bank.

As the crisis evolved, some advisors would switch their opinion before the crisis ended or otherwise remain an enigma. McGeorge Bundy at first was for strong military action and later got cold feet. Robert McNamara flip-flopped depending on the intelligence briefings and the U-2 shoot-down. According to Schlesinger, "Dean Rusk was equally perplexing. At first he was for a strike; later he was silent or absent."[2] Transcripts of the ExComm meetings reveal that Vice President Lyndon B. Johnson contributed very little of substance and rarely took a position.

The following exchange is important because it would have a big impact on the direction President Kennedy would take:

President Kennedy: How effective can the take-out [air strike against the missiles] be, do you think?

Gen Maxwell D. Taylor: It'll never be 100 percent, Mr President, we know. We hope to take out a vast majority in the first strike, but this is just not one thing, one strike, one day, but continuous air attack for whenever necessary, whenever we discover a target.[3]

Sobered by this discomforting military appraisal, the president realized that he could not risk a retaliatory nuclear response by any missiles not destroyed in the air attack. At the conclusion of the ExComm meeting President Kennedy weighed up three options:

– Military: launch air attacks against Cuba (OPLAN 312) followed by amphibious and airborne landings (OPLAN 316).

– Combined military pressure and diplomatic negotiation: aimed at compelling the Soviets to remove the missiles.

– Different combinations of force and negotiations: an emphasis on inducing the Soviets to withdraw their missiles in exchange for US concessions.[4]

Option three was rejected as premature (it was too early to make concessions) and the consensus settled on option two. However, over the following days the president would conclude that an eventual solution would require US concessions – a view that was out of step with many of his advisors, with the exception of Adlai Stevenson, the "super-dove." At this first meeting Stevenson annoyed everyone, including President Kennedy, by advocating removing the US Jupiter nuclear missiles in Turkey, along with evacuating the Guantanamo Naval Base.

As illustrated by the U-2 reconnaissance photos included in this book, it was hard for laymen to discern the details that trained PIs were able to. At one point during his briefing, the president asked Lundahl, "How do you know those are missiles?" Lundahl responded, "By the length, sir."[5] In his posthumous book, *Thirteen Days*, Robert Kennedy describes the reaction to the U-2 photos:

Photographs were shown to us. Experts arrived with their charts and their pointers and told us that if we looked carefully, we could see there was a missile base being constructed in a field near San Cristobal, Cuba. I, for one, had to take their word for it. I examined the pictures carefully, and what I saw appeared to be no more than the clearing of a field for a farm or the basement of a house. I was relieved to hear later that this was the same reaction of virtually everyone at the meeting, including

President Kennedy. Even a few days later, when more work had taken place on the site, he remarked that it looked like a football field.[6]

While the points of interest in the photographs may have appeared to be a "clearing of a field" or a "football field" to the members of ExComm, the expert PIs saw something more ominous – a military installation of the most dangerous kind.

Photo interpretation is both an art and a science. The NPIC analysts could identify an object by its shape, or use libraries of old photos of the military parades in Moscow to determine the lengths of the Soviet missiles and compare them to what they were now seeing in the U-2 imagery. Even so, they were having difficulty distinguishing between the Soviet SS-3 and SS-4 MRBMs (725- and 1,300-mile ranges, respectively). They knew from existing intelligence that the SS-3 was last produced in 1959 and the SS-4 was still being produced. Additionally, the fact that no training firings of the SS-3 had been done since October 1961, whereas 30 SS-4 missiles had been launched so far in 1962, and equipment around the missile site was inconsistent with that required for the SS-3, supported their conclusion. The MRBMs were SS-4 "Sandals" (the Soviet designation was R-12), and they could be operational in days.[7]

The SS-4 was fueled by liquid-storable propellants, guided by a completely autonomous guidance system, propelled by a single-stage rocket, and had a separable reentry warhead. It was 73ft long (with a one megaton nuclear warhead) and 5ft in diameter. Flying at 5,200mph, it would climb to outer-space and the reentry vehicle would disconnect and complete the 1,130-mile trip from Havana to Washington, D.C. in approximately 14 minutes – hardly enough time to evacuate the capital. CIA analysts at the time told President Kennedy that the SS-4 had a 1,200-mile range, but missile historians subsequently discovered that the range had been extended by 1962 to 1,300 miles. In fact, the SS-4 could just reach Manhattan, 1,290 miles from Cuba.

The processed photographic film from the reconnaissance aircraft took the form of a negative image – black and white were reversed in all shades of intensity. The negative film was then duplicated into a positive copy – images were displayed as normally seen by the human eye. PIs worked from the positive film on a light table with a stereoscopic viewer.

The electronics controlling aerial cameras timed their exposures according to the aircraft's speed and altitude such that each frame had a 60-percent overlap of the ground from an adjacent frame. The overlapped images, on each frame, were exposed from a slightly different angle as the reconnaissance airplane traversed its target. For an RF-8A traveling at 500–600 knots (1 knot is 1.2mph) at 500–1,500ft above the target, the cameras could be exposing photos at the rate of three per second. It was literally possible that cameras recycling at such high speed could tear themselves apart. This difference in angle of two adjacent frames provides the PI with a pseudo three-dimensional perspective through the stereoscopic viewer. In 3D everything took on new clarity, allowing the PI to see footprints in the dust and to measure the depths or heights of objects on the ground.

PIs were trained to look for hints that pointed to hidden information. A well trained PI can tell the difference between a housing development and a military installation at a glance.[8] The placement of vehicles, the number, size, and organization of tents, the existence of cables running between buildings, the existence – or absence – of security fences and gates, the shape and placement of storage tanks provide clues that the PI can turn into knowledge.

A PI could determine from the depths of tracks in the mud what kind of truck made them and how heavy the load was. Likewise, shadows and shapes could reveal much about the object being analyzed. Disturbances of the earth could point to underground installations. Infrared film (film sensitive to heat radiation rather than light) could show objects that had been moved or detect camouflage from vegetation. Trees or vegetation that had been cut to cover objects emitted different levels of heat radiation than naturally growing plants, thus exposing hidden objects.

The job was tedious and hours could be spent "checking Cuba's monotonous plains and cane fields looking for signs of new activity: a car parked near a peasant's thatched shack will attract attention – they would strain to spot all major movements of men and any slightest change would come under suspicion."[9] To facilitate this the PI would often go back to look at previous days' coverage of the same area and compare them for changes.

He also used the shadows of objects to gain information, and for that reason photo missions were often flown in the morning or afternoon when the shadows were at their most pronounced. And, PIs were trained in architecture and engineering:

> The layout of objects is important, for it can tell a PI what a building is used for. He can tell what is going on inside by the position of buildings and wings, entrances and loading platforms, the shape of roofs, the position of smoke stacks, or their absence, the position of windows, or their absence, the material of the buildings and roofs. He can even tell in which part of what building each operation is being performed.[10]

These techniques, along with years of experience and training, make PIs the indispensable middlemen in the photo intelligence endeavor. Their track record provides the confidence in their analyses, which in turn produces the hard intelligence that makes aerial photography such a valuable intelligence tool.

Former CIA analyst Dino A. Brugioni describes how VFP-62 got selected for the first *Blue Moon* mission:

> At 1300 hrs on October 16, a meeting was held in McNamara's office to formulate plans for the stepped-up U-2 reconnaissance missions that the president had directed. In addition to McNamara and Gen Carter, CIA officials concerned with the U-2 program and ranking USAF officers were present. The feasibility of low-altitude reconnaissance missions was also discussed. Questions arose as to which organization should fly them, and what numbers of low-altitude missions would be required. The NPIC's Arthur Lundahl was consulted by Carter, and he recommended that the US Navy had the best low-level capabilities. It was no secret in Washington that the US Navy had the best totally integrated low-altitude reconnaissance capabilities in support of the intelligence community.

Lundahl recommended that the US Navy's Light Photographic Squadron No [sic] 62 (VFP-62) be selected if low-altitude reconnaissance was instituted over Cuba.[11]

Adm George W. Anderson, chief of naval operations, concurred with Lundahl's observation that VFP-62 was the finest low-level photo-reconnaissance organization in the US military. Curtis A. Utz writes in his historical account of the Cuban crisis, *Cordon of Steel*, "The men of the Navy squadron were especially skilled in navigation, instrument flying, and intelligence collection techniques, and their aircraft, F8U-1P [RF-8A] Crusaders, were equipped with special cameras."[12]

Brugioni describes some of the US Navy's advantages:

The US Navy had devoted considerable time and effort in developing an effective low-altitude jet reconnaissance capability. Cdr (later Capt) Willard D. Dietz had perceived and pushed for the development of small-format aerial cameras (70mm and 5in) to replace the US Navy's bulky (9 x 9 x 18in format) K-17 and K-38 cameras used in World War II and Korea. His proposal was to reduce the external size of the camera systems so that ongoing fighter aircraft designs could accommodate a viable camera suite without major airframe alterations. His foresight would pay off during the crisis.

Dietz worked with the best research-and-development personnel in the US Navy, and these men collaborated closely not only with the camera manufacturers and research laboratories but also with the reconnaissance units and the fleet. Their efforts had resulted in the development of the Chicago Aerial Industries Inc.'s KA-45 and the KA-46 6in-focal-length framing cameras with a film width of 5in and a capacity of 250ft of film. The system had been installed in the F8U-1P [RF-8A] Crusader and fully tested and proven.

Pilot training in low-level navigation and photographic reconnaissance had been implemented in naval fleet squadrons since 1953. This training, coupled with the proper camera system, onboard computers, and optimized low-level performance of the aircraft, provided a capacity of more than

100 miles of photographic coverage, traveling at 100ft to 500ft above the ground within a 250nm radius from the operating base.[13]

Adm George Anderson, members of his staff and the NPIC drafted a cable to be sent to VFP-62's commanding officer:

Recent U-2 photography of Cuba has revealed the existence of certain installations that may require further evaluation through the use of large-scale, high-resolution photography by LANT F8U-1P [RF-8A] aircraft. A high-level decision whether or not to conduct the required overflights is expected shortly. Once authority is granted for these operations, rapid accomplishment becomes essential. Therefore, operations should be conducted from the closest base to the area of interest, consistent with operational factors. Guantanamo, however, will not be used except for emergencies. Recommend Key West. Your comments/concurrence is desired.[14]

Lt John DeChant, VFP-62 pilot and squadron maintenance officer, took pride in getting the unit ready:

The Cuban Missile Crisis was no crisis for VFP-62 because we could do anything asked of us. We did not have much build-up time for the Cuban missile crisis. We had 29 aircraft, with seven detachments using 20 of them, and two non-flyers that had been cannibalized for parts. We only had two or three jets with the new 5in format Chicago Aerial Industries cameras installed that worked. The mission called for eight camera-ready birds, and we had seven. I had never seen so many FLASH messages [messages with war-time priority – no delay].

We got the word late Tuesday (October 16), and the first mission was set for the following Sunday (October 21) at 0800 hrs for eight camera-ready birds to take off from Key West. It took a minor miracle, but we did it.

We had to ensure that everything would work at high-speed (550–600 knots) and low-level (500ft). We didn't usually operate that way. It was truly an exciting time!

On this first day of the crisis, VFP-62's Lt Cdr Newby Kelt was at the end of the runway at Cecil Field ready to take off in his RF-8A (BuNo 145604) on a routine morning training flight. After a normal departure, Kelt was lowering his wing and increasing speed to about 300 knots when, all of a sudden, he heard a loud "Bang! Bang!" Immediately, his instruments warned of an engine failure (later determined to have been caused by an electrical generator tearing itself apart and flinging metal parts into the engine's turbine blades). Still at low altitude, Lt Cdr Kelt pulled the ejection seat's curtain and departed his aircraft. He made a few swings in the parachute before hitting the ground hard. Although he survived the landing, Kelt injured his back.

Today, the 82-year-old matter-of-factly states, "The ejection seat is not designed to keep you from getting hurt, just to keep you from getting killed." He would return to flight duty in time to fly some of the later Cuban missions. Already short of RF-8As, VFP-62 could have used that airplane in a few days.

At 1430 hrs on October 16 the *Mongoose* Special Group met, with the attorney general opening the meeting. Robert Kennedy expressed the president's "general dissatisfaction with Operation *Mongoose*. In a year results were discouraging: there had been no acts of sabotage, and that even one which had been attempted, failed twice." Kennedy announced he was going to give Operation *Mongoose* more personal attention.[15]

During the following days, U-2 photography continued to provide increasingly bad news. At the October 18 ExComm meeting, Lundahl presented enlargements of photographs taken on the October 15 U-2 missions that showed an even greater threat – two intermediate-range ballistic missile (IRBM) sites under construction at Guanajay, with fixed launchers zeroed in on the eastern USA.

The SS-5 "Skean" IRBM (Soviet designation R-14) had a range of 2,500 miles and carried a one-megaton nuclear warhead. IRBMs would threaten all but a small northwest corner of the USA. McNamara felt that this development demanded more prompt and decisive action.[16] At the time, the CIA incorrectly estimated the range of the SS-5 to be 2,400 miles. In addition a fourth MRBM site had been discovered at San

Cristobal, and PIs counted 21 crates of Il-28 "Beagle" medium-range bombers waiting to be assembled at San Julian airfield. The following excerpt from Lundahl's briefing provides a good example of the intelligence information obtained from the U-2 photographs:

Mr President, gentlemen, the first and most important element I would seek to call your attention to is a new area hitherto never seen by us some 21 miles to the southwest of Havana, which we have at the moment labeled a probable MRBM/IRBM launch complex – sites that look like the things we have been seeing in the Soviet Union. There are two pads, here and here. They are separated by 750ft, and there is a control bunker with cable spars going into a small building inboard of each of the pads. There is no equipment on the pads yet – they are under construction.

The security fence has been superimposed around the place, and on 29 August – the last time we went over this area – the ground just started to be scratched. The orientation of the axis of the pads is 315 [degrees], which will bring you into the central (area) of the United States [Lundahl is pointing out the target of the missiles]. We call it IRBM, sir [Lundahl explains how he came to that conclusion]. The location of the control bunker between the pair of pads might indicate IRBMs.

The impression one would gather is that there is some sense of speed with which they are proceeding with construction [determining the operational status of the missiles was key information for the president].[17]

This insight into the photographic intelligence briefings helps us understand the ongoing tensions and priorities among the intelligence and military organizations, needing continuous photo missions to draw their conclusions, and their political counterparts (State Department) worried about the incursions, the chances of an airplane being shot down, and the resultant international implications. To determine the pace of construction and other intelligence, the PIs had to compare daily photo runs of areas of interest. This technical necessity for intelligence gathering was not always apparent to the decision makers who were empowered to authorize the missions – in particular Dean Rusk, who, as a poor consumer of intelligence, remained a fainthearted supporter of reconnaissance.

A Joint Evaluation of the missile threat, based on U-2 photography from the October 14 and 15 missions, revealed that at least sixteen SS-4s were deployed in western Cuba (two launch sites). The sites contained unriveted, field-type launchers, which relied on mobile erection, checkout, and support equipment. So far there was no positive evidence of nuclear warheads, nor had weapons storage facilities of the standard, highly secure Soviet type, been identified. Nevertheless, the analysts had to assume that nuclear warheads could be available as the sites became operational. They estimated that the SS-4's nuclear warhead weighed approximately 3,000lb and had yields in the low megaton range.[18] The SS-4 and SS-5 were indeed a serious threat, as the following data starkly reveals:

Their nuclear payload was approximately one megaton – equivalent to the explosive power of one million tons of TNT. This made the weapons 80 times more powerful than the Hiroshima atomic bomb – the latter, dubbed "Little Boy", was a 12.5-kiloton (12,500 tons of TNT) weapon – and equal to 48 Nagasaki ("Fat Boy") atomic bombs (21 kilotons each).

The atomic explosion would completely destroy everything within a one mile radius of ground zero.

The temperature at ground zero would briefly be hotter than the surface of the sun and vaporize everything.

The SS-4 and SS-5 had an accuracy of about one-to-two miles, hardly a concern with their immense devastation capability.

What the heat and radiation would not destroy, the blast effects would (generating 600mph winds).[19]

During the Thursday, October 18 briefing, the president questioned Lundahl further if the uninitiated could be persuaded that the U-2 photographs showed offensive MRBM missiles. Lundahl stated "probably not, and that we must have low-level photography for public consumption."[20] Within ExComm, the military representatives were continuing to press for low-level photography. Those missions were delayed several days so that the Soviets would not be tipped off that the US government knew their secrets, thus causing them to expedite construction and installation of nuclear warheads on the missiles. President Kennedy was playing for time while strategies and options were being debated and developed.

By this third day of the crisis there was a growing consensus in ExComm for a blockade, with the exception of a few hawks led by Dean Acheson, who said, "Khrushchev had presented the United States with a direct challenge, we were involved in a test of wills, and the sooner we got to a showdown the better." He favored cleaning the missile bases out decisively with an air strike. Secretary Dillon agreed. Also favoring a strike, Gen Taylor, representing the Joint Chief's view, said, "It was now or never for an air strike. If it were to take place Sunday morning [October 21], a decision would have to be made at once."[21]

It was at this time that Robert Kennedy made his eloquent rebuttal that would greatly influence the president, set the course, and win him respect, even from his adversaries. He said in part:

> It would be very, very difficult indeed for the president if the decision were to be for an air strike, with all the memory of Pearl Harbor and with all the implications this would have for us in whatever world there would be afterward. For 175 years we had not been that kind of country. A sneak attack was not in our traditions. Thousands of Cubans would be killed without warning and a lot of Russians too.

Robert Kennedy favored *action*, to make known unmistakably the seriousness of US determination to get the missiles out of Cuba, but he thought the action should allow the Soviets some room for maneuver to pull back from their over-extended position in Cuba.[22] Many of his contemporaries believed his brother's compelling argument swayed the president's decision for a naval blockade.

At the same time, Pentagon military planners made a first-hand verification of the US Navy's ability to conduct the sustained low-level reconnaissance of Cuba that was required. Cdr Koch, nicknamed "Daddy

Photo," was a hard-nosed, driven individual who always demanded the best of his men and equipment. Koch assured the visitors that VFP-62 had great aircraft, outstanding pilots and maintenance personnel, and a fine technical team, and that the Fleet Air Photographic Laboratory (FAPL) at NAS Jacksonville was a first-rate processing facility.[23]

A few days after the Washington VIPs left, a new Eastman Kodak high-speed film processor arrived at FAPL. It had been requested for months, but *Blue Moon* gave it new urgency. Lt(jg) Bill Kortge recalls the rapid installation of the new equipment:

> Cdr Koch, Lt(jg) H. C. Ogles and I were standing around watching Lt "Red" Haggerty jack-hammer a groove into the floor of the lab for chemical lines. A call came in from the skipper. He wanted me in Key West – a transport was leaving Cecil Field at 1100 hrs.[24]

Blue Moon required a squadron liaison officer to be sent to Washington, D.C. to coordinate last minute details. Lt Cdr Tad Riley describes that part of the story:

> As for me, the missile crisis began in August 1962. I had just returned from a six-month Mediterranean cruise as officer-in-charge of the USS *Saratoga* (CVA-60) VFP-62 detachment [Det 43] and was assigned the position of squadron training officer. As such, I was responsible for the type of training flights we flew. Up to that time, we were more concerned with high-altitude photography, but Cdr Ecker directed me to revise the syllabus to emphasize high-speed low-level reconnaissance. He also told me to familiarize myself with various possible low-level profiles over Cuba from NAS Cecil Field or Key West, and be ready to conduct a briefing at any time. These instructions were classified, and nothing was to be in writing.
>
> Later on the afternoon of October 17, as I was driving out of the squadron's parking lot for home, the Skipper flagged me down and told me to fly to Andrews AFB in Washington, D.C. ASAP. He gave me a phone number to call when I got there. He said he would file a flight plan for me and I could go supersonic in spite of the normal restrictions on

making sonic booms over land. I was airborne in about 30 minutes and landed at Andrews 45 minutes later, which I remember was at about 1800 or 1900 hrs.

Andrews was in the process of conducting a hurricane flyaway because there was a storm heading their way, and things were a little hectic, so I had trouble getting a phone to make my call. A Navy captain answered and when I told him who I was, he wanted to know what was wrong and why couldn't I get to Andrews. He couldn't believe I was already there! Anyway, he had to lean on the base duty officer to assign a driver to deliver me to a back entrance of the Pentagon. They didn't want anyone to see me because I was in flight gear, and some of the press, aware that something was up, were watching the main entrance for unusual activity.

I was taken to a room where there were about four Navy captains. They began asking questions about our capabilities to get coverage of locations they had marked on a map of Cuba. Every once in a while one of them would go to the next room with information that I had given them, and once or twice an officer would look in and ask me another question. I got a glimpse through the open door and saw a bunch of admirals and generals. The only one I was able to recognize was Gen LeMay of the Air Force. At no time was there any reference to what the targets were.

After an hour or so, there was a discussion about whether I was too tired to fly back or should they bring in a cot so I could get some rest. Believe me, there was no way I could have slept at that point, so they marked up a map, with various locations in Cuba indicated with a Magic Marker, for me to take back to Cecil. At Andrews, the duty officer was so adamant that I evacuate my airplane to NAS Memphis that he caused me to finally accept a flight plan for this location. Once airborne, I canceled my plan and proceeded to Cecil, arriving at about 0100 or 0200 hrs on the 18th. I was met by the Skipper and Cdr Bob Koch, who was the squadron photo guru. This started the whole thing as far as VFP-62 was concerned.

Photographic intelligence on October 19 – the fourth day of the crisis – again provided more bleak news. Three coastal defense sites had been identified in Cuba, two of which were considered operational. Observed were cruise missiles that had a range of 35 to 40 miles, and could be fired in about ten minutes in an alert status, with subsequent firings from each launcher at five-minute intervals. By then there were also 24 surface-to-air SA-2 sites, most of which were now operational.[25]

While the crisis continued to heat up, New York attorney James B. Donovan had been tapped by the White House to negotiate with the Castro regime for the release of the 1,113 Bay of Pigs prisoners (some of the captured died of their wounds or were previously released for humanitarian reasons). Donovan had lots of experience negotiating with the communists, having successfully arranged for the release of CIA U-2 pilot Gary Powers in exchange for Soviet spy Col Rudolf Abel (the latter had been sentenced to 30 years and Powers ten years).[26] Castro was demanding $53 million worth of medicine in addition to $2.9 million in cash for prisoners that had already been released.

A poorly kept secret was the government's involvement with the negotiations. Robert Kennedy had secretly gathered a team of lawyers to assist Donovan's efforts. When met by reporters as he returned from Havana, Donovan insisted he was a private citizen representing an organization called Cuban Families Committee for Liberation of Prisoners of War.

Finally, on October 19, Capt Ecker received his orders:

At my location, air intelligence officers, or AIs, began to arrive from Washington with target folders. As the CO, I took the number one target, San Cristobal, plus two others of lesser importance for which I would be responsible. Each pilot available was assigned three targets, with each target being covered by at least three individuals.

At noon on Friday, October 19, I received orders to depart home base and stage to NAS Boca Chica, Key West, Florida. I and 11 other pilots arrived in Key West early on the afternoon of the 19th, and we expected to fly our missions as soon as we refueled. However, we ended up waiting a few days before executing our first mission.

Rear Adm Rhomad McElroy, who was the senior officer present, told me that I was in a standby position, and that we would go nowhere until he personally released us. When I asked him about when we could expect to be released, he merely answered, "I don't know." As soon as I got back to the group I told them to relax, and then called back to Cecil and told the XO, Cdr Bob Coulthard, to send a detachment ASAP, and have them prepared and equipped for an indefinite stay. This was not a big deal as we were used to forming detachments. I then arranged for quarters, transportation, and working spaces for the pilots and the crew. As I recall, all of the accommodations were pretty crude.

Meanwhile, back at the squadron, it had been shaping up into a normal holiday-routine weekend, but after my call all hands were informed that there would be a regular duty section, as well as a standby duty section. This was the first indication to many people that the Cuban Missile Crisis was coming home to VFP-62. Some of the men had made plans for the weekend that involved trips that were personally vital, or pleasure trips with their families. These had to be cancelled if they involved travel more than 50 miles from Cecil. So the men broke dates, canceled appointments and stowed their civilian clothes back into their lockers.

Thus began many long hours of hard work and the formation of additional detachments to be loaded on all the carriers in their home ports – one on just two hours' notice. And the load they left behind was borne by those who stayed home, both at the squadron and in the families. Here it is appropriate to reflect back and to pay special tribute to all the wives who coped so well with the routine chores, but who also prepared for emergencies, setting in stores of food, jugs of water, and gas in the cars, and with never a moment of panic showing as they kept the home fires burning.

In spite of the hardships most unit members were glad that the situation had come to a head. All had sensed that something big was happening with all the unusual activity and visitors. They were ready for the call and eager to answer. This was a total action by the entire squadron, which clearly revealed its capability to accomplish a difficult mission with alacrity!

Naval forces were starting to head for the Caribbean. As reported in *Cordon of Steel*:

On the 19th the world's first nuclear-powered aircraft carrier, USS *Enterprise* (CVAN-65), left Norfolk unexpectedly. A US Navy spokesman stated she sailed to escape the effects of Hurricane "Ella," but the press, always watching for unusual military moves, was skeptical because no other ship left port at the same time. Over the next three days, radar picket destroyers USS *William R. Rush* (DDR-714), USS *Hawkins* (DDR-873), and USS *Fiske* (DDR-842) left NAS Mayport, Florida, to join the carrier as escorts. *Enterprise* joined with the super carrier USS *Independence* (CVA-62) on October 20.[27]

Mrs Kit Ecker tells how she learned that something important was happening:

> Shortly after Bill assumed command of the squadron, I was settling into my new home and assuming the duties as the wife of the commanding officer. Bill seemed to be spending more and more time at the squadron. One day I made a frantic phone call to him to come home as soon as possible – the plumbing was not working and I needed help. I remember him sitting on the edge of the bathtub trying to clear the plumbing. The first indication that I had about something important happening was when Bill looked up with a sense of excitement and told me that many people were coming down from Washington to assess the Cuban situation. He could not tell me more, as it was Top Secret, but that he would be gone for a few days.

The problem of remedying the shortage of airplanes in the squadron was partially resolved by requisitioning the transcontinental record-setting RF-8A (BuNo 144608) at the Naval Air Testing Center at NAS Patuxent River, Maryland, this aircraft having been flown by Marine Maj John A. Glenn (later astronaut and senator) in July 1957. It was acquired and flown to Key West, where it undertook a number of missions over Cuba. Lt Cdr Riley remembers a brass plate in the cockpit designating the airplane's prominence – Maj Glenn had set a new speed record (725.55mph) in the photo-Crusader during "Project Bullet" (he flew faster than a bullet). Glenn's speed run will be discussed in more detail in Chapter 11.

On Saturday, October 20, a CIA National Intelligence Estimate provided an inventory of major Soviet weapons identified in Cuba – it was not good news:

– Four MRBM and two IRBM launch sites in various stages of construction.

– 22 Il–28 jet light bombers, of which one is assembled and three others have been uncrated.

– 39 MiG–21 jet fighters, of which 35 are assembled and four still in crates, and 62 other jet fighters of less advanced types.

– 24 SA–2 sites, of which 16 are believed to be individually operational with some missiles on launchers.

– Three cruise missile sites for coastal defense, of which two are now operational.

– 12 "Komar" class cruise missile patrol boats, all probably operational or nearly so.[28]

Capt Ecker describes the long wait prior to VFP-62 being cleared to fly its first mission over Cuba:

On Saturday, Sunday, and Monday, the 20th, 21st, and 22nd, we anxiously waited to fly our missions. While waiting, we sat around in our flight suits – we had no other clothes. The wives had sent us some money and I had commandeered a few vehicles for the pilots and crew to get around in. While in this holding mode, I remained in contact with the XO, and we kept the squadron functioning in spite of my absence.

While waiting, the photomates at Key West were continuously fine-tuning the camera systems in the airplanes. The photomates were not happy with the vacuum performance in the system as was configured in these aircraft. The vacuum system ensured that the film was perfectly flat against the plate, thus resulting in high-quality photography. Only hours before takeoff on our first mission, one of the photo chiefs, PHC Frank

Wolle as I recall, discovered a "slug" about the size of a nickel in the system. Why it was there no one knew. It had probably been inserted there from some previous camera configuration. The system would still have performed adequately, but now it was perfect for the first mission.

On Monday, October 22, 1962, at about 2000 hrs, President Kennedy addressed both the nation and the world about the crisis, and spoke of his intention to implement a naval blockade – he used the more subtle term "quarantine" – effective from 1000 hrs on Wednesday, the 24th (see Appendices).

EVACUATION OF GITMO DEPENDENTS

Personnelman Third Class George Montgomery, who would not report to VFP-62 until after the crisis was over, found himself caught up in events while assigned to auxiliary seaplane tender USS *Duxbury Bay* (AVP-38), which was on a training cruise in the Caribbean at the time. *Duxbury Bay* was one of four vessels – the others were tank landing ship USS *Desoto County* (LST 1171), stores ship USS *Hyades* (AF-28), and transport USNS *Upshur* (T-AP-198) – assigned to evacuate hospital patients, women, and children. George tells his story:

Monday morning, October 22, four ships were assigned to evacuate 2,400 of the 2,800 dependents at Gitmo, as a second battalion of Marine reinforcements were being put ashore by US Navy amphibious ships – *Duxbury Bay* took on 351. The "Dux" was the smallest of the ships, and the slowest, so the others had to remain with the "Dux" until Wednesday, after getting well out of the area.

The age of the passengers aboard "Dux" ranged from babies in incubators to a couple of senior citizens. Most everyone wore summer clothes, or came from the recreational areas – swimming, playing ball, not from home "neat and clean." Most were not prepared for the evacuation. A full complement of ship's crew numbered 15 officers and 175 enlisted on board – adding 351 more was a tight squeeze.

We had games, potato peeling, movies, more games, and more potato peeling. And when I say "we," I mean that the dependents were working right along with the ship's personnel. The bunks were assigned to the dependents with the exception of one isolated compartment, and only one head [rest room] was available for the crew. Most of us slept topside, and we were able to get to our bunks for clothes at certain times of the day. It was more than cool before we got to Norfolk. The dependents received some cold weather clothing from the Red Cross and support groups when we were close to Charleston, South Carolina. This was transferred over from a supply ship.

It is amazing what people can do when situations arise that are out of the ordinary. Everyone pitched in and attitudes were excellent.

All four ships cleared the docks by 1630 hrs, just hours before President Kennedy went on the air to announce the threat in Cuba. His television address was also broadcast to all ships, including the aircraft carrier USS *Forrestal* (CVA-59) at anchor in the Bay of Genoa, Italy. One hour before the speech, an order went out to place all forces worldwide at increased readiness DEFCON-3 (Defense Condition, with DEFCON-1 being war). On short notice *Forrestal* weighed anchor and set to sea, stranding some crew members who were on liberty tours – they had to be flown out to meet the ship later. VFP-62's photographic intelligence officer Lt(jg) (now Capt) Adam Miklovis had a state room near the ship's forecastle, where the anchor gear was located. Miklovis remembers, "It was late when I was rudely awakened by the sound of the anchor rumbling inbound."

This writer remembers seeing his first nuclear bomb being rolled out on *Forrestal*'s hangar deck, under Marine security guard. They looked "high-tech" – almost an artful shiny-metallic streamlined device – being not very big, but distinctly different from any other bomb belying their incredible destructive capability. The Marine guards, all sporting 0.45cal semi-automatic sidearms, made it clear to stand back. Later, these "special munitions" were hung under jet bombers, cordoned off, and kept under constant Marine armed guard.

The reason for the arming of *Forrestal*'s bombers with nuclear weapons was the concern that the Russians would retaliate by striking the nuclear Jupiter missile sites in Turkey and Italy. The sixteen Jupiter medium-range weapons had a similar range and explosive power as the SS-4, and were owned by the Turks. However, their nuclear warheads were under US control. As a precaution, the president directed the JCS to send the following message to the US Commander-in-Chief, Europe:

> Jupiter [nuclear] warheads in Turkey and Italy are not to be released if the missiles come under attack, and if they are in danger of being taken by our angry allies, destroy them.[29]

An additional concern was that the Russians might also blockade West Berlin. There was a real chance that a nuclear confrontation might erupt in Europe, so Sixth Fleet had to be prepared. *Forrestal*'s commanding officer made an announcement of the ship's increased readiness to execute any mission required by the crisis. We were warned not to make reference to the ship's war preparations in our letters home. All hands knew we were now in dangerous times.

The threat in Cuba that President Kennedy faced, as he sat down to deliver his address, was 24 MRBM launchers at six bases, 12 IRBM launch pads at three bases (still no IRBM missiles per se had been found) and 22 of 24 SAM operational.[30] If one drew an arc with a radius of 1,300 miles (the accepted range of the SS-4) from San Cristobal, the cities of Philadelphia, Pittsburgh, St Louis, Oklahoma City, Fort Worth-Dallas, Houston, San Antonio, Mexico City, all of the capitals of the Central American nations, and the Panama Canal were threatened (this is shown in a map in the Appendices).[31]

As usual with presidential decisions and announcements, the president's address received a varied reaction. Some skeptics believed that after weeks of reports of a military build-up in Cuba from Senator Keating and the media, President Kennedy's announcement was politically timed to influence the midterm elections. Overall, public reaction was supportive and rallied behind the popular president.

When President Kennedy ordered a naval quarantine of Cuba, the US fleet was on its way within hours. One ship's deployment mirrors the *Forrestal*'s rapid setting to sea, the destroyer USS *Blandy* (DD-943) shoving off so quickly from Newport that it left a number of its crew behind, including the paymaster and its money bags. Destroyer Squadron 16, based at Mayport, Florida, canceled all leave and alerted sailors to return to their ships.[32] Adm Dennison ordered all attack submarines in the Atlantic Fleet to load for wartime operations and disperse to waters north of Charleston. In Washington, D.C., Adm Anderson asked Canadian, British, and several Latin American navies for help with locating Soviet ships and submarines in the Atlantic.[33]

People in the Soviet Union learned about the president's speech after the Kremlin propagandists had filtered out certain details. Radio Moscow did announce the president's proclamation of a "blockade" and the US military preparations underway in southern Florida. The US embassy in Moscow boarded up its windows in preparation for any violent reaction to President Kennedy's address. Outside, there were some noisy student demonstrations, otherwise Moscow seemed normal. At the Kremlin, Khrushchev lashed out with the warning, "The Soviet government regarded the violation of freedom of the seas as an act of aggression, which pushes mankind towards the abyss of nuclear missile war."[34]

Watching the president's address in the Bachelor Officers Quarters at NAS Key West, Cdr Ecker and his pilots knew "Fightin' Photo" would be arriving at tree-top level over Castro's Cuba in the morning.

CHAPTER 5

EXECUTING THE MISSION
OCTOBER 23, 1962

Navigation in the early 1960s was somewhat primitive by today's standards. There was no Global-Positioning System to assist pilots to find their targets. The RF-8A did not even have radar and the U-2 pilots occasionally used celestial navigation – steering by the stars in an age of nuclear weapons, supersonic aircraft, and satellites! We will see later that a U-2 pilot's navigational error almost triggered tragic consequences during the most critical day of the crisis. Each *Blue Moon* mission required a flight plan that had been approved in Washington, D.C.

As a senior VFP-62 officer and flight leader, Lt Cdr Tad Riley describes how he led his wingman to the assigned target:

> The flight plan plotted a track on maps to the designated latitude and longitude of the point of interest. Prominent landmarks, such as roads, bridges, railroads, and factories, showed up on standard aerial charts. Flying low and fast, as we did, we navigated by looking for those landmarks. I had a little trouble because a highway on our maps of Cuba that would have indicated a freeway at home turned out to be the equivalent of our country roads. Also, our maps showed only a few railroads, but in fact there were many railroads that serviced the sugar cane plantations.
>
> It was basic piloting to use a compass and second hand to time each leg of the flight plan. These were the same methods used in those days by our bomber crews training to deliver nuclear weapons.

Since in most cases we were only "feet dry" [over land] for 15–20 minutes, we had enough film to allow us to turn on our cameras when we crossed the beach and leave them on until we were "feet wet" [over water]. That simplified things a little, and let us keep our heads out of the cockpit. We kept our speed up to about Mach 0.96 [96 percent of the speed of sound, which is 738mph at sea level] because that was the maximum speed we were told the Cuban MiG-15s, MiG-17s, and possibly MiG-19s could go in level flight. Those airplanes were only supersonic in a dive, and were alleged to be hard to handle at, or near, Mach 1.

What is amazing about Riley's account is that VFP-62 pilots (and probably no one else in the squadron) had no access to U-2 photos of their assigned targets for the early missions. U-2 photography was given a Top Secret *Talent* security classification – *Talent* was the classified codename (even the codename was classified!) for distribution control of U-2 photography. Access to U-2 photos of the targets would have been extremely useful. Instead, mission pilots were told to "look for suspicious activity, such as construction sites, military vehicles, or other unusual goings on." Looking back on this bizarre situation, one would think that these pilots, risking their lives, would have been provided with all they needed to accomplish their missions.

When the September and early-October U-2 photography started to show an increase in SAM construction, President Kennedy tightly restricted distribution of the intelligence, hence the security classification *Talent* granting access to only those with "a need to know." Apparently, that did not include US Navy photo-pilots flying over Cuba. Understandably, the president was trying to avoid leaks to the press, public, and senators who were trying to score political points in the midterm election. For example, when a SAM site was identified, only the coordinates of the location were transmitted to the aircraft carrier commanders.

The AIC provided intelligence support, including photo interpretation, to Adm Robert L. Dennison, Commander-in-Chief Atlantic and Atlantic Fleet (CINCLANT and CINCLANTFLT). The following unpublished account written by Chief Petty Officer William T. Hocutt, who was then assigned to AIC, recounts one of the many strange events associated with the crisis:

> We learned that the USAF's Tactical Air Command [TAC] had printed annotated [U-2] photographs of the missile sites in Cuba without *Talent* classification. These photographs were being provided to all USAF pilots who might be called on to bomb Cuba. They sent one copy of these pictures to AIC too. The photographs were marked "Top Secret, No Foreign Dissemination." We assumed that the USAF had received authorization to downgrade the classification of these photos.
>
> The photos were sent to the NAS photo lab with a request to make copy negatives and enough prints for all of the aircraft carriers. The photo lab worked all night, and the next morning we had a stack of prints 4ft x 4ft and 3ft high. We planned to send these photos to various US Navy commands, particularly the aircraft carriers, but ran into a problem. The AIC executive officer said that he was told by someone on the CINCLANT staff that he would be court-martialled if we sent out those photos. The XO was told by the staffer that HE KNEW that the photographs had a higher classification than what was marked on them.
>
> As a result, those photos sat in our office for several days. They served as a reminder that USAF pilots had photographs of their major potential targets in Cuba, but US Navy pilots did not.[1]

Talent security restrictions provided obstacles for the VFP-62 mission planners as well. The job of a mission planner is to provide a detailed plan for the pilot to follow as he navigates toward the target. It starts with the location of entry and takes the optimum approach to the target, avoiding SAM sites, large cities, and obstacles of all kinds (power lines, antennae, mountains, and so on). Good maps are essential, but having actual photos of the target area would be optimum. The following account, attributed to Lt Cdr Bernard W. "Bill" Kortge (then a Lt(jg) VFP-62 photo interpretation officer) in Chief Hocutt's memoir illustrates the problem:

On Tuesday, October 16, 1962, Capt Ecker called: "Bill, there is a plane due here at 1100 hrs. A Lt(jg) Joe Parker from the AIC is on it, and I want you to meet him." I responded, "All right Commander, I will be there. Joe and I have been bumping into each other since 1949."

I am at the tower as the airplane taxies up, and I meet Joe as he walks toward the building. I divert him toward the hangar [VFP-62's administrative offices and ready room were in the squadron's hangar]. "It is not a long walk to the hangar Joe, and on the way how about telling me what is happening?" "Not here Bill," Joe responded, indicating something big was up.

In Cdr Ecker's office I get through the formalities and then the skipper asks Lt(jg) Parker the purpose of the visit. Joe gives a brief on the fact that offensive weapons have been detected in Cuba, that there are three MRBM sites under construction and that VFP-62 is being asked to obtain low-level photographs for the intelligence community. Parker continues, "Commander, I have the information on the sites and will stay to help you prepare flight plans." I had a feeling that not all of what Joe had to say was news to Cdr Ecker.

Cdr Ecker gave us our orders: "Bill, you and Joe get started on this, and let me know in a couple of hours how you are doing."

On the way to the PI space, I told Joe I wanted him to meet Cdr Koch, and as we passed the PI office I stuck my head in and told the crew to take off for lunch and to not come back until the next morning. After introducing Joe, I mentioned that he and I had some work to do planning some missions. Cdr Koch didn't blink an eye. He knew. I turned to Joe, "Okay Joe, let's go to work."

In my office, I locked the door behind me and asked Joe for the material he had. He walked to the other side of an 8ft x 10ft table, set his briefcase up with the back of the lid towards me, took out a folded sheet of paper, locked his case, walked back to where I was and handed it to me. I glanced at the numbers on the sheet – three sets of coordinates. "Joe, is this all that you have for me?" "That's it Bill, it should be all you need." I believe that I was upset at this point. I told him no it wasn't all I needed. I would need some maps.

Our map case had 25 copies of all the maps that covered Cuba, and it didn't take long to figure out which ones I would need. With the site plotted, I then looked for a feet dry and a feet wet point, then started planning the route. It was shortly after 1400 hrs when I finished the first route. Several times during the afternoon when I made a change on a turning point, I would ask Joe what he thought. He would go to his briefcase, look at something, then come back and tell me it looked good to him.

"Joe, I am going to go get a cup of coffee and ask the skipper to come and look at this. I want his opinion before I spend all afternoon and evening on the next ones." It took about a half-hour to brief the flight – the skipper was satisfied. About 1615 hrs the skipper called to tell me that he was going home, and that he wanted a call an hour before I finished. It was a little past 1900 hrs when I called the duty officer and a little before 2000 hrs when Cdr Ecker showed up in his flight gear. After briefing him on the second and third plans, the three of us walked out of the hangar together, the skipper to head north [here Kortge is inferring that Capt Ecker flew to Washington, D.C. with the plans] while Joe and I headed home. As I drove toward home, I thought, "Why didn't they just send a message with the coordinates?"[2]

The next morning (Wednesday, October 17) at 0700 hrs, Lt(jg) Kortge received a call and learned that Washington had rejected VFP-62's flight plan. Lt Cdr Kortge continues the story:

The VFP-62 duty officer called, "Bill, the commanding officer wants to see you, and where is Mr Parker?" "Joe is with me, we will be right out."

The skipper gave us the bad news, "Bill, they did not like it – you need to do a different plan." I was shocked, "What didn't they like sir?"

"Bill, I don't know and I couldn't get anyone to say what the problem was." "All right sir. I will look at it from a different direction."

Late that night the second set of flight plans were flown to Washington, D.C. by a VFP-62 pilot. The next morning Kortge learned the plans had been rejected again. He tells how the flight plan problem was finally resolved:

I started to think. There is something that I don't have and I need it. Back in my office I sent the crew home again, sat down at my desk, lit up a cigarette, enjoyed my smoke and coffee then started in a new direction.

"Joe, get Cdr Boroughs (Operations Officer at AIC) on the phone. I need to talk with him."

"Bill, I have Cdr Boroughs on the line."

"Commander, Bill Kortge here. It's been a long time, and I don't have very much time right now. I've had two sets of plans turned down for no reason that I've been given. I want to see the [U-2] pictures that Joe has in his case. You know that I know what they are, and unless I can see them and figure out what is wrong, then we are looking at more lost time."

"Bill, you've got them. Put Joe back on." When Joe hung up the receiver I said, "I am going to the ready room and I am going to drink a cup of coffee before I come back. There are razor blades in that drawer. I expect to see the pictures when I return." He sanitized the pictures by removing the caveats [the classified codename *Talent* and notations, which Kortge was not cleared for] and burned them.

I asked Joe, "Did they change the code word [security codename that allowed access to U-2 photography in 1960] after Powers was shot down?" I was a little more than upset.

I pulled out a set of fresh maps and started drawing in the target detail from the [U-2] photos. Then I plotted the coordinates of the target – they did not fit!

"Come on Joe, help me out here! Get Boroughs again!" [Boroughs came back on line.] "Commander, give me the map reference that your people are using. I think we have wasted two days due to stupidity."

"I will call you right back Bill."

In a very short time he called back, and as he read off the reference I could have cried. "Commander, we are using the wrong map edition. Where do I get the correct one?" Boroughs responded, "They are at the map and chart supply at NAS Jacksonville." [NAS Jacksonville was about 10–15 miles from Cecil Field.]

"Thank you Commander, it should work this time."

I started filling out a requisition, asked Joe to go tell the duty officer I needed a driver right now, and then left to see if Cdr Koch was in the office. He was. I explained what was going on, got his signature, and went to the ready room, where the duty driver was waiting. I told the driver that if there was any problem that he was to call me.

The driver called from NAS Jacksonville and said, "Mr Kortge, they say you cannot have the maps you ordered." [In the US Navy, "Mr" is an appropriate title to address an officer below the rank of commander.]

"Okay, fine, now I want to talk to whoever is in charge over there, the Department Head or Division Officer."

A lieutenant came on line and I asked him what the problem was and why I couldn't get the maps that I ordered. His response: "They are pre-positioned war material and therefore cannot be distributed." [This indicates that the maps were associated with the air strike or invasion OPLANs.]

"Fine Lieutenant, I need your full name and file number." Then I gave him mine. "Lieutenant, I am going to make a telephone call and then I expect that you will receive a call. The caller will ask for you by name and I suggest that you be there to take the call. If after I make my call I find out that you will not be getting a call, then I will call and apologize. Do you have any questions?" He had none and said he would wait for a call.

"Quick Joe, get Cdr Boroughs again." I explained my latest problem to Cdr Boroughs, and when I finished he said, "Bill, it is taken care of." In a short time the driver called to say, "They are getting your maps now, and I will be out of here." I responded, "Don't speed and thank the Lieutenant for me."

I used the initial [October 16 flight] plans, transferred to the new maps, recalculated the turns and headings, and briefed Lt Cdr Jim Kauflin [Kauflin was one of the pilots that made the first mission over Cuba]. Joe and I went home and had a few.[3]

Receiving the news that Washington had finally approved the flight plans, Kortge triumphantly exclaimed, "It's a go! Joe is on his way back to Norfolk, 30+ men (the groundcrew) are on a transport headed for Key West and the photo-airplanes will leave this afternoon [October 19]."

This rather long, interesting but frustrating chain of events illustrates how security classifications and bureaucratic hurdles – in this case the clearance requirement *Talent* for U-2 photography – can hinder critical functions during an urgent military operation. Without Kortge's diligence and perseverance, VFP-62's first *Blue Moon* mission could have been jeopardized. Sometimes, one man can make a difference between success and failure. Bill Kortge and Joe Parker rose through the ranks from enlisted photomates – US Navy photographers – to so-called "mustang" officer rank. There were a few mustang VFP-62 pilots also. All were held in particularly high esteem by the enlisted men.

On October 23 at 1057 hrs, during the JCS meeting, the chiefs were told the White House had approved six (VFP-62) *Blue Moon* sorties. At NAS Key West Lt(jg) Kortge received the orders:

We were in the ready room, open for business. The groundcrews are swarming around the aircraft like bees around a hive. Our airplanes take up the ramp adjacent to the tower. The windows have been covered with sheets of plywood and they are covered with maps. Initially there were only three points plotted on the maps [longitudinal and latitudinal coordinates for the first day's targets].

After 0800 hrs our phone rings. I answered with, "VFP-62 ready room." Voice on the phone: "Do not hang up your phone." Me, "Okay, whom am I talking to?" There is no response. The line is open but not responding. During the next hour or more, a voice came on and said, "You can man your aircraft and start your engines." Shortly after, not certain that there was someone on the other end of the line, I said to the voice, "We have eight aircraft ready for launch – six go-birds and two spares." Shortly, the voice came back and said, "Launch your aircraft."[4]

On the flightline the VFP-62 groundcrew of plane captains, maintenance personnel and photomates had checked and rechecked the Crusaders – some even sleeping under the aircraft overnight, waiting for the signal to begin flight operations. For the ground support team, time drags before and after flight operations – there's nothing to do except wait for the pilots to arrive and the order to launch aircraft. These long periods of downtime provides opportunities for "creative" activity. One VFP-62 metal-smith stamped out a stencil and painted in large black letters under the jet's air intake, "Smile, You're on Candid Camera," referring to a popular television program famous for catching the antics of people while off guard.

Then, finally, the tempo sped up like the frenzied last movement of a Beethoven symphony. The pilots arrived at their aircraft and the nervous anticipation surrounding the preflight inspections began. Some pilots showed their anxiety as they mounted their aircraft. It took three steps to get into the RF-8A. The first, a one-rung pull-down ladder for the left foot. Above it, two small steps popped out from the fuselage, just big enough for the soles of the right and left feet. Finally you grabbed the canopy rail and swung your right foot over the control column in front of the seat, being very careful not to hit any switches or levers, particularly the ejection seat. Then you slid into the snug, but comfortable cockpit.

The pilots were strapped in and the groundcrew brought the NC-5 start-up vehicles (one at each end of the flightline) alongside each aircraft and plugged them in, starting one and then moving on to the next. The turning up of the powerful Pratt & Whitney J57 engine that could generate a thrust of 10,200lb (16,000lb in afterburner) started first with a low, groaning howl, and as the turbine blades started to whirl faster, it became a loud, deafening high-pitched whine. The kerosene smell of JP-4 jet fuel filled the air and the heat blasting from the tailpipe warned of the fiery hell within. Everyone was brought to their peak of alertness as adrenalin pumped, paying attention to their responsibilities for anything that would "down" an aircraft.

Soon the roar of the eight Crusader engines (two spares) penetrated the groundcrew's ear protection, as the pilots and the plane captains went through their functional tests. This was a dangerous time to be around the Crusader. The engine's man-sized intake was low and menacing, giving the jet the nickname "The Gator" – it could easily suck a man into the engine, even at idle power. On a mission as important as this, the final check was for the pilot to start each camera and a photomate to check for proper shutter action through the camera bay windows. Once checked, a "thumbs-up" was given.

The US Navy places a high level of trust in its teenaged enlisted sailors who are responsible for the serviceability of the multi-million dollar equipment that it uses on a daily basis. Many of these young sailors are freshly out of high school and Navy technical schools. All are given responsibilities far beyond their years – each personally responsible for the pilot's life. As a consequence, strong bonds develop between the officers and enlisted crew. Relationships were more casual than in the traditional "black shoe Navy," while still adhering to respect for rank and military courtesies. Air Group personnel are issued special brown, rugged work shoes for use on slippery flightdecks, as opposed to the traditional black dress shoes worn by the regular surface US Navy, hence the nickname "black shoe Navy."

Finally, the RF-8s taxied to the runways and all was silent on the flightline. The first missions of *Blue Moon* were underway. Dino Brugioni describes VFP-62's tactics:

> The US Navy had found through experience that high-speed low-level reconnaissance could be best performed with two aircraft working closely together. The lead aircraft would be flown by a veteran pilot who was also an experienced navigator and pathfinder. The second aircraft, with a junior officer as pilot, would follow about 0.5 miles behind and about 0.25 miles to one side of the lead aircraft. The second aircraft would then maneuver as necessary to capture targets or objects that the lead pilot might have missed.
>
> VFP-62 was prepared to launch six aircraft per mission, flying three separate flight tracks, two aircraft per track. Each aircraft had [six] cameras: a forward-firing KA-[45 or] 46, three trimetrogen cameras providing

A fresh-faced Aviation Cadet William B. Ecker, wearing his winter flying suit. This photograph was taken in 1943 during the early stages of his flying training. *(Capt William B. Ecker collection)*

Recently promoted Lt(jg) Ecker (second from left) joined F4U-1D-equipped VF-10 in September 1944. He is seen here with fellow Corsair pilots Lt(jg)s Porter, Cordray, and Hays. These men all transferred to VBF-10 when it was established on January 2, 1945. Ecker sortied with Lt(jg) Wes Hays and two other pilots when the Condition 10 fighters were launched from USS *Intrepid* (CV-11) on April 16, 1945. *(Capt William B. Ecker collection)*

Ens Ecker (squatting, bottom right) poses with fellow neophyte fighter pilots in front of a war-weary F6F-3 Hellcat at NAS Vero Beach, in Florida, after completing his Operational Flight Training course in the summer of 1944. *(Capt William B. Ecker collection)*

USS *Intrepid* (CV-11) prepares to launch aircraft from CVG-8 during 1944. Weighing in at 27,100 tons, and capable of embarking up to 82 aircraft, the *Essex* class carrier *Intrepid* was commissioned into the US Navy on August 16, 1943. Decommissioned 31 years later, the vessel has been the home of the Intrepid Sea, Air and Space Museum in New York City since 1982. *(via Tailhook Association)*

Seen just off Okinawa on March 10, 1945, this F4U-1D Corsair from VF-10 was conducting an anti-kamikaze patrol when photographed. Lt(jg) Ecker flew a number of missions in similarly marked Corsairs from the deck of *Intrepid* prior to the vessel being badly damaged by kamikaze attacks on April 16, 1945. *(via Tailhook Association)*

Shepherded by an *Iowa* class battleship to left and several "small boy" destroyers, USS *Intrepid* (CV-11) turns into wind prior to launching a trio of F4U-1As from VF/VBF-10 in April 1945. *(via Tailhook Association)*

Debris litters the flightdeck of *Intrepid* following the kamikaze strike that effectively knocked the carrier out of the war on April 16, 1945. Lt(jg) Ecker had launched on a rescue mission for a downed aviator prior to CV-11 coming under attack. *(US Navy)*

Lieut. (j.g.) William B. Ecker
Bill would cease to be a fighter pilot on the deck if his hands were tied behind him. On the deck he flew every section maneuver so realistically with his two hands that his left hand spun in once and fractured two of his fingers. Bill, who expects to make the Navy his career, calls his home port Omaha, where, as Technical High's star all-around athlete, he developed the physique known in Boystown as "The Body." He was in the first eager group of ensigns awaiting to commission the squadron in AC in September 1944, after training at Corpus and Vero Beach.

This rather lighthearted pen portrait of a young Lt(jg) William B. Ecker appeared in the *Intrepid* cruise book at the end of the vessel's eventful 1944–45 combat deployment. *(via Robert Gandt)*

As this photo roster clearly shows, VBF-10 was a big squadron – typical of carrier-based fighter units in the last 18 months of the Pacific War. *(US Navy)*

Wearing a cumbersome and restrictive C-1A partial pressure suit during evaluation testing, Lt Cdr Ecker climbs aboard an F8U-1 Crusader of VF-174 at NAS Cecil Field in January 1958. This unit had become the East Coast replacement air group squadron for the Crusader just two months prior to this photograph being taken. Following his promotion to the rank of commander, Ecker served as VF-174's executive officer, prior to reporting to VFP-62 as its prospective commanding officer in January 1962. *(Capt William B. Ecker collection)*

Lt Cdr Ecker was a part of the pre-commissioning crew for the US Navy's first "supercarrier", USS *Forrestal* (CVA-59). This photograph was taken during the ship's Caribbean shakedown cruise in early 1956, when CVA-59 embarked Air Task Group 181. *(Capt William B. Ecker collection)*

VFP-62 F9F-6P Cougars fly over Malta in 1958 during Det 43's Sixth Fleet deployment with CVG-3 embarked in USS *Saratoga* (CVA-60). Note the jets' two starboard camera oblique windows. *(vfp62.com collection)*

The F2H-2P Banshee was the US Navy's first photo-reconnaissance jet. With three rotatable cameras, the Banshee gave VC-62 the first naval aircraft fully dedicated to aerial photography. Here, the port camera bay is open and a variety of aerial cameras are on display – note their size. In future years cameras would be made considerably smaller. *(vfp62.com)*

This photo shows the glossy sea blue scheme initially worn by VFP-62's F2H-2P Banshees at NAS Jacksonville. Note the wingtip external fuel tank and two oblique camera bay windows. *(vfp62.com)*

The RF-8A cockpit showing at top-center (round bluish lens) the viewfinder that the pilot used for centering his cameras on his target. In front of the control column is the camera bay control panel. The camera bay controls (clockwise, starting at the top left corner) are bay 1, bay 3, bay 4, and bay 2 (lower left). The bay 3 and 4 controls have a square rotary switch with various degrees of obliquity settings. Two round lights on each panel indicate status conditions – green (power on), red and amber indicating photos being taken. The film counters indicate the amount of film used and, finally, the toggle switches turn each camera on or off.

The Master Control panel for altitude and speed input is on the cockpit side console to the right, out of view. *(Ken Jack collection)*

Photographers Mate Second Class Bill Newby threads film into the bay 1 KA-45 camera. Note the film cassette of supply and take-up reels beneath his right arm. The camera mount above his right hand was specially fabricated by VFP-62 to fit the bulky camera in the tight quarters of bay 1. The camera bay cover is to the right and the window is just visible in the top-right corner of the photograph. *(Art Scarborough, PHC collection)*

A photomate prepares the KA-45 film cassettes for installation into the cameras. There is a film container in his right hand, while his left hand is touching the film mechanism that would be attached to the top of the camera. *(Art Scarborough, PHC collection)*

Right: A photomate installing a camera bracket in camera bay 4. This photo was shot from camera bay 3 (port side of the jet). Cameras shared space with other aircraft wiring and tubing, and they were heated to avoid condensation on the camera lens. The vertical window is under his right elbow. *(Cdr Peter Mersky collection)*

Below: A photomate sitting in the cockpit of an RF-8A checks out the jet's cameras. His left hand is on a control panel that is fitted with on-off switches, status lights, film footage meters and knobs for rotating the oblique cameras in bays 3 and 4. All four camera bays could be controlled from this panel. At the top center is the viewfinder lens that gave the pilot a complete view of the ground beneath his aircraft. *(Cdr Peter Mersky collection)*

The Lockheed U-2, with its distinctive long wings, was not a sturdily built aircraft. It was designed for one purpose only – long flights at very high altitudes (exceeding 70,000ft) and at relatively low speeds. Labeled the "Dragon Lady" by pilots for its dangerous flight handling characteristics, the U-2 discovered the first ballistic missiles in Cuba. This aircraft is a U-2F, one of only two involved in the crisis – most USAF airplanes at this time were original A-models, which lacked the U-2F's bigger engines and more advanced equipment. *(USAF)*

Most of the U-2s involved in the Cuban Missile Crisis were A-models identical to this particular aircraft. They were also operated in natural metal finish, as seen here. Delivered to the USAF in March 1957, 56-6701 served with the CIA and various reconnaissance wings. Upgraded into a B-model, the airplane was further modified into a U-2C in 1968. Following its retirement in 1982, the spyplane became an exhibit within the SAC Museum at Offutt AFB, Nebraska. *(USAF photo courtesy of Norman Polmar)*

F8U-1P BuNo 146864 served with VFP-62's Det 42 as part of CVG-8 embarked in USS *Forrestal* (CVA-59) during the carrier's Sixth Fleet deployment in 1960. Photographed here in March of that year, the jet bears VFP-62's distinctive "filmstrip" decals on both its wingtips and tail. The airplane's night photography flare compartment is shown above the national insignia on the forward fuselage, with the oblique windows for camera bays 2 and 4 below. Under the fuselage, the vertical windows for camera bays 2, 3, and 4, and the bay 1 forward-firing camera "bubble," can also be seen. Upgraded into an RF-8G, this aircraft (then assigned to VFP-62's Det 38) was destroyed in a midair collision with an SP-2H Neptune of VP-30 near Jacksonville Beach, Florida, on September 27, 1967. The pilot of the Crusader was killed, as were all five crew in the Neptune. *(Cdr Peter Mersky collection)*

The Chicago Aerial Industries Inc KA-45 5in format, 6in focal length camera. It had a between-the-lens shutter. The metal bracket bolted to the top and sides of the camera was not included in the VFP-62 installation in camera bay 1. *(Owen Miller, Battleship Park, Mobile, Alabama)*

This view of the KA-45 shows the film cassette mounted to the back of the camera. The cassettes could contain either 100ft or 250ft rolls of film. *(Owen Miller, Battleship Park, Mobile, Alabama)*

This photograph, taken by a U-2 on October 14, 1962, shows construction of the MRBM site that was designated San Cristobal No. 1 by the Pentagon. Located two nautical miles from Los Palacios, it was the second set of MRBMs found in Cuba. The small size of the objects of concern made it difficult for laymen to discern what they were seeing – a common problem with U-2 photography throughout the crisis. *(Dino A. Brugioni collection at National Security Archives, George Washington University)*

This U-2 photograph, taken on October 14, 1962, shows a truck convoy approaching a deployment of Soviet MRBMs near Los Palacios at San Cristobal. This was the first image identified by NPIC PIs on 15 October that showed Soviet medium-range ballistic missiles in Cuba. *(Dino A. Brugioni collection at National Security Archives, George Washington University)*

VFP-62 pilots and officers at NAS Key West, Florida, on October 22, 1962 – the evening of President Kennedy's television address to the nation. Cdr Ecker is holding the Cuban flag. The next day, six of these pilots would fly the first Blue Moon mission over Cuba. These individuals are, in the back row (from left to right), Lt Gerald Coffee and Lt(jg) William L. Taylor, center row (again, from left to right), Lt(jg) Terry V. Hallcom, Lt Thomas Cook, Lt(jg) John J. Hewitt Jr, Lt(jg) Barnard W. Kortge, Cdr William B. Ecker (CO), Lt Edmund M. Feeks, and Lt Arthur R. Day. In the front row (from left to right) are Lt(jg) Robert W. Chase, Lt Bruce C. Wilhelmy, Lt Cdr Tad T. Riley, and Lt Cdr James A. Kauflin. *(Capt William B. Ecker collection)*

A CIA reference photograph of a Soviet medium-range ballistic missile (designated an SS-4 by US intelligence and known as an R-12 in Soviet use) in Red Square, Moscow. *(CIA photo at National Security Archives at George Washington University)*

Robert Kennedy's handwritten note from the first ExComm meeting on October 16, 1962 shows his concern for the discussions on attacking Cuba. The note reads, "I now know how Tojo felt when he was planning Pearl Harbor." This note was sent to Mrs John F. Kennedy on November 15, 1966 to be given as a Christmas present to Ethel Kennedy, (RFK's wife). *(JFK Library and Museum)*

Cdr Ecker describes a Blue Moon mission. This photograph hangs in the National Air and Space Museum in Washington, D.C. *(Cdr Peter Mersky collection)*

Reviewing the mission photos at the FAPL Fleet Air are (from left to right) Lt(jg) M. Cox (VFP-62 PI), Cdr Robert Koch (VFP-62's senior photo officer), and two unidentified personnel. *(Cdr Peter Mersky collection)*

Cdr Ecker (left) reviews his mission photographs with Capt Harry G. John and Cdrs Robert Koch and R. Coulthard (VFP-62's executive officer). *(Cdr Peter Mersky collection)*

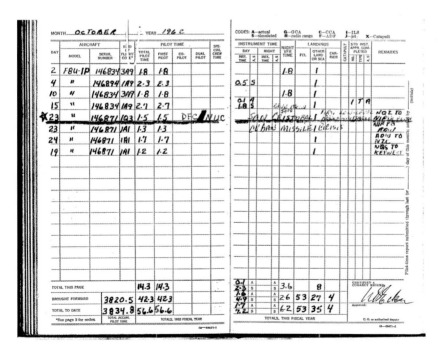

Cdr Ecker's flight logbook shows two entries for October 23, 1962 documenting the flight to and from Cuba, as well as the flight to Andrews AFB for his Pentagon debrief. The log of October 24 is the return trip to NAS Cecil Field and the one on October 19 (out of order) is his trip to NAS Key West. *(Cdr Peter Mersky collection)*

American, Cuban, and Russian delegates gather on the 40th anniversary of the Cuban Missile Crisis (Havana, October 10–12, 2002) outside the weapons bunker at San Cristobal MRBM site No 1, which had been photographed by Capt Ecker on October 23, 1962. *(Capt William B. Ecker collection)*

An October 23, 1962 VFP-62 low-level photograph of San Cristobal MRBM site No 1, showing the construction of a weapons bunker. Note the men on top of the bunker. *(Capt William B. Ecker collection)*

Another photograph from the highly successful series of low-level reconnaissance missions flown by VFP-62 on October 23. This photo of MRBM launch site No 1 at San Cristobal reveals in incredible detail missile erectors, cables, a missile shelter tent, fuel tank tractors, and other vehicles. *(Dino A. Brugioni collection National Security Archives George Washington University)*

A USAF RF-101C Voodoo photo–reconnaissance aircraft. A forward-firing camera port can be seen in the jet's nose, with an oblique window just forward and below the US titling. *(USAF)*

This undernose view of a VFP-62 RF-8A accentuates the jet's massive air intake, the small window in the nose cone for the cockpit viewfinder, the camera bay 1 window, and the stenciled message to Castro's armed forces, "SMILE YOU'RE ON CANDID CAMERA," *(Capt William B. Ecker collection)*

While this photo, taken in May 1963, suggests harmony between Soviet Chairman Nikita Khrushchev and Cuban President Fidel Castro after the Cuban Missile Crisis, Castro never forgave Soviet willingness to withdraw the nuclear missiles from Cuba. A marriage of convenience existed afterwards between the Soviet superpower and its communist satellite in the Caribbean. *(AFP/Getty Images)*

NPIC official David Parker points out photographic evidence at the UN Security Council on October 25, 1962. Ambassador Adlai Stevenson, seated second from right, describes the photos to Soviet Ambassador Valerian Zorin on the extreme left. The image that Mr Parker is pointing to is clearly a low-level photo taken by VFP-62 on October 23. *(National Security Archives at George Washington University)*

horizon-to-horizon coverage, and [two] vertical KA-45s. There was approximately 100ft of film [250ft was also used] in each camera; some 3,600ft would therefore be exposed by the six aircraft. The commanding officer of the squadron, Cdr William B. Ecker, along with Lt Cdr Tad T. Riley, Lt Cdr James A. Kauflin, Lt Gerald Coffee, Lt Bruce Wilhelmy, and Lt(jg) John Hewitt, were tapped to fly the first low-level mission over Cuba. They were briefed on their penetration and exit points, checkpoints, targets, and possible opposition. Communication and electronic procedures were also reviewed, as well as escape and evasion.[5]

Lt Cdr Tad Riley describes mission preparation for the VFP-62 pilots involved in the first *Blue Moon* operation:

While still at Cecil Field, before deploying to Key West, the *Blue Moon* crew was issued "war time" khaki flightsuits to replace the orange ones we had previously worn. We were also told to strip our wallets of everything but our Geneva Convention Cards and a small amount of cash ($10–15). We were briefed about the mission and assigned our routes and targets. Lt Jerry Coffee and I got central Cuba. There were three flights of two airplanes each (east, west, and central Cuba). The senior pilot led and No 2 followed a couple of hundred yards astern so that he could be directed right or left to get better coverage of targets of interest as we passed by.

Call signs were "Red", "White," and "Blue" – I was "Red 1" and Jerry was "Red 2." Up until that time, targets weren't identified as IRBM sites. We were only briefed to look for suspicious, major construction activity, and we'd "know it when we saw it." One clue was big piles of what appeared to be prefabricated cement fence posts. They were white and really stood out.

Capt Ecker describes his first mission:

During the Cuban Missile Crisis, only US Navy and USAF tactical reconnaissance jets and U-2s were allowed to fly over the island of Cuba

– all aircraft were unarmed. It should also be noted at this time that there were other types of aerial reconnaissance conducted by the US Navy during the missile crisis. However, none of these squadrons was allowed to fly over the island of Cuba. They conducted their missions from a stand-off position offshore.[6]

The only weapon the pilot had was a 0.38cal pistol in a shoulder holster. It only had tracer bullets for signaling if one were forced down.

On October 23, 1962 (eighth day of the crisis), my wingman, Bruce Wilhelmy, and I took off on our mission to obtain pictures of the missile base at San Cristobal. At the same time four other pilots in my squadron departed on their missions to obtain pictures of two other high priority missile sites in Cuba.

While taxiing, we had no verbal communication with the control tower. We had previously arranged that our duty officer (who was one of the pilots not flying that day) would phone the tower and alert them that we were scrambling. We would use their Aldis Lamp signals for our control (green for go and red for stop or hold). It was all green for us! Other aircraft taxiing or flying in the area maintained routine communication with the tower, and they were all subordinated to us as we prepared to take the runway. Any Cuban eavesdropping would not be alerted to our operation via control tower communications.

In just a few minutes we were at the head of the duty runway. We taxied into position, and getting a green light from the tower, we hit our "burners" [afterburners in jet aircraft provide maximum thrust for takeoff and also for combat or emergency operations]. Once safely airborne, we raised the landing gear and lowered the wing to the down-and-locked or retracted position – actually, the fuselage of the airplane was flown up to the wing.

Takeoff was in a generally westerly direction, and thus in order for us to set course for the target, it required only a moderate turn to port after we were airborne. Since Cuba was only about 90 miles away, I expected landfall in about eleven or twelve minutes. We flew low-level through showers and restricted visability. These showers were actually a blessing. Because we were flying so low, we were picking up salt spray off the sea, and the showers washed most of it off our windscreens and camera bay windows. We flew mostly VFR (Visual Flight Rules), but from time-to-time we would go momentarily onto instruments.

After nine or ten minutes we broke out of the shower activity, and upon doing so passed over a large number of small craft, probably fishing boats. My immediate thought was, "Oh great, just what we need to alert the damn Cubans." However, looking back on it, I doubt if any of those particular craft had radios, and even if they had, the crew would probably not have known what to do anyway. Also, at this time we broke out into clear skies and bright sunshine – and there at 11 o'clock [a clock code is used to denote directions away from the aircraft, with 12 o'clock being straight ahead on the nose and 6 o'clock dead astern] was the Havana skyline. My initial point [IP] of land was farther to the west. So much for my initial compass heading. Obviously, the wind was stronger from the west than had been predicted for us. Havana Radio surely did not turn on their homer to accommodate us.

I immediately climbed to about 1,500ft, reoriented our position and headed for the IP which was the port of Mariel [Mariel was later to become famous, or infamous, as the embarkation port for the 1980 Cuban refugee sea-lift]. But, since Mariel had an airstrip and port facilities, and was directly on my course, it was included in the mission. I learned later that Mariel was actually one of the major ports where the missiles were off-loaded (after dark), but saw nothing of significance on this daylight pass.

Bruce and I turned off our cameras and made a 90-degree port turn to a heading of about 180 degrees south. After a minute or so, we made a turn of 90 degrees to starboard, and now we were again on a generally westerly heading.

The best way to describe our altitude and speed during all of our missions is tree-top level and very fast. I must qualify this statement somewhat, because when flying photographic reconnaissance missions there are certain physical restrictions or natural laws which must be obeyed in order to allow the cameras to recycle properly and to maintain a 60 percent ground coverage overlap between successive images.

This overlap is required in order to provide the photo interpreters with stereometric or three-dimensional viewing. To say it another way, the higher you are, the faster you can go, and, conversely, you must slow down if you decrease altitude.

In today's age of digital photography, where the camera does all of the "thinking" for us – light control, focus, and speed of exposure – one can easily take for granted the complexity of getting a good, focused, and well-lit picture. Only a few years ago, those of us using more sophisticated cameras of the time had to understand that the lens aperture (adjustable opening, known as the "f" setting) and speed (how much light it gathered, the so-called maximum "f" number), as well as shutter speed (duration of exposure compensating for movement of the subject), had to be adjusted by the photographer. Aerial cameras, including the advanced KA-45/46, did not have automatic exposure control, the photomate having to preset these prior to the mission being flown.

Other factors that predetermined the altitude and speed at which pilots could fly over a target and get good photos were the camera's focal length (the distance between the center of the lens and the photographic film – in the case of the KA-45, it was six inches), the resolution desired (measured in lines per millimeter), and the so-called hyper-focal length (the distance to the nearest object desired to be in focus – the distance to the ground object). Thus, based on all of this, the optimum altitude to fly over the target with the KA-45/46 was between 1,000ft and 1,500ft. That could be altered dependent on the various factors mentioned. The KA-45/46 cameras had a high recycling rate (how many photos per second that could be taken) and could obtain the desired overlap.

Capt Ecker continues his account:

Once on this heading, we were paralleling a range of small mountains on our right, or north side, when all of a sudden the San Cristobal missile complex appeared! I called to Bruce to move out farther to the right so that we would get maximum coverage of the target area, rather than flying close together or in tandem.

The missile complex included the missile build-up or assembly equipment, the fuel-tank trailers, the missile-erector sites, the launchers themselves, and so forth. Naturally, I could not identify each of these components in detail at the instant that we passed over them, but it was all there, and recorded in the few seconds' duration of the run. These were the pictures that Ambassador Adlai Stevenson would use on October 25 when he would confront Soviet Ambassador Zorin in the Security Council of the United Nations [see Chapter 8].

We came off the target but continued to let our cameras run to pick up any residual intelligence that might be on our flightpath as we came starboard onto a northeasterly heading. Actually, we did photograph what appeared to be the first stages of some kind of construction. The ground was plowed and it was being cleared and leveled. I never did find out if it was destined to be another missile site, and whether it was important or not. Once we went "feet wet" – got over the water – we began a climb to 40,000ft. Higher altitudes conserve fuel in jet aircraft.

Shortly after we began our climb to 40,000ft, we could see a build-up of extreme thunderstorm activity in both forward quadrants – from our 9 o'clock position to our 1 o'clock position. Thunderstorms of this magnitude, if entered, can literally disintegrate aircraft under certain sets of circumstances. I elected to return to low altitude and to continue on course, trying all the while to penetrate the storm safely. The whole mission would have been in vain if the pictures were lost either by our running out of fuel by circumnavigating the storm area or by being torn to pieces in the storm – Key West was completely covered by this granddaddy of storms. We entered it at very low altitude and went on instruments at once.

Capt Ecker was right to be concerned, as Capt Ron Knott noted in his book *Supersonic Cowboys*. He describes the loss of two VF-62 F-8Bs (only one pilot was recovered) from a flight of seven that entered a storm cell whilst flying from NAS Cecil Field to Guantanamo Bay on August 25, 1962:

Vertical wind shears or engine icing could cause an [engine] flameout. The F-8 was a great airplane to fly as long as the engine was running. However, an engine flameout causes instant electrical and hydraulic power loss. This makes the great Crusader not too "user-friendly," to say the least. All flight instruments go ape, the airspeed decreases rapidly, and the flight controls freeze since there is no hydraulic power. In a situation like this, the pilot is just along for the ride, but he is frantically trying to regain control of that hunk of metal falling through space by instant recall of his emergency procedures. All the while, he is being slammed around in the cockpit like a sock in a washing machine.[7]

Capt Ecker continues the story:

Then all of a sudden, by the grace of God (or the Virgin Mary, who is the patron saint of Naval Aviators), a small sun hole appeared high at our 10 o'clock position. I called for the burners and, in a matter of seconds, Bruce and I popped through the tiny hole into bright sunshine, and with clear skies all around.[8]

Once on top, we set a course back to Jacksonville. Although the squadron was based at NAS Cecil Field, which is about 18 miles to the west, my main photographic laboratory was at NAS Jacksonville, or what we called Mainside. At this time, Bruce and I looked over each other's airplane for bullet holes, leaks, or whatever would be out of the ordinary but both jets were sound. The only casualty experienced was mechanical – my air conditioning system failed while over the target area, and although it was damn hot for a while at low altitude, things were much more comfortable once back at 40,000ft. Speaking of bullet holes and looking back to the target area, I can't confirm if we were fired upon or not, but on most later missions we would see the "popcorn" flak (37mm AAA fire which exploded in white puffs) in our mirrors. It was definitely a combat environment!

Because of the clouds and storm conditions, I'm not exactly sure of just where we hit the Florida coast, but I estimate by time, speed, and heading that it was somewhere around the Naples area. Incidentally, when we did finally penetrate the storm area, we popped up behind the ADIZ – Air Defense Identification Zone – well into territorial United States. This caused much concern within the USAF's Air Defense Command, as we, at this time still unidentified, had penetrated its forward line of defense. Fortunately for them and the country, we were not Cuban or Russian bombers, which were at this very time being uncrated and assembled in Cuba.

A short while later we landed at JAX, and while taxiing in I saw that the other four aircraft had already made it home. Because their targets were farther to the east, and also clear of the storm area, it was a straight shot for them to come up the east coast of Florida, and they had beat us back handily. On arrival at the flightline, it was only a matter of a couple of minutes until all the film was unloaded and on its way to the "soup" – the developing fluid [actually, as we will see in the next chapter, the film in Capt Ecker's airplane was not unloaded at NAS Jacksonville].

Lt Cdr Tad Riley describes his first mission:

The Russians were busy installing security fences around their installations. They were also constructing large Quonset type buildings and laying cement launch pads. A lot of vehicles would be scattered around and, of course, people.

In regard to the people, on later missions there was interest in whether they looked Mongolian, or if we could see if they had shoulder patches to identify their units. Needless to say, at our speeds and altitudes that was a little unrealistic, but later one of us got a picture (we seldom saw the product of our efforts, so I don't know which flight it was) of a headquarters building that had a garden of colored rocks around the flag pole that showed a unit patch. I personally never saw the picture so I can't vouch for the truth of the matter [intelligence agencies were trying to determine if the sites were under Russian or Cuban control].

From the first mission, we were briefed that once we had covered our target assignments and were running for home, we should "let them know we were there." In other words, "flat hat" so they could see our insignias, and to make a lot of noise with our afterburners. We called it "flushing their toilets" [as we will see later, this was a purposeful strategy to intimidate and harass the Cubans and Soviets].

The previous accounts put us into the cockpit of the US Navy Crusaders. The following excerpt from the *Washington Post* gives an excellent impression of what it must have been like on the ground watching the fast-moving jets fly over:

> On a blue-green morning in October, while Cuba was climbing into a warm bath of Caribbean sun, a speck appeared close in on the sparkling horizon and grew within seconds into a United States Navy jet traveling at almost 1,000mph. It shot across the treetops with high-speed electronic cameras flicking – and vanished.
>
> To any Castro militiaman who might have been sprawled on the beach munching a section of sugar cane, the jet was just an ear-splitting screech. Before the neat Russian engineers laboring a few miles inland realized what had happened, the airplane was far out to sea again on the other side of the island.
>
> What did happen in those few streaking seconds startled the world. The events that followed revealed a scope of United States intelligence operations so all-seeing and sophisticated that dark alley cloak and dagger spying has become as outmoded as Capt Marvel and Shazam.[9]

It would be an exaggeration to say the skies belonged to the US Navy jets, but their intrusions went largely unnoticed until they arrived over their targets. Those on the ground had little warning as the supersonic jets outraced their sound, flying different routes, and making good use of the terrain to arrive before anything could be hidden.

Adm Joseph F. Carson, Commander of Fleet Air Jacksonville, waited for the Crusaders to return from their first reconnaissance mission over Cuba. Mrs Kit Ecker describes the admiral's enthusiasm:

> The admiral was due to retire when the crisis erupted. He kept a close watch on the developments and movements of VFP-62 during the crisis.

He was thrilled that this opportunity arose for the US Navy to display its skills. Around the squadron, the word was that the admiral seemed suddenly rejuvenated by the exhilarating developments. He greeted all the "Washington brass," including the Secretary of the Air Force (Joseph Charyk), and later pinned the Distinguished Flying Crosses on the six pilots who flew the first mission over Cuba.

Richard Crowe, a photomate second class stationed at FAPL, was in the control tower when the jets returned. "All flights in the Jacksonville area had been either re-routed or grounded to facilitate the arrival of our birds. That was really impressive for a 22-year-old to see."

President Kennedy was counting on the support of the Organization of American States (OAS) to back his decision for the quarantine that would go into effect on October 24. On October 22, before his address, the president met with the Congressional leadership to discuss the crisis. Senator Saltonstall brought up the question of the legality of the blockade. A great many senators expressed concern over the proposed action with the OAS, indicating that they felt it would delay, rather than act. Saltonstall then asked whether the blockade would be legal if the OAS did not support it. In full candor, the president answered, "It would probably not [be legal]. However, we would proceed anyway."[10]

At 0900 hrs on October 23, Secretary of State Rusk addressed the Special Meeting of the Council of the OAS and asked them "to take all measures necessary to remove the threat to the hemispheric security."[11] The Council continued its deliberations to approve or disapprove the USA's unilateral action until 1700 hrs. When the Council finally voted, it passed with one abstention (Uruguay lacked instructions from home). Later, Uruguay changed its vote and made it unanimous – a victory for Rusk and the United States.[12]

The film from the returning jets had to be processed at the FAPL at NAS Jacksonville, given a cursory look by VFP-62 PIs, and then flown by courier jet to NPIC in Washington, D.C. for detailed analysis.

Lt Cdr George Custer was a pilot in VC-62 (VFP-62's predecessor squadron) during 1954–57, flying Banshees and Cougars. In a strange twist of fate, his naval career brought him full circle back to complement his old squadron during the Cuban crisis. He was now an F-8 Crusader fighter pilot assigned to US Navy Utility Squadron 4 (VU-4), and officer-in-charge of a detachment sent to NAS Jacksonville to fly the film to Washington, D.C. after processing. George recalled that he flew just under the speed of sound so as not to break windows with his sonic booms. He was kept on radar control the entire trip, and given priority in the airspace up to Washington, D.C. His fastest time was 54 minutes from Jacksonville to Andrews AFB, where he was met by armed individuals who took the film to NPIC. Custer claims to be related to Gen George Armstrong Custer of the battle of Little Big Horn fame.

At FAPL, Cdr Robert Koch, the principal photo officer of the squadron, carefully inspected the negatives. "They're beauties," he said. "Run the duplicate positives and let's get them to Washington."[13]

CHAPTER 6

PENTAGON BRIEFING
OCTOBER 23, 1962

There is no doubt that the first *Blue Moon* missions caused great anxiety in Washington, D.C. Evidence of that is when the JCS ordered Cdr Ecker, immediately after his mission, to the capital so that he could brief them in person. Here, Ecker describes his experiences of briefing both them and the various intelligence agencies:

> Once the airplane was in the chocks and the engine secured, I was starting to unstrap and leave the jet when Bob Koch climbed up on the side of the RF-8 and said, "Stay put. You're going to Washington." My reply was, "How come?" The answer came back, "They want to talk to you personally is all I know." While the airplane was being refueled, Bob provided me with a ham sandwich and a small carton of milk, and we discussed the mission briefly – I told him that the missiles were all there as advertised!
>
> The aircraft's refueling and mine were complete almost simultaneously, and Bob assured me that I was legally filed for D.C., and to just get going. Flight plans must be filed for all but local flights. Those flight plans are filed with Air Traffic Control, and along with radar following, they track you all the way. However, from Key West to Cuba and back to Jacksonville, we were not on a flight plan of any kind. The weather was perfect all the way to Washington, D.C., and in less than an hour (I was peacefully cruising at 0.88 Mach) I landed at Andrews AFB, on the outskirts of the city (in Camp Springs, Maryland) and taxied to the Navy side of the airfield.

Waiting there were two (not one, but two) Air Force helicopters. Both had their engines running, ready for takeoff. As soon as I deplaned, an Air Force colonel, who introduced himself as [Col] Doug Steakley (Photographic Reconnaissance Chief for the JCS), tried to hustle me into one of the choppers. However, there are certain post-flight procedures that must be performed within two minutes after engine shut-down, and since no one at Andrews knew how they were performed, I had to do them. This caused a bit of heated conversation with Steakley, but I prevailed and the delay was really not that long.

Once in the helicopter, I removed my torso harness, and for the first time that day – it was now somewhere between 1300 and 1400 hrs – tried to relax, but the chopper flight was too short. I did have time to notice that Steakley had still not informed me of where we were going or who we were going to see. We landed at the Pentagon helipad and got into a big, black limousine that was waiting there for us. We cleared the pad and drove toward the entrance of the Pentagon. Then, suddenly, Steakley pushed me down on the floor of the back seat. "Hey, what are you doing?" I shouted. Steakley then explained that he had just spotted about 200 reporters and a lot of TV cameras out there, and he didn't want them to see me in flight gear.

Once inside the Pentagon, we proceeded to a meeting room, where we were confronted by a Marine sentry and a blank door. The sentry opened the door, stuck his head in, and made some sort of announcement into the guarded room, and then resumed his post.

A moment later, a four-star admiral emerged, shook hands with me, and escorted us inside. It was then that I realized that we were in the secure meeting space of the JCS, and that the admiral was the Chief of Naval Operations Adm George Anderson – he never did identify himself. As Steakley and I followed the CNO, Steakley whispered to me, "Take off the gun!" I had already dropped my helmet, G-suit, nav-bag, and torso harness into a convenient corner, but one just doesn't leave one's gun lying around. I quickly decided that I was in pretty darn good company, so I complied.

The next person to welcome me and to shake my hand was a four-star general with a name tag on his right breast that read TAYLOR. Needless to say, this was the CJCS Gen Maxwell Taylor – a fine gentleman. After his congratulatory handshake, the Chairman asked me if there was anything I wanted. I guess I looked rather raunchy because after losing my air conditioning system in the airplane and sweating as a result of it, I was pretty dehydrated. When I croaked out, "I'd sure appreciate a drink of cold water." He chuckled. After my drink, I followed him to the only two vacant chairs situated around a perfectly square table in this relatively small room. There was no head and no foot to the table, which seated about eight persons per side.

As I went to pull out one of the two available chairs, I was somewhat restricted by a four-star Air Force general sprawled out to my right. As I pulled at the back of the chair, I said, "You'll have to pardon me, General, I'm kinda smelly and sweaty." His retort, as he took a big cigar out of his mouth, was, "You've been flying an airplane haven't you? You ought to sweat and smell. Sit down!" This was my first encounter with the very flamboyant Gen Curtis LeMay.

My debrief to the JCS was relatively short – only ten or twelve minutes – during which time Gen Taylor assisted me by holding up the left side of my navigation chart. I showed the audience the route that I had flown, where I engaged my cameras, and what I saw in the fleeting moments of the fly-over. I explained that the missile complex was there, but that it was camouflaged, and that I could not identify everything precisely, but that it was all there, and that the pictures would answer all their questions in detail. I was somewhat surprised that about one-third of the individuals in the room were in civilian clothes, and two of them asked a couple of rather irrelevant questions. When the briefing was over, the group murmured its thanks and I departed.

Capt Ecker's reference to civilians in the JCS briefing room was confirmed during the 2002 conference in Cuba, where the key players of the crisis visited a bunker photographed by the Ecker-Wilhelmy flight on October 23. "I have these extremely strong feelings standing on this site where the photos were shown in the briefing room," said former Kennedy aide Ted Sorensen, who was present when Ecker was summoned to Washington, D.C. "It could have been the end of the world, but here we are 40 years later, Americans, Cubans, Russians."[1]

Capt Ecker resumes his account:

After Steakley and I left the room, we proceeded to a large, highly classified area which I later learned was the Joint Reconnaissance Center (JRC). This area was so highly classified that when Steakley took me in, he had a very heated argument with a guard who controlled access. Even though Steakley was the boss, or officer-in-charge, of the center, I did not have the proper clearances for admission, and therefore was not on the list of persons authorized for entry. So, the guard promptly placed us both on report [a formal complaint for an infraction] for a security violation as I followed Doug into the center.

This was proper and routine procedure but, as far as I know, after review of the circumstances, nothing ever came of it. A year or so later, when I was assigned to duty in the Pentagon in OPNAV [Office of the Chief of Naval Operations] and had all the necessary "tickets," I was in the JRC and the NRO [National Reconnaissance Office] on a daily basis, with occasional visits to NPIC – all three areas are highly classified, above Top Secret! [Pulitzer Prize author Neil Sheehan writes in his marvelous account of the development of the US Intercontinental Ballistic Missile (ICBM), *A Fiery Peace in a Cold War*, "Eisenhower established a new ultra-clandestine office to jointly manage reconnaissance satellites with the CIA. Under President Kennedy, it was named the National Reconnaissance Office, and kept so hush-hush that its very existence was secret."[2]]

This interlude was only to give me a place to rest and enjoy a Coke and sandwich until Bud Edminston, the previously mentioned naval officer assigned to the NRO, was able to leave work. He took me home with him and introduced me to his wife, Carolyn, who fixed dinner for us while Bud and I grilled some steaks and also enjoyed a libation or two. After dinner and a call home to my wife, Kit, I spent the night with them.

I had no identification, little money, and my only clothing was my summer flightsuit. The latter get pretty dirty and greasy around airplanes. and I remember sitting on their living room floor after dinner. They had just gotten new, light colored furniture, and although they offered to throw a sheet over it, I preferred to sit on the floor. The next morning, Bud outfitted me in one of his sets of "Blues" (standard US Navy uniform for that time of year and the geographic area) and I accompanied him to work. Fortunately too, the uniform fit fairly well and had the proper rank. The morning was spent visiting various US Navy offices that were concerned and involved with the crisis.

I described my flight many times over and received a multitude of congratulations for my conduct of the operation, and the outstanding pictures which many had seen by now. This was the US Navy's day! These accolades were particularly nice to hear from my former air group commanders Capts Sid Bottomley and Bert English, who were now senior officers stationed in the Pentagon. Each was really thrilled when I said, "What else could you expect from a (his name) trained man?"

What really impressed every one was the way the US Navy stole the show! There is a great deal of professional jealousy among the services, especially in the Washington, D.C. area. I'll speak more of this later.

Within an hour after I had dropped the film off at Jacksonville, it had been developed, given a cursory analysis, and then transported by a standard Crusader to Washington. The pictures were in the hands of the president, the JCS, the JRC, NPIC, and the secretary of defense within a few hours after I left the meeting with the JCS. The president later directed that the pictures be sent to Ambassador Adlai Stevenson at the UN. As the American representative to the UN, he would use these pictures to show the world that the Soviet Union had, indeed, based missiles in Cuba.

At this point, a minor correction to Capt Ecker's account of how the film in his cameras was handled explains how the first *processed* mission photos were received on the desks of intelligence officials just hours after they were taken. Capt Howard Skidmore (VC-62's executive officer in

1953–54 – see Chapter 1) was assigned to the Pentagon – he was responsible for who had security clearance for reconnaissance information – when Capt Ecker flew up to brief the JCS. He remembers that the film in Ecker's RF-8 was unloaded at *Andrews AFB*, not Jacksonville, and processed at the Naval Photo Intelligence Center (NAVPIC), in Suitland, Maryland. This has been confirmed by Dino Brugioni, the CIA photo analyst quoted so many times in this book.

When one thinks about it, this was the fastest way to get the film to Washington, D.C., bypassing the need for a separate courier airplane. NAVPIC would certainly have the expertise and equipment to process the film. Also, Capt Ecker explained at the beginning of this chapter that he never left his jet while it was being refueled. So, with the excitement of the mission and the quick turnaround, he understandably assumed that his film had been unloaded at Jacksonville, as had been the case with the other aircraft that overflew Cuba that day. Also, being strapped in the cockpit, his view of any activity around the camera bays was extremely limited.

Kit Ecker remembers the public response to the news of VFP-62's missions:

> Bill arrived home on October 24, tired but elated that the whole mission had gone so well. The next morning the local newspaper ran the story, and as I opened the paper a note fell out. Our young paperboy had enclosed a carefully hand-printed note for Bill. It read, "Congratulations Commander Ecker."
>
> Our sons Richard and Michael went to school that day. Richard was in Mrs Fowler's math class, as was Frank Kauflin (who was the son of Jim Kauflin, one of the original six pilots to fly over Cuba). After the children were seated, Mrs Fowler announced that there were "children of very important people in the room." All the students (including Richard and Frank) looked around in bewilderment – no one knew who she was talking about.

Later, in Chapter 15, the motion picture *Thirteen Days,* and its portrayal of Cdr Ecker's Pentagon briefing, is discussed. What is clear from the account earlier in this chapter is that there was a multitude of intelligence agencies interested and anxious about the outcome of the first low-level mission – all of them wanted to debrief Cdr Ecker. There is no record that Maj Richard Heyser (the USAF U-2 pilot of October 14) attracted the same attention in Washington, D.C. – U-2 photography was familiar and accepted by then. Now, it was recognized that VFP-62 had advanced the collection of photo intelligence to a new and exciting level. The weeks of hesitation for authorizing low-level flights on the part of Secretary McNamara gave way to the recognition that the U-2 and the RF-8A would both be key assets for the resolution of the crisis.

Capt Skidmore adds that a USAF colonel approached him demanding access to NAVPIC's darkroom as Capt Ecker's film was being processed. He denied the request – apparently the USAF was extremely interested in the first US Navy photos too. When the film from the Ecker mission of October 23 arrived in Washington, D.C, the intelligence officials were expecting 70mm film from the old (as-delivered) RF-8A cameras because they were not aware of the new, recently installed KA-45 cameras, which used a 5in format film.

VFP-62's photos were also being prepared for Ambassador Adlai Stevenson's UN presentation (on October 25) of the photographic evidence.

CHAPTER 7

THE USAF GETS ITS CHANCE
OCTOBER 24, 1962

Researchers are struck by how sparse records of the USAF's participation in the Cuban Missile Crisis are. Michael Dobbs notes in his riveting book, *One Minute to Midnight*:

> Together with the Marines, the US Navy has done the best job of the four armed services in making its missile crisis records available to the public, despite the fact that its budget for historical research is only a fraction of the amount available to the Air Force. In contrast to the US Navy, the USAF has done a very poor job of documenting its role in the crisis in a way that is accessible to outside scholars. In many cases, they [declassified Air Force records] were designed to make the Air Force look good, rather than provide an accurate account of what took place during the missile crisis.[1]

Aviation author Robert F. Dorr, writing about the USAF participation during the crisis, gripes that the US Navy's selection for the first missions on October 23 may have been a result of military politics:

> With a naval officer, Adm Robert L. Dennison, commanding Atlantic Fleet forces, it was no accident that the first tactical reconnaissance missions over the island were flown by RF-8A Crusaders (known as F8U-1P until the previous month) on October 23, 1962.[2]

As previously discussed, VFP-62 was recommended by the CIA's Director of NPIC with good reason. In fact, after some practice runs, the USAF discovered that its camera system and tactics were only suitable for middle-to-high-altitude aerial photography.

Its 363rd Tactical Reconnaissance Wing flew the McDonnell RF-101C Voodoo within TAC. The RF-101C was the photo variant of the F-101 fighter. It was a large single-seat, twin-engined, supersonic high-performance aircraft, and it had a centerline ejector pod with flash cartridges that gave it a limited night photo capability. Further, it could carry a centerline nuclear weapon, which enabled it to perform a secondary strike mission. This offensive weapon capability was never used in combat, and it certainly would have weakened any argument against shooting at "unarmed" reconnaissance aircraft if indeed it had been.

While the RF-101C and the RF-8A entered service during roughly the same time period (1956–57), the C-model Voodoo was designed to be an improvement over the A-model. The latter had "a notorious fault which caused some to argue that the Voodoo might never prove itself to be combat ready – its pitch-up problem," Dorr noted in his book *McDonnell F-101 Voodoo*. He continues to explain:

> The T-tail configuration of the F-101A was the cause: at high angles-of-attack the wing disrupted and blocked the airflow over the horizontal tail, causing it to lose lift, resulting in a severe nose pitch-up, sometimes followed by a potentially fatal spin. The root cause of this problem was not resolved in later versions, but a "stick shaker" was implemented to force the stick forward at the onset of a pitch-up.[3]

All aircraft, including the RF-8A, have flight envelopes which have to be respected, but "the pitch-up problem caused doubt about the F-101's dogfighting capability, and some in the Pentagon began to view the *Voodoo* as "better suited for other roles – reconnaissance and interception – where the pitch-up problem would be less threatening than in air-to-air engagements with other fighters. More than a decade after the first steps were taken to design it, the Voodoo was still an airplane in search of a mission."[4]

VFP-62 stood down on October 24 to give the USAF its turn over Cuba. Dino Brugioni writes:

> When photography from the Air Force low-level mission was totally unusable, a SAC PI tried to help the pilots to make sure that their velocity/altitude settings on the cameras were correct – a number of pilots admitted that they were flying at 200–250ft with a camera setting of 500ft.[5]

This pilot error caused the IMC, previously discussed, to incorrectly compensate for the ground motion.

The Cuban Missile Crisis accented the RF-101C's limitations, and the USAF's lack of a satisfactory reconnaissance system. In a panic it tried to procure Chicago Aerial Industries KA-45 and KA-46 cameras as fitted into the RF-8A, but found that the only ones available were being shipped to the US Navy! Gen Curtis LeMay, the Air Force chief of staff, cajoled CNO Adm George Anderson to agree to split the shipment with the USAF. According to Dino Brugioni:

> The story of the Navy bailout of the Air Force's low-level predicament became a muted classic of the Cuban Missile Crisis[6] . . . Not only were Air Force cameras and pilot training lacking, its PIs were poorly trained and understaffed. When, at last, interpretable imagery was received, Gen Walter Sweeney, the TAC commander, hurried over to see it. He asked the TAC major in charge to point out the missiles on the film. Reyes Ponce, an expert SAC interpreter [who accompanied Sweeney], was flabbergasted. Finally, he could resist no longer, "Sir, what the major is showing you is a fallen palm tree." Needless to say, the major was quickly replaced.[7]

The USAF would not fly again until October 26.

By the end of the crisis, the USAF and US Navy had flown about the same number of missions. Dorr explains the Voodoo pilots' frustration with their role in the crisis:

[The Cuban crisis] was a far from gratifying experience for most of the RF-101 pilots. Few got to fly more than a mission or two over Fidel Castro's terrain, and some experienced nothing more exciting than going from MacDill [AFB] to the Florida Keys as a "spare," only to turn around and head home while a wingman went in. With everybody thinking that a world war was about to explode around them, with a mission waiting to be performed and no one able to do the job better, the Voodoo pilots itched to fly and fight – and had not nearly enough opportunity.[8]

Not all Air Force SNAFUs were related to low-level reconnaissance inadequacies, as we will see in the following chapters. VFP-62 pilot (now) Capt Jerry Coffee tells of a USAF fighter wing's arrival at Key West:

One of my lighter memories of the Cuban missile crisis was hearing that an Air Force squadron commander in California had lobbied hard to get his F-104 Starfighter jets deployed to Key West – to get in on the action, needed or not. He succeeded.

Upon the squadron's arrival, my fellow US Navy pilots and I watched as the twelve airplanes circled to land. The lead jet landed short, sheared off its landing gear, and slid up the runway on its belly in a cloud of smoke and sparks, coming to rest half on the runway and half in the grass. The other airplanes waved off and headed to a nearby air force base to refuel and return when the wreckage was cleared.

When the smoldering airplane didn't explode and the pilot was safe, we started planning the welcoming "happy hour" for the Starfighter pilots, which would of course include embarrassing posters and songs reminding them of their snappy arrival. The party was a relaxing moment in an otherwise serious and intense incident in the service of America's national defense.

Ken Walling of US Navy F-8 fighter squadron VF-32 picks up the story:

We heard that our boys in Greyhound blue [a slur on their uniforms] were being put up in the Holiday Inn while we were in condemned

World War II barracks. Some of the more creative guys, like Jerry Coffee and others, got a roll of Kraft Paper and made a mural depicting the incident that must have been 15–20ft long. They also wrote a song called "Hitting the Lip." We converged on the bar at the Holiday Inn where a large group of the Air "Farce" boys were lounging around in their flight suits and ascots. We anticipated that and wore our flight suits. The mural was carefully pinned up on the wall. Then the song was sung. One unknown major didn't like it too much because he was the guy who "hit the lip." He lunged at one of our guys but his buds pulled him back. A lot of beer was consumed and we all became friends. We were never able to get those F-104 drivers to engage us in a little aerial combat maneuvering. Of course, with their turning radius of a couple of counties, they were smart to ignore us.

Capt Ecker reminds us how serious October 24 was:

Robert Kennedy said that the ExComm meeting held on Wednesday, October 24, was one of the two most stressful meetings during the Cuban Missile Crisis. The first part of the meeting covered the information in the photos taken by VFP-62 pilots the day before. He describes the briefing: "The U-2s and low-flying airplanes had returned the previous day with their film, and through the evening it was analyzed. The results were presented to us at the meeting. The launching pads, the missiles, the concrete boxes, the nuclear storage bunkers – all the components were there, by now clearly defined and obvious. Comparisons with the pictures of a few days earlier made it clear that the work on those sites was proceeding, and that within a few days several of the launching pads would be ready for war."[9]

Later events at this same meeting provided the stress referred to by Kennedy. By that time, the quarantine barrier around Cuba had been established by the US Navy. The president and his advisors now waited to see the reaction by the Soviet Union. After many tense minutes, a messenger brought the news that "we have a preliminary report that some of the Russian ships have stopped dead in the water. A short time later, the report came that the 20 Russian ships closest to the barrier had stopped and were dead in the water, or had turned around."[10] Robert Kennedy concluded his chapter describing this meeting by saying, "For a moment the world had stood still, and now it was going around again."[11]

Lt Cdr Tad Riley adds:

When the USAF got into the act, the missions started to be alternated – one day US Navy, the next day USAF. We heard by the grapevine that they weren't hacking it, and from then on we were sometimes assigned the same mission they'd flown the day before. This even included identical launch, route, and target times.

Once the USAF installed US Navy cameras in its RF-101s, the quality of the photography improved. While US Navy pilots were told that the missions were classified, and not to discuss them, their USAF counterparts discussed the missions freely with the press. Consequently, the press – looking for details to print – made it seem as if the USAF had done it all, much to the ire of the US Navy pilots (more on this later).

On this ninth day of the crisis, the president and ExComm were preoccupied with the approaching ships nearing the quarantine boundaries. Wednesday, October 24 would be a day when attention would be diverted away from the mainland of Cuba to the high seas, where the Soviet response to the waiting US Navy was unknown. The naval quarantine was massive, with approximately 46 ships, 240 aircraft, and 30,000 personnel directly involved in the effort. By the time the crisis would end, the US Navy would come alongside 55 Cuba-bound ships and let them pass through after establishing that they carried no proscribed material. US Navy planes and ships also detected and tracked a half-dozen Soviet submarines.[12]

Facing the unknown as the quarantine took effect, President Kennedy turned to his CNO. "Well Admiral, it looks as though this is up to the Navy." "Mr President, the Navy will not let you down," Adm George W.

Anderson confidently responded.[13] However upbeat, the CNO had grave concerns for the possibility of a submarine attack, and warned his fleet commanders "I cannot emphasize too strongly how smart we must be to keep our heavy ships, particularly carriers, from being hit by surprise attack from Soviet submarines. Use all available intelligence, deceptive tactics and evasion during forthcoming days. Good luck."[14]

Khrushchev's memoir reveals his indifference to the tightening American military noose:

> In our estimation the Americans were trying to frighten us, but they were no less scared than we were of atomic war, but we had installed enough missiles already to destroy New York, Chicago, and the other huge industrial cities, not to mention a little village like Washington. I don't think America had faced such a real threat of destruction as at that moment.[15]

On October 24, VFP-62's photos were distributed to various intelligence agencies in Washington, D.C. Chief Hocutt remembers receiving the images:

> We [AIC] received copies of the VFP-62 low-altitude photography of Cuba [on October 24], and they were great. We previously had photographs of much of the Soviet equipment, but most of our pictures were from high altitude, without much detail. We now had excellent pictures.
>
> We did not receive any USAF low-altitude photographs until about a week later. I assumed that, as a US Navy command, we weren't on the distribution list for the USAF Photography. It was not until 1991, when *Eyeball to Eyeball* by Dino Brugioni was published, that I found out why. The USAF had not developed cameras and procedures for high-speed low-altitude photography. They had to ask the US Navy for cameras so that they could play also.
>
> On the morning of October 23, we received a message authorizing the downgrading of the security classification of all U-2 photography from "Top Secret *Talent*" to "Top Secret No Foreign Dissemination."

We immediately shipped the annotated [U-2] photographs of the missile sites in Cuba to the aircraft carriers and other commands.[16]

The Guided Missile and Astronautics and Atomic Energy Intelligence Committees and the NPIC issued the following joint statement on October 24:

> The quality of the recent [VFP-62 October 23] low-level photography permits positive identification of many types of missile-associated equipment, and confirms previous estimates of the general characteristics and rate of construction of the probable nuclear warhead bunkers at several sites, but we are unable to determine whether the bunkers are for storage or checkout of the warheads.[17]

On the third day of *Blue Moon*, Lt(jg) Kortge reminded pilot Lt Cdr Art Day, "In North Korea, if you flew attack missions repetitively in the same pattern, eventually they shot someone out of the sky. We reversed our flights – the imagery showed manned AA facing in the wrong direction."[18]

After the USAF's failed missions on October 24, VFP-62 flew ten sorties (five two-airplane missions) on October 25.[19]

CHAPTER 8

SHOWDOWN AT THE UNITED NATIONS
OCTOBER 25, 1962

The discovery of the missile sites was a closely guarded secret until October 22, when President Kennedy gave his television address. Earlier that day, American ambassadors had met with allied heads of government and presented each of them with a personal letter from the president, a copy of his speech, and copies of U-2 photos. ExComm must have had some concern about the credibility of the photographic evidence, as an intelligence officer from the CIA accompanied the presentations to the British, French, German, and Canadian governments to brief and answer questions as necessary.[1]

The US government recognized early on that it had to gain the confidence and support of its allies and the foreign press – both essential to winning the moral high ground for its unilateral military response. Sherman Kent, the CIA Chairman of the Board of National Estimates, wrote the following assessment of how the photo evidence was viewed among America's western allies:

> On the morning after the president's address, the British press was almost universally skeptical of the president's claim that the USSR had established offensive bases in Cuba. References were made to the forthcoming election, and to "failures" of past US intelligence efforts re[garding] Cuba."[2]

Also, the after-effects of the Bay of Pigs experience (cover-ups, distortions and falsification of US involvement in the invasion) and President Eisenhower's cover-up of the U-2 incident on May Day 1960 caused worldwide skepticism of the recent US claims of missiles in Cuba. Nor was the United States getting much sympathy from some of its key allies. Kent goes on to describe the first reaction of Britain's prime minister, Harold Macmillan:

> The British people, who have been living in the shadow of annihilation for the past many years, had somehow been able to live more or less normal lives, and he felt that the Americans, now confronted with a similar situation, could, after the initial shock, make a similar adjustment. "Life goes on somehow."[3]

Realizing that his statement might be misinterpreted as his not being concerned or shocked at the presence of nuclear missiles in Cuba, Prime Minister Macmillan reassured the US ambassador "that if the president was convinced that a meaningful offensive capability were present, 'That was good enough for him.' But he went on to say that he felt that a blockade would be difficult to enforce, and that the US would have problems getting solid UN support."[4]

Mr Kent outlines the challenges of presenting the photo evidence:

> As a source of information, overhead photography has always won high marks. Any viewer of an air photo is likely to bring with him some associative apparatus. For example, he has seen airfields from above and he can tell the difference between a picture of an airfield and one of a freight yard. All viewers, however, took on faith, or on the say-so of the purveyors, that the pictures were what they were claimed to be – scenes from Cuba taken a few days ago.
>
> The public affairs officer in our embassy in Paris was worried about the French press, and [was] concerned about how proof of the missiles could be demonstrated to the world.[5]

As a result of these concerns, approval was requested, and granted, for the release of sanitized copies of the photos to the press for publication.

On the other hand, there was universal acceptance of the veracity of the U-2 photos by the heads of government, mainly because the President of the United States had issued them. For instance, France's President Charles de Gaulle, when presented with the U-2 evidence, studied them with intense interest and declined a briefing from an intelligence officer who was waiting outside the room. Not so for some in the public, who had to contend with low-resolution TV images or poor reproductions of the photos. All had to accept on faith that long-covered tents, as analyzed by PIs, were missile preparation facilities.[6] All of this was why the upcoming presentation of the photographic evidence at the UN was so important.

The Soviet response to President Kennedy's speech was to deny US claims. This set the stage for the high-drama confrontation at the UN, where, in addition to U-2 photos, VFP-62's October 23 imagery was prepared on presentation boards. The Soviet claims that only defensive weapons were being provided to Cuba would soon be quashed.

It was at the afternoon session of the Security Council of the UN, on October 25, 1962, that Soviet Ambassador Valerian Zorin made the mistake of challenging UN Ambassador Adlai E. Stevenson to produce hard evidence to support his allegation that the Soviets had installed offensive missiles in Cuba (see Notes for a reference to a complete transcript).[7]

He mocked the questionable photos that Stevenson had shown the council just before the Bay of Pigs invasion. Those photos were of the B-26 that the CIA had painted up to look like a Cuban Air Force airplane that had landed in Miami. The CIA ruse, not disclosed to Stevenson, was that the pilot (actually a member of the CEF) had defected from the Cuban Air Force and bombed his own airfields, before escaping to the USA. The problem was, however, the CIA had not done enough homework, and some features of the B-26 clearly were not remotely close to those fitted to the airplanes in Castro's air force. The botched plan backfired, with much embarrassment for everyone, especially Stevenson.

Zorin caustically remarked, "One who has lied once will not be believed a second time. Accordingly, Mr Stevenson, we shall not look at your photographs." In response, Ambassador Stevenson, at his most acerbic best, began an undiplomatic condemnation. "I want to say to you Mr Zorin, that I do not have your talent for obfuscation, and for double talk. And I must confess that I am glad that I do not!" He then began to unveil the evidence. "Well, let me say something to you, Mr Ambassador – we do have evidence. We have it, and it is clear and incontrovertible. And let me say something else. Those weapons must be taken out of Cuba. You, the Soviet Union, have created this danger, not the United States. And finally, Mr Zorin, I remind you that the other day you did not deny the existence of these weapons. But, today again if I heard you correctly, you now say that they do not exist, or that we haven't proved that they exist, with another fine flood of rhetorical scorn."

Stevenson proceeded to pursue his quarry. "All right, sir, let me ask you one simple question. Do you, Ambassador Zorin, deny that the USSR has placed, and is placing, medium- and intermediate-range missiles and sites in Cuba? Yes or no? Don't wait for the translation. Yes or no?"

Zorin (after a short, non-humorous chuckle as he played for time) shot back, "I am not in an American courtroom, sir, and therefore I do not wish to answer a question that is put to me in the fashion in which a prosecutor puts questions. In due course, sir, you will have your answer."

Stevenson replied, "You are in a courtroom of world opinion right now and you can answer yes or no. You have denied that they exist and I want to know whether I have understood you correctly."

Zorin demurred, "Continue with your statement. You will have my answer in due course."

Exasperated, the non-confrontational Stevenson blurted what would become an iconic statement in the Cuban Missile Crisis. "I am prepared to wait until hell freezes over, if that is your decision. And I am also prepared to present the evidence in this room." The phrase, "until hell freezes over" brought the typically polite and serene ambassador new celebrity – finally someone was answering back to the Soviets. Adlai enjoyed the favorable response to it, but he realized that it was not literally true. The United States was not prepared to wait endlessly for the Soviets to come to grips with the crisis they created and start to deal with its consequences.

Nevertheless, it had the dramatic effect he had hoped for, and came to characterize Stevenson at his rhetorical best – his finest hour – as many would agree. The former governor of Illinois and presidential candidate in 1952 and 1956 was not fully trusted by President Kennedy. However, the president did have high praise for his performance that day.

And with that, Stevenson turned to an easel behind him and had its covering shroud removed, revealing a group of aerial photographs. He proceeded to explain them:

> The first of these exhibits shows an area north of the village of Candelaria, near San Cristobal, on the island of Cuba, southwest of Havana. The first [U-2] photograph shows the area in late August 1962. It was then, if you can see from where you are sitting, only peaceful countryside.
>
> The second [U-2] photograph shows the same area one day last week. A few tents and vehicles had come into the area, new spur roads had appeared, [and] the main road had been improved. The third [U-2] photograph, taken only 24 hours later, shows facilities for a medium-range missile battalion installed. There are tents for 400 or 500 men. At the end of the new spur road there are seven 1,000-mile missile trailers. There are four launcher-erector mechanisms for placing these trailers in erect firing position. This missile is a mobile weapon, which can be moved rapidly from one place to another. It is identical to the 1,000-mile missiles that have been displayed in Moscow parades. All of this, I remind you, took place in 24 hours.

Stevenson then moved on to explain a second exhibit:

> Three successive photographic enlargements of another missile base of the same type [MRBM] in the area of San Cristobal. These enlarged photographs *clearly show* [emphasis added] six of these missiles on trailers and three erectors.

U-2 photos would not reveal such detail – enlarged or not – to non-experts, and these photographs were most likely taken at low-level by Cdr Ecker and Lt Bruce Wilhelmy on October 23.

Another exhibit showed a series of photos of an IRBM site near Guanajay (southwest of Havana, close to San Cristobal), and this included two U-2 images most likely taken on October 15. Stevenson continued to the next exhibit:

> The next photo shows a *closer view* of the same intermediate-range launch site. You can *clearly see* one of the pairs of launch pads, with a concrete building from which launching operations for three pads are controlled. Other details are visible, such as fuel tanks [emphasis added].

The Ecker-Wilhelmy mission on October 23 had a primary target of San Cristobal and a secondary target of Guanajay. A photo of the Guanajay site, taken on October 23, is included in the plates section of this volume, and it is most likely the third photo from this exhibit.

Ambassador Stevenson concluded his presentation of the photographic evidence with what clearly is a collection of VFP-62 photographs of an MRBM site:

> These photographs are on a *larger scale* than the others, and reveal many details of an improved field-type launch site. One photograph provides an overall view of most of the site – you can see *clearly* three of the four launching pads. The second photograph displays details of two of these pads. *Even an eye untrained in photographic interpretation can clearly see* [emphasis added] the buildings in which the missiles are checked out and maintained, ready to fire, a missile trailer, trucks to move missiles out to the launching pad, erectors to raise the missiles to launching position, tank trucks to provide fuel and vans from which the missile firing is controlled. In short, all of the requirements to maintain, load, and fire these terrible weapons.

Zorin ridiculed the evidence, but it was a bleak, unauspicious performance at best. He tried to attack the credibility of the aerial photographs but Stevenson laid down a confident challenge:

> As to the authenticity of the photographs, which Mr Zorin has spoken about with so much scorn, I wonder if the Soviet Union would ask its Cuban colleague to permit a UN team to go to these sites. If so, I can assure you that we can direct them to the proper places very quickly.
>
> We know the facts, and so do you, sir, and we are ready to talk about them. Our job here is not to score debating points! Our job, Mr Zorin, is to save the peace. And if you are ready to try, we are.

At 1925 hrs, October 25, 1962, the Security Council adjourned, not to meet again until after the crisis.

The impact of bringing aerial photographs onto the Security Council floor was best described by author DeWitt S. Copp:

> No other proof could have been more irrefutable, and no other proof would have been more acceptable to many among ourselves, our allies, and, of course, those unsympathetic to us. The UN could not debate away the iron reality of the aerial photographs, nor could the world.[8]

Down through the decades, many have claimed credit for the low-level photographs shown at the UN on October 25. It is certain that the USAF could not have provided them because of their failed missions the day before. Even if their photos had been useable, processing time and interpretation would have been impossible to complete by then. Furthermore, the photos could not have been attributed to VMCJ-2, as its first operations were flown on the very day of the UN presentation. Some knowledgeable observers even doubt if VFP-62's low-level photos of October 23 were part of the UN exhibits. The evidence is not concrete. However, we have Capt Ecker's version of events, and some poor-quality photos of the presentation boards in the Security Council (one is shown in the photo plates section). There are some features on those photos that seem too large for U-2 imagery.

In addition, Dino Brugioni, in an interview for this book, also substantiated that both U-2 and VFP-62 photos were used for the UN presentation. So, to some extent, the evidence is circumstantial. In support of the RF-8 photography, we have used Ambassador Stevenson's words, as he described the exhibits, to support the premise that low-level photography was used. Phrases such as, "Even an eye untrained in photographic interpretation can clearly see," "These photographs are on a larger scale than the others," "These enlarged photographs clearly show," and "The next photo shows a closer view" persuasively demonstrate that he was referring to low-level photographs.

Most importantly, the question has to be raised, why wouldn't they use the low-level photographs to dispel doubters' skepticism, especially since they had them? It would make no sense to rely totally on U-2 photos in a forum where the purpose was to convince everyone – all laymen as far as photographic intelligence goes – that the evidence supporting the US assertions was clear and unshakeable.

Of course the media covered the showdown at the UN, with photographs of the presentation boards and interested council members reviewing them. *Washington Post* article "The Day Adlai Stevenson Showed 'Em at the UN" (February 5, 2003) by Michael Dobbs compared Stevenson's Cuban evidence presentation to Secretary of State Colin Powell's presentation (February 5, 2003) of US "evidence" of the existence of Iraqi weapons of mass destruction. With the same forum and imperatives, Powell's objective was to persuade as many governments as possible to support a US-led invasion of Iraq, or at least have them get out of the way while the United States did what it believed it had to do. The *Washington Post* article included a close-up photo of delegates looking at two aerial photographs of Cuba, both clearly produced by low-level reconnaissance aircraft – VFP-62's Crusaders. All attempts to obtain the *Washington Post* photo for inclusion in this book sadly failed.

After the UN display of photos, the press tried really hard to find out who was flying the *Blue Moon* missions. Lt Cdr Tad Riley remembers one incident related to this:

> They [press] would sit outside the Key West fence and count the number of airplanes that took off, then call JAX for someone to count the number that landed. Once, one of the airplanes had a problem that could only be fixed at Cecil, so it was diverted there. Then the film was driven over to the photo lab at JAX. The press assumed that one of us had been shot down, which created a stir for a while.
>
> We didn't want to be identified during the crisis because we heard a rumor that Fidel had offered a $10,000 reward for the "Yankee War Criminals – Dead or Alive."

CHAPTER 9

THE MARINES JOIN *BLUE MOON* MISSIONS
OCTOBER 25, 1962

VFP-62's commanding officer needed help to meet his *Blue Moon* commitments, and the Marine Corps was ready to give it. VMCJ-2 was the composite reconnaissance squadron for the 2nd Marine Aircraft Wing based at MCAS Cherry Point, North Carolina, in 1962. The squadron flew both RF-8A Crusaders and EF-10B Skyknights, the latter being Korean War-era passive electronic counter measures (ECM) aircraft. The squadron had been involved with reconnaissance missions over and around Cuba since 1960, when the Soviets started their relationship with Fidel Castro's government.[1]

The EF-10Bs, operating around the island's periphery, were credited with one of the first intercepts of Soviet early-warning radar in Cuba. The squadron also monitored the build-up of the Soviet-designed radar-controlled AAA and SAM air defenses in the months before the October missile crisis. No ground-based radar could search the sky without being recorded, as the EF-10B's ECM electronic "black boxes" monitored and recorded every electromagnetic signal coming from Cuba.

In addition, the Marine Corps' RF-8As had been providing monthly photographic coverage of the fence line at Guantanamo Naval Base for some time, as well as performing some undisclosed overflight missions on at least two occasions dating back to 1960.[2] Lt Col Dick Conway, a VMCJ-2 pilot from the period in question, confirms this history:

VMCJ-2 was involved with Cuba long before the crisis became history. Passive ECM missions were flown monthly around the island collecting the electronic "fingerprints" of the sites. We flew as close to the land as allowed, trying to entice the radar operators to "come up" and electronically look at us. When they did, the frequency was logged and the location documented. In addition to the ECM flights, the squadron was routinely tasked with photo-reconnaissance missions directly over Gitmo. Their purpose was to detect any Cuban military build-up in the immediate vicinity of the base.

Shortly after *Blue Moon* commenced Capt Ecker found himself short of airplanes and pilots. He explains how the Marine Corps was brought in to help:

From the 25th onwards, I spent from 18 to 20 hours a day planning for the next day's missions, staging the airplanes and pilots to Key West and still doing the routine, day-to-day job of being the squadron's commanding officer.

Because I had to cover all the decks of all the Atlantic Fleet aircraft carriers, two of which were in the Mediterranean on assignment to Sixth Fleet and three or four others that had been alerted for the blockade, plus anywhere from eight to ten pilots and airplanes at Key West, I soon ran out of both RF-8s and pilots.

To fill the void, four Marine Corps pilots from VMCJ-2 were assigned to me. Along with the pilots came four RF-8As. VMCJ-2 was the designation of the Marine fighter photographic squadron on the East Coast. The Marines remained with me until November 17 when the pressure eased off and I was again able to cover all of the requirements with my own airplanes and pilots.

The VFP-62 augmentation detachment was composed of Capts Fred Carolan, Dick Conway, John Hudson, and Edgar Love, with Dick Tinsley as the back-up pilot. The four pilots flew their RF-8As, with VMCJ-2's "CY" tail code and distinctive *Playboy* Bunny logo, into NAS Cecil Field on October 21 to have their cameras checked out. They then flew on to Key West to join VFP-62 on October 22. The remainder of their parent squadron also deployed to Key West to support contingency operations on the 22nd. A two-airplane RF-8A detachment was then despatched to Guantanamo to support base defense operations. LCpl Jack Hayden remembers VMCJ-2's arrival and setting up operations:

I recall the misappropriation of a jeep from the Navy motor pool. When we got off the transport airplane in Boca Chica very late, SSgt L. L. Smith charged me with procuring a jeep from the motor pool at Boca Chica. I got on the horn and called the motor pool, advising them that I was calling on behalf of Col White [not real name] assigned to Squadron such-and-such [not a real name] and needed to check out a jeep for a few days to move equipment and supplies. I was advised to come down and sign one out in the colonel's name. We kept the jeep the entire duration of the conflict, but had to keep it hidden during the day because the Navy continued to look for it.

We used the jeep mainly to transport officers and men to and from various eating and drinking establishments in Key West. One night in Key West I was driving a couple of captains from a bar and was running out of gas. One of the captains advised me to pull into the next gas station I saw. I pulled in and had the attendant fill the tank, and the captain signed the bill and told the attendant to send it to the Navy motor pool at Boca Chica! I still have a picture of myself and the jeep.

On a more serious note, Hayden remembers what it was like to be in the racially segregated south:

I don't want to get political, but one thing still bothers me. During the crisis, the military took over many of the hotels and motels in the Key West area because there was not enough space on the base to house all of the troops that were being sent to the area. I remember a couple of black Army enlisted men that were sent to bunk with us because the motel that their unit was staying in did not allow blacks. I was just a young kid from the mountains of Colorado and could not grasp the depth of segregation in the South. I could not fathom a man serving his country not being allowed to stay in a motel with his own outfit because of his skin color. Being of Native American descent and a member of the Cherokee Nation, I have never forgotten that incident.

The Marine pilots on the augmentation detachment were briefed on the *Blue Moon* targets and merged into VFP-62 operations.

Shortly after the Marines' arrival some "midnight painters" from VMCJ-2 stenciled red *Playboy* bunny logos on VFP-62's RF-8As. Cdr Ecker, in a thoughtful gesture to "his" Marines, let them stay.[3] Remembering this daring act, (now) Col Edgar Love adds that the infamous VMCJ-2 painters got carried away one night and snuck over to where the USAF F-104s were parked. They tried to repeat their bunny painting on the Starfighters, but on this occasion met with little success. Jack Hayden picks up the story:

I was one of the "midnight painters" from VMCJ-2. The only thing I might add is that we were not successful in painting our bunny on the Air Force F-104s. Just as we stood up to apply the stencil and spray paint on one of the jets (I held the stencil and Cpl Don Lockner was to apply the paint) we were challenged by Air Force Security armed with shotguns. We were arrested and taken to the Air Force Security Officer and questioned for about an hour. We were then escorted to VMCJ-2's hangar and turned over to WO Stone, who gave us a dressing down in front of the Air Force Security people. After the Air Force left the hangar, WO Stone advised us to clean the black grease off our face and hands, get out of our Ninja costumes and await a conference with the CO in the morning.

We were summoned to the CO's office in the morning and given a severe dressing down for our activities, and advised that the bunny stencils were to be put on hold. He also mentioned that President Kennedy would be arriving in Boca Chica to give the Navy Unit Commendation to VFP-62 and VMCJ-2.

We left the CO's office and contacted some friends in the photo lab and gave them a heads-up on President Kennedy and Air Force One being in Boca Chica. The photo boys superimposed a bunny on a picture of Air Force One and slipped a copy under the CO's office door. Those in the office recalled, when the CO was handed the photo, that they had never heard the old man in such a state. He wanted the men responsible arrested and charged (I can't recall the charges he mentioned). It took the office boys a lot of talking to calm the old man down and advise him that it was just a joke, and no damage had been done to Air Force One! The rest is history.

Col (then Capt) Love concludes the story:

The next day, the Air Force colonel in charge "invited" the VMCJ-2 CO over "for a discussion." While the angry Air Force colonel was trying to decide what to do about it, the VMCJ-2 CO argued plaintively, "it wouldn't look good to have the publicity get out that the Air Force security was so poor." The Air Force colonel dropped the charges.[4]

Hayden adds, "I still have my well used bunny stencil."

The Marines began flying *Blue Moon* missions on October 25, first as wingmen and later as section leaders with their US Navy counterparts. Col Love tells what it was like operating over Cuba:

On one mission we were told that the pictures from our vertical cameras were blurry due to water spray from [salt water] sea chop – we were flying close to the water to avoid radar detection. On another mission, flying behind and off the wing of the leader, I observed the [Cuban] site operators running toward their positions to arm their weapons – we were long gone before they could do us any harm.

On the October 27 mission, while ingressing over the beach resort of Varadero and flying southeast for about eight minutes until we picked up the Calabazar de Sagua SS-4 missile site, near some low humpbacked hills above the fields of sugar cane, I took oblique [photos] shots of the site and then headed for Santa Clara. As we passed the airfield, I saw a flight of MiG-21s (40 were based there) about to land, and I banked steeply to my left to avoid them. Luckily, they either didn't see us or chose to ignore us. We turned back north toward the SS-5 IRBM site at Remedios, and as we popped up to take our photos, I saw puffs of smoke from AAA fire from my right. I broke sharply away from the fire and nearly collided with my Navy wingman, who had come in too close. We both switched to afterburners, and soon were safely out over the water heading to Jacksonville.[5]

Capt Love's photos showed that the SS-4 MRBMs at Calabazar were fully operational. With their nuclear warheads, these weapons were capable of destroying New York City.[6]

CHAPTER 10

THE CRISIS MOUNTS
OCTOBER 25–29, 1962

On October 24 (the ninth day of the crisis) SAC was placed at DEFCON 2 at the direction of the JCS – the highest state of alert before war, and the first time in its history. The US war machine was primed for battle. On October 27, the United States detonated a test hydrogen bomb over Johnston Island, in the northern Pacific. Tensions between the Soviets and the Americans were intensifying over the quarantine and approaching Soviet vessels. On top of that, a massive US invasion force was being assembled in southern Florida, and photo intelligence showed increased activity at the missile sites. The prospects for a peaceful settlement of the crisis were growing ever dimmer.

During those critical days, low-level missions were going to be utilized to do more than photograph missile sites. During the 1000 hrs October 25 ExComm meeting, the secretary of defense recommended several recurring low-level surveillance strikes of multiple aircraft in an operation "*that would resemble an air strike*, that should pursue surveillance in the interests of gathering intelligence, *camouflaging the possibility of a later low-level attack, emphasizing our concern with offensive installations already in Cuba, familiarizing ourselves with camouflage* [emphasis added] and to determine whether the Soviets were building additional sites." The recommendation was approved and eight low-level sorties (plus two U-2 missions) were ordered to cover the nine missile sites, airfields holding Il-28s and MiG-21s, nuclear storage sites, "Komar naval vessels," coastal installations, and selected SAM sites.[1]

Clearly the unarmed RF–8As and RF–101Cs were now projecting US power and will. Each screaming Crusader overhead brought the explicit threat of an aerial attack on Soviet military hardware, whenever the United States chose to do so. As we will see later, it also had the effect of rattling the Soviets and Cubans into becoming more aggressive in the way they responded to the overflights.

At noon on October 25, Lt Jerry Coffee was flying *Blue Moon* mission number 5012 as wingman to Lt Cdr Tad Riley toward an IRBM site that was under construction at Remedios. Both men had participated in the first *Blue Moon* missions on October 23. Coffee had the rugged good looks of a fighter pilot, natural and imposing in his G-suit, with unforgettable deep, dark penetrating eyes that would make him easily recognizable when his image as a prisoner of war in North Vietnam was flashed across television screens in 1966 – he would spend seven years in the "Hanoi Hilton." In VFP-62 Coffee was admired and respected by the enlisted groundcrew. Michael Dobbs' *One Minute To Midnight* describes what happened next:

> About two miles to the north of the missile site was a large military-style camp. Coffee could see rows and rows of tanks and trucks, many of them under camouflage. On this mission, he had to make a quick decision. As wingman to a more senior pilot, he was to fly in lockstep with the lead airplane along a pre-assigned track. But the target was too tempting to miss.[2]

Today, (now Capt) Coffee describes in his own words what happened next:

> I actually spotted the motor pool late – I had to slam the control column to the left and pull hard through the turn to over-fly the target. In the turn, I switched on the cameras to "ALL," activating my forward, vertical and side oblique or panoramic cameras. I barely got the wings level in

time, but with all those cameras activated I suppose it wouldn't have mattered that much. I was so fast and so low that I could only get a quick impression of what was below me – tracked vehicles, trucks, and equipment. I rolled back right until I spotted my leader, now about a half-mile ahead of me, and caught up just before we crossed the Remedios missile site – our primary target.

Mission completed, we turned north to go feet wet. Our path took us across a beach-side village, over which my flight leader, Tad Riley, said with a note of triumph, "Let's let 'em know we're here – burner . . . NOW!" We both nudged our throttle handles to the left, selecting afterburner . . . WHUMP-WHUMP . . . as we pulled up the noses of our Crusaders to climb out over the Straits of Florida. I'm sure it sounded to the locals like a humongous clap of thunder right in their village square. In reviewing the film at NAS Jacksonville lab, the village chickens were flapping all over the place, and one guy was literally diving head first out the window of his hut.

It wasn't until weeks later that the Marine Commandant's letter arrived at the squadron detailing the strategic implications of my impetuous action. Actually, had the photos not revealed significant information, I could have been in trouble for an unauthorized deviation from our planned and approved route.

In due course a letter of appreciation arrived from Gen David M. Shoup, commandant of the Marine Corps, commending Coffee's "alertness in a rapidly changing situation." The letter went on to praise "the most important and most timely information for the amphibious forces, which has ever been acquired in the history of this famous Navy-Marine fighting team."[3]

At the 1700 hrs ExComm meeting on October 25, Secretary McNamara briefed the group on the technique of night photo-reconnaissance using flares. He suggested that dropping flares on an IRBM site at night would be highly effective. Gen Taylor thought that the psychological effect of night reconnaissance would be entirely favorable, as well as serving to keep up the pressure and providing more information about the readiness status of the strategic missiles (night photography is described in detail in Chapter 12).

McNamara also explained that Soviet missiles have an eight-hour countdown, and that low-level reconnaissance could give intelligence if the missiles were being placed in position to reduce the length of the countdown. Walt Rostow, from the State Department, said "any reconnaissance flights would have a beneficial effect on developments in New York [talks between UN Secretary General U Thant and Ambassador Zorin, as well as talks between U Thant and Ambassador Stevenson]." Secretary McNamara concluded by "recommending the continuation of daytime reconnaissance, and to add night reconnaissance, not only to gain information, but to convince the public that we are increasing pressure on the Russians."[4] No decision was made on McNamara's recommendation for night photography.

Early Friday morning on October 26, Arthur Lundahl arrived at his NPIC office to review the photos taken the previous day by US Navy Crusaders over the Remedios area of central Cuba. Teams of PIs had analyzed the photos overnight. The details of what they found are described by Michael Dobbs:

After weeks of studying high-altitude U-2 imagery, it was a relief finally to examine the low-level photos. Everything was so much clearer and more detailed. Even laymen could make out the telltale features of a Soviet missile camp – the long missile shelter tents, the concrete launch stands, the fuel trucks, the bunkers for nuclear warheads, the network of feeder roads. It was possible to see individual figures strolling among the palm trees for cover as the US Navy Crusaders flew overhead.

Coffee did not know it [at the time], but he had just discovered a new class of Soviet weaponry on Cuba. A low-level photograph of the Remedios area of central Cuba showed row after row of T-54 tanks, electronics vans, armored personnel carriers, an oil storage depot, and at least a hundred tents. From the layout of the site and the precise alignment of the tents and vehicles, it was obvious that this was a Soviet military encampment, not a Cuban one. These were clearly combat troops, not "technicians," as US intelligence had previously described them. And there were many more than anyone had suspected.

The PIs drew attention to an oblong object with shark-like fins, some 35ft long, alongside a truck. Lundahl recognized the object as a FROG (Free Rocket Over Ground, the official Soviet name was "Luna"). It was impossible to tell whether this particular FROG was conventional or nuclear, but military planners had to assume the worst.

There was now a frightening possibility that, in addition to the missiles targeted on the United States, Soviet troops on Cuba were equipped with short-range nuclear-tipped missiles capable of destroying an American invading force.[5]

In subsequent years, it has been confirmed that these battlefield "Luna" missiles had nuclear warheads that yielded approximately 2 kilotons of explosive force and had a range of 16 to 20 miles.

The US Navy's October 25 photos of four MRBM sites showed that the Soviets were working overtime to make their MRBMs operational, and the San Cristobal MRBM site No 2 would probably be operational by October 26. Also, road construction at Remedios suggested that possibly another IRBM site was being planned for missiles that could reach most of the United States.[6]

All of this new information caused more concern that a peaceful resolution to the crisis was becoming less likely. Potentially, if nuclear war broke out, the 1,300-mile range MRBMs would threaten the lives of 92 million Americans if the United States launched an attack and four or five SS-4s were expended in return. A report from a Department of Defense spokesman delivered the somber assessment that there were enough fall-out shelters, but they were only equipped for 40 million people. The president asked what emergency steps could be taken, but ExComm came to the stark conclusion that with respect to civil defense, "not much could or would be done . . . that whatever was done would involve a great deal of publicity and public alarm."[7]

Relations between the Soviet and Chinese communists had not been good since the Gary Powers shoot-down, and they were not improving with the Cuban crisis. The Chinese were publicly stating that the Soviets should take stronger measures to counter the US actions. Khrushchev in his memoir wrote, "The Chinese were making a lot of noise publicly, as well as buzzing in Castro's ear; 'Just remember, you can't trust the imperialists to keep any promises they make!' In other words the Chinese exploited the episode to discredit us in the eyes of the Cubans."[8]

President Kennedy saw value in McNamara's recommendation to use the low-flying jets as psychological weapons of intimidation and agreed to apply further pressure by increasing the frequency of low-level incursions over Cuba from twice a day to once every two hours. VFP-62 flew fourteen sorties until dusk on October 26. Presidential advisor McGeorge Bundy now realized that photo intelligence was key to the crisis too, with the analysis of aerial photography "often precursing [sic] analytical thinking."[9]

With the discovery of the IRBM sites, ExComm pressed for more U-2 missions, but weather would become a negative factor. Prior to the crisis, high-altitude missions had been flown by CIA pilots in specially modified CIA U-2s (fitted with more powerful engines that allowed them to fly higher and electronic counter measure electronics that alerted the pilot to the presence of SAMs), or SAC U-2s flown by USAF pilots. As previously noted in this volume, the Kennedy administration had decided that all U-2 missions were to be flown by USAF pilots only. Apparently, President Eisenhower's mandate that only CIA pilots would fly U-2 missions so as to circumvent international legalities associated with the intrusion of sovereign airspace by aircraft flown by uniformed military officers was no longer a concern.

Just flying a U-2 is very tough on pilots, not to mention operating the airplane in a combat environment whilst being tracked by SAM radar. The long hours in the cockpit and the difficulty of keeping alert at the boundary of space and earth, while always exposed to the risk of hypoxia (not enough oxygen and too much nitrogen in the blood), caused the early deaths of many excellent pilots. These challenges are exquisitely described here by Cholene Espinoza, a former U-2 pilot:

The U-2 is nicknamed the "Dragon Lady" for good reason. You never knew what to expect when you took it into the air, no matter how experienced you were. This was the unfortunate consequence of its design. The trade-off with an airplane built light enough to fly above 70,000ft is that it is almost impossible to control. And 13 miles above the ground, the atmosphere is so thin that the "envelope" between stalling and "over-speed" – going so fast that you lose control of the airplane, resulting in an unrecoverable nose dive – is razor thin, making minor disruptions, even turbulence, as deadly as a missile. The challenges are even greater near the ground, since to save weight, the airplane doesn't have normal landing gear.[10]

Of the USAF pilots qualified to fly the CIA U-2s, two who had flown the jet during its early flights with the agency – Majs Rudolf Anderson and Richard Heyser – were tapped for many more missions. Consequently, as the number of missions increased, concern grew for pilot fatigue, as well as their vulnerability to being shot down by the deadly SA-2 SAMs, which were now operational. Nevertheless, USAF Gen LeMay, in his standard mode of promoting SAC, insisted that no CIA pilots should be used.

48-HOUR DEADLINE

It appears that by Friday, October 26 (the eleventh day of the crisis), President Kennedy was concluding that a 48-hour moment for decision was approaching. The length of this window of opportunity was partly based on the assessment that no Soviet ships would cross the quarantine line for 48 hours. The president also knew that there was mounting stress building within his own team of advisors for a strike on Cuba no later than Monday, October 29.

At the morning ExComm meeting the president stated, "We are going to have to face the fact that, if we do invade, by the time we get to these sites, after a very bloody fight, they [the missiles] will be pointed at us. And we must further accept the possibility that when military hostilities first begin, those missiles will be fired."[11] At the 40th anniversary conference of the Cuban Missile Crisis in Havana, this possibility was indeed confirmed by Russian and Cuban delegates.

In the following telephone conversation with Prime Minister Macmillan, the president updates a key ally on the state of affairs:

President Kennedy: Hello, Prime Minister.

Prime Minister Macmillan: Hello, what's the news now?

President Kennedy: Well Governor Stevenson saw U Thant this afternoon and made our proposals about the import of arms ceasing, and work on these bases stopping and leading to eventual dismemberment. We are continuing the quarantine. The build-up of the sites continues, however. And I put a statement out this afternoon describing how the build-up is going on, so that unless in the next 48 hours we get some political suggestions as to the dismantling of the bases we're then going to be forced with a problem of what to do about this build-up. So, I would sum it up, Prime Minister, by saying that by tomorrow morning, or by noon, we should be in a position of knowing whether there is some political proposal that we could agree to, and whether the Russians are interested in it or not.[12]

Finally, by this stage in the crisis, VFP-62 mission planners were getting copies of U-2 photos to help them develop the best approach to their targets. Around the 26th or 27th, Capt Edwin ('Ed') Dankworth from the JRC met Lt(jg) Kortge at Key West, who provides this account of the meeting:

Capt Dankworth came down from Washington, D.C. with an example of the Air Force's first [low-level] efforts. I didn't know how the Air Force could have the nerve to say they had a low-level capability. I asked if we could get some of the good stuff [U-2 photos] to use for briefing purposes. After that he was good about sending tubes of enlargements several times a week.[13]

October 27, referred to as "Black Saturday," was the twelfth day of the crisis. Intelligence assessments were based more and more on low-level photography, focused on missile site readiness, pace of construction, and any significant changes at the offensive missile sites. The October 25 and 26 reconnaissance missions revealed that:

> – As of 25 October there was no evidence indicating any intention to halt construction, dismantle or move the sites.
> – Five of six MRBM sites were believed to have full operational capabilities, and the sixth was estimated to achieve that status on October 28.
> – The Soviets had the capability of launching up to 24 MRBMs within six-to-eight hours of a decision to do so, and a re-fire capability of up to 24 additional MRBMs within four to six hours.
> – A total of 33 MRBMs had been observed.
> – No IRBMs, missile transporters, erectors, or associated equipment had been observed to date.
> – No high-altitude coverage suitable for searching the Remedios area [where IRBM sites were being constructed] had been conducted since October 22.[14]

A CIA report on October 27 revealed that – at this late date – world sentiment towards the US position was mixed:

> Official London seems intent on checking premature optimism, which is showing up in widely scattered parts of the world, particularly among the neutrals, French support for the US is hardening, and there are reports that anti-US demonstrations have broken out in several Latin American capitals, including Buenos Aires, Caracas, and La Paz.

The report also provided the grim news that there were four MRBM sites at San Cristobal, two MRBM sites at Sagua La Grande, two IRBM sites at Guanajay, and one IRBM site at Remedios.[15]

At 1600 hrs President Kennedy was meeting with ExComm, and Secretary McNamara was reporting on the day's reconnaissance – one mission aborted for mechanical problems, according to preliminary reports, one airplane was overdue, and several had encountered ground fire. Again, McNamara recommended night reconnaissance. The president delayed a decision on night flights pending a full report on the day's daylight missions (the night mission was later called off).

While this was going on, Secretary of State Dean Rusk interrupted and reported that a U-2, flying near the North Pole, had accidentally strayed over the Soviet Union due to a navigational error (the pilot used an incorrect star to navigate by). In response, the Soviets scrambled fighter jets to intercept the spyplane and the United States responded by scrambling its F-102 Delta Dagger fighter jets armed with nuclear-tipped missiles. The U-2 eventually made it safely back to a US base, where the pilot had a lot of explaining to do. The president decided not to make the incident public.[16]

Following this news, the president brought his advisors back to the task of untangling two recent proposals from Chairman Khrushchev. The first, dated October 26, was received via diplomatic channels and not made public. It was obviously written by Khrushchev – very lengthy, often rambling and drifting into philosophical rationalizations for the Soviet introduction of the nuclear weapons. At times it portrayed a man groping for relief. A few key excerpts of that letter are reproduced here to give the reader the essentials of its content (see Notes for source of its full content):

I see, Mr President, that you too are not devoid of a sense of anxiety for the fate of the world, and not without an understanding of what war entails. What would a war give you? You are threatening us with war. But you well know that the very least which you would receive in reply would be that you would experience the same consequences as that which you sent us. And that must be clear to us, people invested with authority, trust and responsibility. We must not succumb to intoxication and petty passions, regardless of whether elections are impending in this or that country, or not impending. These are all transient things, but if indeed war should break out, then it would not be in our power to contain or stop it, for such is the logic of war. I have participated in two wars and know that war ends when it has rolled through cities and villages, everywhere sowing death and destruction.

I assure you that on those ships, which are bound for Cuba, there are no weapons at all. The weapons which were necessary for the defense of Cuba are already there. If assurances were given by the President and Government of the United States that the USA itself would not participate in an attack on Cuba, and would restrain others from actions of this sort, if you would recall your fleet, this would immediately change everything. Then the necessity for the presence of our military specialists in Cuba would disappear.

Mr President, we and you ought not to pull on the ends of the rope in which you have tied the knot of war, because the more that each of us pulls, the tighter that knot will be tied. And a moment may come when that knot will be tied too tight that even he who tied it will not have the strength to untie it, and then it will be necessary to cut the knot. And what that would mean is not for me to explain to you, because you yourself understand perfectly of what terrible forces our countries dispose.

These thoughts are dictated by a sincere desire to relieve the situation, to remove the threat of war.

Respectfully yours,

N. Khrushchev[17]

Thus, Khrushchev was willing to withdraw his missiles in exchange for the United States' commitment not to invade Cuba and end the quarantine.

The second proposal from Khrushchev, dated October 27, was not delivered, but printed in *TASS* (the leading Soviet news agency at that time) and broadcast over Radio Moscow. It took a harder line, with the addition of a quid pro quo of trading Turkish for Cuban missiles. An excerpt is provided below:

Dear Mr President,

You are worried over Cuba. You say that it worries you because it lies at a distance of 90 miles across the sea from the shores of the United

States. However, Turkey lies next to us. Our sentinels are pacing up and down and watching each other. Do you believe that you have the right to demand security for your country and the removal of such weapons that you qualify as offensive, while not recognizing this right for us?

This is why I make this proposal. We agree to remove those means which you regard as offensive [weapons]. We are willing to carry this out, and to make this pledge in the United Nations. Your representatives will make a declaration to the effect that the United States, for its part, considering the uneasiness and anxiety of the Soviet state, will remove its analogous means [Jupiter missiles] from Turkey. Let us reach an agreement as to the period of time needed by you and us to bring this about. And, after that, persons entrusted by the United Nations Security Council could inspect on the spot fulfillment of the pledges made. Of course, the permission of the governments of Cuba and Turkey is necessary to the entry into those countries of these representatives, and for the inspection of the fulfillment of the pledges made by each side.[18]

Interestingly, he had offered ground inspection of the missile withdrawal, but added the caveat that Cuba would have to agree to such an undertaking. This latter technical point would prove troublesome in the coming weeks. What's startling about this history is that at a time when the United States and the Soviet Union were toe-to-toe in a struggle over nuclear weapons, there was no direct line of communication between Moscow and Washington, D.C. – the fastest method of transmittal was through public media. One of the outcomes of the Cuban Missile Crisis was the addition of a direct line between the two heads of state.

Khrushchev's addition of the removal of the Jupiter missiles in Turkey was not unexpected, as it had been assumed from earlier discussions that he might do so, but it created new complications for ExComm. Following this request by the Soviet leader, McGeorge Bundy pointed out that there would be a serious reaction in NATO countries if the United States appeared to be trading the withdrawal of missiles in Turkey for the withdrawal of missiles from Cuba. The president responded that if the United States refused to discuss such a trade and then took military action in Cuba, it would also be in a difficult position. President Kennedy then left the room to talk to NATO Commander-in-Chief, Gen Lauris Norstad, on the secure phone to Paris.

In the president's absence, Secretary McNamara pointed out, in connection with the current military situation, that "a limited air strike on Cuba was now impossible because reconnaissance airplanes were being fired on." He felt that ExComm must now look to the major air strike to be followed by an invasion of Cuba. "To do so," he said, "we would need to call up the reserves."[19]

Despite Khrushchev's conciliatory proposals, the JCS were alarmed by a briefing on the day's reconnaissance at the 1940 hrs meeting. "The canvas is off the launchers," Mr Hughes from the DIA announced, "and the missiles are on the launchers. There is a reload capability ready."[20]

Developing a response to the Soviet proposals was proving difficult. The president found he was in a minority (with the exception of his brother Robert) when he expressed that Khrushchev's proposal for a quid pro quo on the missile trade was reasonable, and because it was public, so would the world. His advisors did not agree.

The transcripts of the ExComm discussions show John F. Kennedy at his best – tolerant of dissent, keen on his grasp of the details (his advisors would mistakenly interpret the text and he would clarify it) and empathetic with the necessity to avoid Khrushchev's humiliation in any negotiated settlement. Most importantly, Kennedy realized that time was running out, and history would not be kind in the event nuclear war broke out when a compromise could have prevented it. To him, Khrushchev's logic was clear – why would the United States object to nuclear weapons 90 miles from Florida, while not recognizing the same concern of the Soviets for the Jupiter missiles in Turkey, much closer to their border?

Of course NATO and Turkish concerns added to the complexity. At one point the president lost patience with both his secretary and undersecretary of state (George Ball), as illustrated by this exchange (emphasis in original):

President Kennedy: How much negotiations have we had with the Turks?
Rusk: We haven't talked with the Turks.
President Kennedy: Well, have we gone to the Turkish government before this came out this week? I've talked about it now for about a week. Have we had a discussion in Turkey, with the Turks?
Ball: This would be an extremely unsettling business.
President Kennedy: [the president came close to dressing them down] Well, *this* is unsettling *now* George because he's got us in a pretty good spot here, because most people will regard this as not an unreasonable proposal, I'll just tell you that.
Bundy: But, *what* most people, Mr President?
President Kennedy: I think you'll find it very hard to explain why we are going to take hostile military action in Cuba, against these sites – what we've been thinking about. The thing he's saying is, "If you'll get yours out of Turkey, we'll get ours out of Cuba." I think we've got a very tough one here.[21]

The dilatory State Department was clearly more interested in maintaining good relations with the Turks than following presidential orders or priorities. A missile trade was one of the options (Adlai Stevenson had originally proposed it, much to the chagrin of those in ExComm) available from the first day of the crisis, and no work had been done to prepare for it. President Kennedy had not dismissed this option on October 16, but he thought it too early to make such a concession.

The stakes were high. If these final negotiations with the Kremlin failed, an air strike on the missile sites followed by an invasion seven days later were being planned and anticipated by some advisors. The original JCS strike plan called for a 500-sortie air attack no later than Monday, October 29, followed by an invasion of more than 125,000 soldiers seven days later.[22] The actual number of air strikes and the size of the invasion force differ in various references, with McNamara, in his book *In Retrospect*, stating "The first-day air attack of 1,080 sorties" and "an invasion force totaling 180,000 troops was assembled in southeastern US ports."[23] The number depends on whether you count those troops in reserve or other troops staged to set up a government in Cuba after the invasion. Certainly, it would be as large as the Normandy invasion of World War II. Reacting to the steady drumbeat for attacking Cuba, the president responded angrily, "I'm not going to war over any damned useless missiles in Turkey."[24]

During ExComm's discussion, Gen Taylor announced, "Flak came up in front of the surveillance [low-level aircraft]." McNamara responded, "Now the first question we have to face tomorrow morning is, are we going to send surveillance in? I think we have basically two alternatives. Either we decide not to send them in at all, or we decide to send them in with proper cover [fighter escorts]." He went on to say, "If they are attacked, we must attack back – either the SAMs or MiG aircraft that come up against them, or the ground fire that comes up." Gen Taylor supported this with, "I'd say we must continue surveillance. We must not fail on surveillance." The president voiced his opinion that he was "against responding to an attack [on our aircraft]" and the issue remained unsettled.[25] Some of the doves were becoming more hawkish.

Fidel Castro was becoming more impatient with the reconnaissance airplanes violating Cuban air space. According to Michael Dobbs:

> There was a huge psychological difference between high-level and low-level flights. For most Cubans, the U-2s were merely dots in the sky, distant and impersonal. The Crusaders were a national humiliation. It was as if the Americans were taking sadistic delight in flying over Cuba whenever they wanted. Some Cubans saw – or thought they saw – the *yanqui* pilots rock their wings in derisory greeting.[26]

Castro describes his attempts to shoot down the low-level reconnaissance airplanes:

> On the morning of October 27, a couple of airplanes, or several couples of airplanes, appeared in low-level flight over different places, and our batteries began to fire. The inexperience of our artillerymen, who had recently learned to operate these pieces, probably made them miss as they fired on the low-flying aircraft.[27]

153

Gen Joseph Carroll (DIA) briefed the JCS at the Pentagon on October 27. "There is evidence of possible Soviet ground forces with modern equipment [including] surface-to-surface missiles [the FROGs detected by Lt Coffee's October 25 photos]." At 1403 hrs Col Steakley announced to the JCS that "The U-2 over-flying Cuba is 30–40 minutes late." Returning low-level reconnaissance pilots had reported an increase in AAA fire over their targets that day, but the fast Crusaders had eluded damage. There is a widely written account that "One of the low-flying jets was hit by 37mm AAA, but managed to limp back to its base." This is almost certainly a false report. There is no documented evidence that any RF-8As were ever hit, and it is undetermined if an RF-101 was. Col Steakley continued, "all but two airplanes were fired at."[28]

Back at the ExComm meeting, in a stroke of brilliance, the attorney general made the suggestion to write a response addressing Khrushchev's first proposal and ignore the second proposal that included the missile trade. He and Ted Sorenson were given the task to draft a response.

Suddenly, the meeting was interrupted again by the secretary of defense: "The U-2 was shot down!" Bobby Kennedy reacted, "The U-2 shot down?" Gen Taylor provided the latest information. "It was shot down [over a Russian-controlled SAM] site near Banes in eastern Cuba. It's on the ground – the wreckage is on the ground. The pilot's body [Maj Rudolf Anderson] is in the airplane." Much discussion followed on how to retaliate, with McNamara advocating taking out the SAM sites.

The president's first reaction was, "This is such an escalation by them isn't it?" A confused but interesting exchange then took place. Again the president, "How can we put a U-2 fellow over there tomorrow unless we take out *all* the SAM sites?" From the meeting transcripts, an unidentified voice shouts, "They've fired the first shot!" The president asks, "We can't very well send a U-2 over there, can we, now? And have a guy killed again tomorrow?" Gen Taylor responded, "We certainly shouldn't do it until we retaliate, and say that if they fire again on one of our airplanes then we'll come back with great force." The president responds, "Well, except that we still got the problem of – even if you take out *this* SAM site – the fellow still is going to be awfully vulnerable tomorrow from all the others, isn't he?" McNamara responded back, "We can carry out low-altitude surveillance tomorrow."[29] Robert Kennedy's own reflection on that moment in his book sums up the group reaction:

> There was sympathy for Maj Anderson and his family. There was the knowledge that we had to take military action to protect our pilots. There was the realization that the Soviet Union and Cuba were apparently preparing to do battle. And there was the feeling that the noose was tightening on all of us, on Americans, on mankind, and that the bridges to escape were crumbling.[30]

The president, seeing the direction this discussion was going in, abruptly brought the advisors back to the task of finishing the response to Khrushchev. The tragedy caused a temporary stand down of U-2 missions.

According to Tad Szulc, Castro disavowed Cuban involvement with the shoot-down of the U-2:

> Fidel told me, "It is still a mystery how it happened. We had no jurisdiction, no control over Soviet anti-aircraft batteries [SAMs]." He said, "We had simply presented our viewpoint to the Soviets, our opposition to low-level flights, and we ordered our batteries to fire on them. We could not fire against the U-2. But a Russian there – and for me it is still mystery, I don't know whether the Soviet battery chief caught the spirit of our artillerymen and fired, too, or whether he received an order – did fire the rockets [SA-2s]. This is a question that we do not know ourselves, and we didn't want to ask much about this problem."[31]

At an 1830 hrs meeting, Gen Taylor briefed the JCS members on the White House meeting. "The president is seized with trading Turkish for Cuban missiles – he was the only one in favor of it." Taylor went on, "The president has a feeling that time is running out." Now, photo-reconnaissance was tasked "to get a better background for attacking Cuba."[32]

With the brazen U-2 shoot-down, policy-makers in Washington, D.C. were now greatly concerned about what seemed to be an escalation in the Soviet response to US reconnaissance aircraft. However, such concerns did little to alter the way VFP-62 went about its daily routine of *Blue Moon* missions. By now the unit was conducting overflights of Cuba on a regular basis, although with a little interference from Washington, D.C. as Capt Ecker explains:

> The US Navy flew low-level missions on October 25, 27, and 29. The pilots who were not on the first mission spent their time at Key West while they waited for their sorties to come up. So we were settling into a more-or-less routine schedule. I would receive the targets from Washington on the evening prior to the flights. We would then plan the routes to best accomplish the mission, while staying out of the missile and antiaircraft envelopes. Initially, Washington tried to do the mission planning, with some chairbound "SOB" making operational decisions for us. I soon put a stop to this nonsense, but they still insisted that we give them all the details of the various routes as soon as we had finalized them.
>
> They also demanded that the pilots give a running report or account while flying the mission. That's all we needed was for the whole damn world to know where we were heading and the time that we would be there, including the enemy gun and missile crews. A sample report would be something like this: "1141 feet dry (that is over the Cuban land mass) 1147 entering run, heading 197 degrees; 1151 off target, took 37mm flak no apparent damage; 1152 outbound, heading 012 degrees; 1201 feet wet, returning to home base; ETA 1234." I know why they wanted this information in Washington. Everybody and his brother wanted to get into the act, and each wanted to show how knowledgeable and important he was by being able to come up with an immediate answer to any question that might be put to them.

Lt Cdr Tad Riley comments on mission planning:

> Whoever was setting up the missions at the other end also got very nervous about how long we were feet dry. They even started questioning our mission planning. They invariably came up with shorter times for our

missions, and we figured out they weren't accounting for the time necessary to make turns so that the targets were approached from the optimum direction. They also required that once we were feet dry and could break radio silence, we would have to report over each assigned target.

We didn't think it was real smart to come over our targets from the same direction and time as the previous day, so I for one (I probably wasn't the only one) decided to fly my missions in the opposite direction from the way I had flown them the day before (clockwise or counter clockwise). I still reported "times over target" when they expected it, no matter where I really was! Once I saw a manned gun position pointing in the opposite direction from my approach. The gunner was looking over his shoulder and frantically cranking his gun around to track me.

Here, Capt Ecker describes how the intense mission schedule started to develop a routine, and the unique way the unit marked the accumulation of missions on its jets:

Bob Koch or I would plan the flights at either NAS JAX or Cecil. The flight plan would then be relayed to Washington, the mission pilots would be notified, and maintenance would be alerted to have X number of aircraft available, plus one or two spares.

At about 0400 hrs the mission aircraft and pilots would depart Cecil and fly to Key West, getting there at first light. Depending on the mission, sometimes we would stage the evening before. At Key West the airplanes would be refueled, and just minutes before takeoff the film loaded into the cameras. Four or five hours might elapse after arrival at Key West before executing the mission. This could be for any number of reasons – delays from Washington, weather, aircraft malfunction, and so forth. Because of the high humidity factor, we did not want the film to get moisture soaked by being in the cameras for long periods.

Each mission originated at Boca Chica and terminated at NAS Jacksonville. We used VAP-62's ramp facility there. The unit flew the RA-3, the reconnaissance version of the twin-engined Skywarrior jet attack bomber. Cdr Bob Roemer was the unit CO, and he was usually part of the reception committee, along with Adm Carson and myself.

The US Navy had two types of photographic squadron at this time, with VFP-62 designated as a "light or fighter" aircraft unit and VAP-62 a "heavy or attack" aircraft unit. The RA-3 was a huge aircraft with a full crew – pilot, co-pilot, navigator, and photomates to operate the camera. VAP-62 had superior capability when it came to mapping photography, but its Skywarriors would have been very vulnerable to ground defenses over Cuba. The aircraft was nicknamed the "flying coffin" for its difficulty to evacuate in an emergency.

Capt Ecker continues:

After the film was dropped off, it was the pilot's option to either return to Cecil at once or to go to the Lab and view his pictures as soon as they were developed. Most pilots opted to stay, and in either case there was no need to refuel, as it was only an eight-to-ten minute flight over to Cecil.

On all missions after the first day, a unique thing happened at the termination of each sortie as soon as the engine stopped turning. Following a successful aerial engagement, a fighter pilot would paint an enemy flag symbol onto his airplane for each enemy machine he had shot down. Similarly, bomber crews painted a bomb on their aircraft for each mission completed. During the Cuban Missile Crisis, we initially marked every aircraft that had completed a mission with a caricature of a pot-bellied Castro smoking a big cigar and holding a dead chicken by the feet. Subsequently, after each additional mission a two-inch "dead chicken," hanging upside down, was added [the "Castro & Chickens" stencil was the handiwork of squadron PI Don Jusko].

This recording method was derived from the time that Castro, having just taken over from the previous dictator, Fulgencio Batista, made his first trip to the UN in New York City. I remembered reading that because he and his staff feared being poisoned, they brought live chickens into their suite in the Waldorf Astoria. There, the chickens were killed, plucked, and cooked – over an open fire yet! [Castro was a target of numerous CIA assasination attempts.]

Sometimes, I would meet the returning pilots and watch the chalking-up of another chicken. Other times I might be back at Cecil catching up on the daily routine.

One of my daily concerns was money. AIRLANT alloted a certain amount of money each month to each of its squadrons. The amount varied with the size of the unit, its operational commitments, training phases and other factors. This fund was called the squadron's OPTAR. We had to stay strictly within the balance. The squadron had to buy everything from this fund including fuel, spare parts, flight pencils, and paper clips – everything, except food and pay. A graph was posted in my office that was updated daily to show at a glance if we were on, over, or below the OPTAR at that particular instant. If off the balance line, adjustments would be made to bring us back on target.

Woe be it to any commanding officer who had to go "hat-in-hand" to AIRLANT and ask for additional money to meet his required operations. Fortunately, with the importance of our stepped-up operations (and the attention focused on VFP-62), I had no need to worry about the OPTAR for quite few months.

While President Kennedy and ExComm waited for Khrushchev's next move on the evening of October 27, at squadron level in VFP-62 morale was soaring thanks to all of the importance and activity surrounding the Cuban missions. Officers of all rank up to rear admiral were commonly looking over the shoulders of the groundcrew maintaining the aircraft. The US Navy stresses high maintenance standards for all of its equipment, and VFP-62 took it to the highest level. Lt Cdr Tad Riley remembers, "Our RF-8s had the best maintenance, and I would have stacked them up with the airplanes of any other Navy or Marine squadron." Chief Aviation Structural Mechanic Richard Flake concurs. "The Navy birds got a good cleaning regularly because of their deployment aboard ships." Aviation Mechanic Vinnie Zabicki adds, "I can only remember one aborted flight at Key West – smoke in the cockpit, probably due to a generator failure." Zabicki goes on, "Another time we had a small incident of a tailpipe fire – great balls of fire! [This happens when you have a wet start – no ignition, and raw fuel in the tailpipe.] The tower called the crash crew when we restarted the aircraft."

The plane captain is usually a junior enlisted man, but he has the huge responsibility of looking after the airplane. Long hours are part of his daily routine, especially aboard ship. One of his duties is to sit in the cockpit and "ride the brakes" in case the airplane has to be moved. In recognition, only he and the pilot get their names stenciled on the airplane – it is the plane captain's machine.

One of his most important tasks is to climb up next to the pilot and remove the safety pins from the ejection seat. There are about five pins preventing an accidental ejection while the airplane is on the ground, and they have to be removed by the plane captain after the pilot is seated in the cockpit. Some pilots are so paranoid about this being done properly that they insist on holding the pins in their hands and counting them. There have been fatal incidents where a pin left in the seat prevented a pilot from escaping a doomed airplane.

One of the senior officers at Key West, Lt Cdr Art Day said, "The crew down there was so dedicated that some of the plane captains even slept in the engine intakes of the aircraft, using their jackets as pillows, in order to be instantly ready for a launch."

Richard Flake adds, "We spent some nights under the wing of one of the airplanes keeping 'watch' and resting. About dawn we preflighted the birds, checked the fuel, and cleaned the windscreen and canopy, then waited for the pilots to come down. Initially they were anxious. I was trying to do the pre-taxi-launch checks and the pilot started giving me the 'pull chocks' sign. I pulled the chocks and he was gone. Later they calmed down and allowed us to perform the checks." Capt Ecker fondly remembers his maintenance crew:

From early on, the Key West detachment, or Det, was known as the "Rotten Cotton Ball" Detachment (RCB Det) of VFP-62. The individuals were referred to as "RCBs" or "Keating's Kids." The "Rotten

Cotton Ball" reference came from a song with a catchy melody that was popular in Key West at the time. The name of the song was "Cotton Fields," and it was playing on almost every jukebox any time you'd walk into a joint. ["Oh when those cotton balls get rotten and you can't pick very much cotton in those old cotton fields back home."]

The "Keating's Kids" handle came from Senator Kenneth Keating, a Republican from New York, who tried to get the administration to recognize his charges that there were Soviet offensive missiles in Cuba. Prior to our pictures, official Washington did not believe him. It was also Keating that early on had urged an embargo that was dismissed by then Vice President Lyndon B. Johnson. Although he was vindicated by our photographic evidence, we never did hear from him.

Seldom in one's career does a situation arise where you can be doing a job of such worldwide importance and magnitude. Even with all of its challenges, the very best job in the whole, wide, world is to be the commanding officer of a US Navy fighter squadron.

Back at the Pentagon, the JCS met at 1830 hrs on October 27 to discuss the grim news of the U-2 shoot-down, and the photo intelligence showing an increasing number of missiles reaching operational status – the JCS were starting to change their strategic thinking. When CJCS Gen Maxwell Taylor asked his colleagues, "Should we take out a SAM site?" he got some surprises. Gen LeMay replied, "No, we would open ourselves to retaliation and a lot to lose." Gen Earle G. Wheeler, chief of staff of the Army, said, "I feel the same way – Khrushchev may [let] loose one of his missiles on us." In frustration, the chairman railed, "Gentleman, you all recommended retaliation if a U-2 was downed. If this was wise on the 23rd, it should be just as wise on the 27th."[33]

With time running out, on October 27 Robert Kennedy met secretly with Soviet Ambassador Anatoly Dobrynin to alert him to a new proposal being offered to Khrushchev that could end the conflict. It would require the Soviets to cease work on offensive bases, render all offensive weapons inoperable, and remove them from Cuba. In exchange, the president was willing to end the quarantine and give an assurance not to invade Cuba. Kennedy also hinted at the eventual removal of US Jupiter missiles from Turkey within four to five months, but this could not be a public commitment.

The attorney general ended with a stern warning. "If the Cubans shoot at our airplanes, then we are going to shoot back. We can't stop these overflights," he explained. "It's the only way we have to quickly get information about the state of construction of the missile bases on Cuba, which pose a serious threat to our national security. But if we start to fire in response, a chain reaction will start that will be very difficult to stop." Kennedy finished with the caution, "Time is of the essence, and we shouldn't miss the chance."[34]

GOLDEN SUNDAY

At 1110 hrs on Sunday, October 28 (the thirteenth day of the crisis), members of ExComm received the text from the Soviet news media reporting Khrushchev's agreement to remove the missiles under UN supervision, in exchange for President Kennedy's commitment to halt the quarantine and not invade Cuba. In a letter to President Kennedy, the Soviet leader pronounced his agreement:

> In order to eliminate as rapidly as possible the conflict which endangers the cause of peace, to give an assurance to all people who crave peace, and to reassure the American people, all of whom, I am certain, also want peace, as do the people of the Soviet Union, the Soviet government, in addition to earlier instructions on the discontinuation of further work on weapons constructions sites, has given a new order to dismantle the arms which you described as offensive, and to crate and return them to the Soviet Union. I regard with respect and trust the statement you made in your message of 27 October 1962 that there would be no attack, no invasion of Cuba, and not only on the part of the United States, but also on the part of other nations of the Western Hemisphere, as you said in your same message. Then the motives that induced us to render assistance of such a kind to Cuba disappear.

It is for this reason that we instructed our officers – these means as I had already informed you earlier are in the hands of the Soviet officers – to take appropriate measures to discontinue construction of the aforementioned facilities, to dismantle them, and to return them to the Soviet Union. As I had informed you in the letter of 27 October, we are prepared to reach agreement to enable UN representatives to verify the dismantling of these means. Thus in view of the assurances you have given, and our instructions on dismantling, there is every condition for eliminating the present conflict.

In conclusion, I should like to say something about a détente between NATO and the Warsaw Treaty countries that you have mentioned. We have spoken about this long since, and are prepared to continue to exchange views on this question with you and to find a reasonable solution. We should like to continue the exchange of views on the prohibition of atomic and thermonuclear weapons, general disarmament, and other problems relating to the relaxation of international tension.

I should like you to consider, Mr President, that violation of Cuban airspace by American airplanes could also lead to dangerous consequences. And if you do not want this to happen, it would be better if no cause is given for a dangerous situation to arise. We must be careful now and refrain from any steps that would not be useful to the defense of the states involved in the conflict, which could only cause irritation and even serve as provocation for a fateful step. Therefore, we must display sanity and reason, and refrain from such steps.

In connection with the current negotiations between Acting Secretary General U Thant and representatives of the Soviet Union, the United States, and the Republic of Cuba, the Soviet government has sent First Deputy Foreign Minister V.V. Kuznetsov to New York to help U Thant in his noble efforts aimed at eliminating the recent dangerous situation.

Respectfully yours,

N. Khrushchev[35]

In recognition of the resolution, McGeorge Bundy said "that everyone knew [those] who were hawks and who were doves, but today was the doves' day." Secretary McNamara said that Soviet ships would not attempt to cross the quarantine barrier, and he also made the recommendation that no reconnaissance missions be flown. It was suggested that surveillance could be done by the UN. The president agreed, but warned "The United Nations must carry out reconnaissance or else we will."[36]

At the JCS meeting held earlier that same day, Gen LeMay announced that he wanted a meeting with the president to convince him that the United States had to attack the missile sites in Cuba before they became fully operational. The Army chief of staff, Gen Earle G. Wheeler, backed him up. "My people tell me that all MRBM sites are now operational. If the warheads are with the missiles, they can be made ready to fire within two to five hours." Soon after this discussion, a ticker tape arrived with Moscow Radio's announcement that Khrushchev had agreed to remove the missiles. The chiefs were unanimously skeptical, with Gen LeMay voicing his concern. "The Soviets may make a charade of the withdrawal and keep some weapons in Cuba." Adm Anderson was equally upset. "The no-invasion pledge leaves Castro free to make trouble in Latin America." Gen LeMay still wanted to go to the White House, but the others decided to wait and see whether the reconnaissance flights met opposition, and what their pictures showed.[37]

Not yet made public (and it would not be until Robert Kennedy wrote *Thirteen Days* seven years later) was the understanding that the United States would withdraw its Jupiter missiles from Turkey at a later date. Another point not specifically mentioned in the agreement was the American requirement for the removal of the Il-28 bombers and MiG-21 fighters, which the United States considered offensive weapons. These unresolved issues would keep diplomats busy, and frustrated, for months ahead.

Over the next few days, non-stop low-level reconnaissance would continue far and wide over Cuba, covering all of the missile sites. VFP-62 photo missions continued at a furious pace with a new purpose – the verification of the removal of missiles. Lt Cdr Tad Riley illustrates how mission planning responded to the quickly changing events:

> I was taxiing out when one of the PIs came after me in a car. I stopped
> and he came up and handed me a scrap of paper that had literally been

ripped out of a sectional map of Cuba. On it was a big "X" and "No 1" had been circled in black ink. It was obvious to me that the priority of one of my secondary targets had been upgraded.

President Kennedy accepted Khrushchev's offer in a return letter on October 28 (reproduced here in part):

I am replying at once to your broadcast message of October 28, even though the official text has not yet reached me, because of the great importance I attach to moving forward promptly to the settlement of the Cuban crisis. I think that you and I, with our heavy responsibilities for the maintenance of peace, were aware that developments were approaching a point where events could have become unmanageable. So, I welcome this message, and consider it an important contribution to peace.

The distinguished efforts of Acting Secretary General U Thant have greatly facilitated both our tasks. I consider my letter to your October 27 [message] and your reply of today as firm undertakings on the part of both governments that should be promptly carried out. I hope that the necessary measures can at once be taken through the United Nations, as your message says, so that the United States in turn will be able to remove the quarantine measures now in effect. I have already made arrangements to report all these matters to the Organization of American States, whose members share a deep interest in a genuine peace in the Caribbean area.

I agree with you that we must devote urgent attention to the problem of disarmament, as it relates to the whole world and also to critical areas. Perhaps now, as we step back from danger, we can together make real progress in this vital field. I think we should give priority to questions relating to the proliferation of nuclear weapons, on earth and in outer space, and to the great effort for a nuclear test ban. But we should also work hard to see if wider measures of disarmament can be agreed on and put into operation at an early date. The United States government will be prepared to discuss these questions urgently, and in a constructive spirit, at Geneva or elsewhere.

John F. Kennedy[38]

President Kennedy's agreement to suspend the quarantine and to assure that the United States would not invade Cuba was based on several conditions being met by the USSR. Firstly, the weapons systems would be removed under appropriate UN observation and supervision, and secondly, there would be established adequate arrangements through the UN to ensure the carrying out and continuation of Soviet commitments. The slow imposition of these conditions by the communists ultimately delayed the full implementation of the agreement for a month, and required both the US Navy and the USAF to continue aerial surveillance over Cuba.

By Monday, October 29 (the day after the agreement had been reached between Khrushchev and President Kennedy), ExComm realized that it could not depend on the UN to adequately provide surveillance over Cuba. Secretary Rusk felt that more up-to-date reconnaissance was required, and several missions were duly approved that day.[39] He also reported that U Thant would not go to Cuba on October 30–31 if the United States conducted aerial reconnaissance overflights during his visit. On another matter, Robert McNamara announced that he had grounded all U-2 flights (worldwide) until a procedure was developed to avoid the navigational error that had seen one of the spyplanes stray over the Soviet Union on October 27. The president agreed to discontinue reconnaissance until November 1.[40]

During the meeting with U Thant, Fidel Castro would not agree to on-site inspectors to verify the dismantling of the missile sites. This in turn meant that high- and low- altitude photography would again become a top priority. American negotiators in New York were tasked with asking the Soviets not to fire on reconnaissance airplanes. The superpowers had reached an uneasy détente without consulting Fidel Castro. Apparently, his concerns counted for nothing. Castro was furious with his Soviet ally, and 20 years after the crisis he expressed his "irritation," as he put it:

> It had never crossed my mind that the option of withdrawing the missiles was conceivable. This incident, in a certain way, damaged the existing relations between Cubans and Soviets for a number of years – many years elapsed.[41]

Fidel, living up to his concept of military honor, describes his visit to a Cuban antiaircraft artillery battery:

> That day [October 29] I was at San Antonio AFB, where we had some batteries, and that was where every day, at 1000 hrs, these airplanes were flying over. I went there, and I waited for the airplanes at 1000 hrs. I knew that there would be a counterstrike, and that possibly we would have many casualties, but I thought it was my duty to be there, in a place that surely would be attacked, but the airplanes did not come that day. [Szulc writes, "Fidel sounded almost wistful."][42]

At around 1800 hrs on the 29th, Adm Dennison called Adm Ricketts and informed him that all *Blue Moon* missions flown during the day had been successfully completed. However, he said that one airplane had been fired on by a 37mm weapon as the pilot was on his way out near San Julian. Over the next few days pilots noticed that they were still being tracked by Cuban radar at times – the danger for reconnaissance aircraft was not yet over. The Cuban Missile Crisis was entering a new and still-dangerous phase.

That same day, in the White House, Arthur M. Schlesinger witnessed the feeling in the White House immediately following the détente with the Soviets:

> In Washington most of us felt a sense of limitless relief. Even the original hawk, Dean Acheson, was confounded. On October 29 he congratulated Kennedy on his "leadership, firmness, and judgment," adding that the denouement "amply shows the wisdom of the course you chose – and stuck to." On that Sunday [October 28] the president said to his brother that this was the night he should go to the theater, like Lincoln. Robert Kennedy answered, "If you were going to the theater, I would go too," having witnessed the inability of [Vice President] Johnson to make any contribution, of any kind, during all the conversations. Frequently, after the meetings were finished, he would circulate and whine and complain about our being weak, but he never made any suggestions or recommendations.[43]

This is a fair complaint by Schlesinger, for when one reads the transcripts and declassified reports, the vice president is rarely engaged.

Four days after the U-2 was shot down, Castro ordered that the body of its pilot, Maj Rudolf Anderson, be returned to the United States for a dignified burial at home.[44]

CHAPTER 11

UNARMED, UNESCORTED, & UNAFRAID

The Vought RF-8A Crusader was aerodynamically different from the F-8 fighter version that sired it. A flat fuselage bottom, necessitated by the vertical camera bay windows, and a shorter tail with less drag, gave the reconnaissance jet a boost in speed over the fighter version. More importantly, it had a greater fuel capacity – all advantages for an unarmed reconnaissance aircraft making speed runs over hostile territory.

And speed was the goal when Marine Corps Maj John Glenn (a future astronaut who was the first man to circle the globe, and also a future US Senator) used an F8U-1P – the aircraft was redesignated the RF-8A in 1962 – to perform his record-setting flight during *Project Bullet* on July 16, 1957. At a time when speed records were deemed to be an important thing for aircraft to achieve, the US Navy was excited to try and beat the previous USAF transcontinental speed record (averaging 672mph) held by the Republic F-84F Thunderstreak. More importantly, the F8U-1P was able to prove that its J57 turbojet engine could handle maximum combat power (in afterburner) for long periods of time at high altitude. Lt Cdr Charles F. Demmler flew an F8U-1 fighter as a backup during the record attempt.

The pilots had to refuel three times during the flight using US Navy piston-engined AJ-2 Savage tankers, which had a ceiling of 25,000ft and a top speed of 300mph. That meant the Crusader pilots had to reduce their speed from more than 1,000mph and descend from their cruising altitude of 50,000ft to refuel. On one of the tanking evolutions, Lt Cdr Demmler damaged his refueling probe and had to land, leaving Maj Glenn to finish the race alone.

The flight took off from NAS Los Alamitos in California and landed at Floyd Bennett Field in New York City. Glenn turned his cameras on to produce photo coverage of the coast-to-coast 2,446-mile course. He achieved a new speed record by averaging 725.55mph (Mach 1.1 at 35,000ft) during the flight's duration of 3 hours 23 minutes. This meant that Glenn had completed the crossing faster than a bullet.

Flying at supersonic speeds (the speed of sound varies at different altitudes, being 761mph at sea level and 68 degrees Fahrenheit, and 670mph at 30,000ft), the F8U-1P was laying down sonic booms along the way. When an aircraft travels through the air, it produces pressure airwaves much like the bow of a boat makes waves as it plows through the water. As the jet approaches the speed of sound, the waves are forced together and merge into a single shock wave traveling at the speed of sound (Mach 1). This is perceived on the ground as a loud boom, and the shock wave is visible. Altitude and atmospheric conditions can affect the strength of the sonic boom, which can break windows if strong enough.

As previously mentioned, *Project Bullet* F8U-1P BuNo 144608 was acquired by VFP-62 for Cuban missions in October 1962. After its assignment to *Blue Moon* and the NATC, it was transferred to VFP-63 (the West Coast photo squadron). Unfortunately, the jet was lost in a flightdeck crash aboard USS *Oriskany* (CVA-34) in the South China Sea on December 13, 1972. Its pilot, Lt Thomas B. Scott, survived. Had it not been so, BuNo 144608 would certainly have been a strong candidate for preservation in the Udvar-Hazy National Air and Space Museum at Dulles Airport, Virginia.

Beyond the *Project Bullet* accomplishment, the Crusader won the coveted Collier Trophy for its design and development in 1956 (the first fighter recipient in the 73-year history of the award). The prototype XF8U-1 was also the first aircraft of any type to break the sound barrier on its maiden flight, winning the Thompson Trophy for its speed. And, finally, it was the winner of the first Certificate of Merit from the Bureau of Aeronautics.

The Crusader was a really hot jet, and fighter pilots loved it. The manufacturer, Vought, celebrated aviators who exceeded 1,000mph in the aircraft by providing them with a pin and a certificate that welcomed them into the "Thousand Miles-Per-Hour Club" – a right-of-passage so to speak. VFP-63 pilot John "Lightnin'" Davison fondly remembers, "I flew 'Vigs' [RA-5C Vigilantes] and A-4s as well – all fun. But I don't think there is a pilot alive who flew F-8s who won't say that it was the most fun to fly – I considered it to be the Harley Davidson of airplanes." Retired US Navy Capt Larry "Deacon" Sein adds, "Having flown most fighters in the Navy inventory, I can honestly call the F-8 my One True Love in aviation. There are those who flew her, and those who wished they had." Equally fervent, fighter pilot Bruce Martin affirms his adulation. "The F-4 Phantom II was an enormously capable aircraft, but in my experience, there was never anything like the F-8 for the pure joy of flying a beautiful airplane."

It could also be a dangerous aircraft for both groundcrew and pilots, having one of the highest accident-to-hours-flown ratios of most modern fighters. Many of those accidents occurred bringing Crusaders back aboard carriers. During flightdeck operations, the jet's low, man-sized intake was feared and respected. Indeed, the only things potentially deadlier were whirling propellers, especially at night. It was always exciting to watch a Crusader poised for launch on a wet catapult, pulling against its hold-back restraints at full power and sucking moisture off the deck into an upward-swirling mini-cyclone – visible evidence of its awesome power. US Navy fighter pilot Capt Ron Knott describes the love and fear that surrounded the Crusader:

> The pilots that flew this supersonic machine loved her with a passion, having both admiration and respect for the jet. The Crusader was unorthodox. This sleek fighter commanded the respect of all that were fortunate enough to take her screaming through the skies at the speed of heat. This bird would kill you as quick as an enemy missile if you didn't stay within her performance envelope, however. She was a touchy thoroughbred that demanded fair treatment. With the latter, she would

give you awe-inspiring performance. But just lead her onto the forbidden path and she would throw you into eternity very quickly. Many excellent US Navy and Marine Corps F-8 pilots were handed the fate of death because of this temperamental beast.[1]

Cdr Newby Kelt thought that the Crusader was the "best airplane" in the US Navy at that time, being "very capable. But in some flight scenarios the pilot could encounter 'departure' – the Crusader's version of a spin. Like many fighters, the Crusader didn't have a lot of wing surface, and an indication of departure was when the airplane could buck and shutter, rotate right or left, lose air speed, and enter a flat spin – other times flipping ends and even fire or smoke coming out the intake." All survivable events, if handled with care.

Lt Cdr Tad Riley concurs, "I liked the handling characteristics of the RF-8A. You had to keep on top of it, but fighters have to be a handful if they are any good. You had to be careful going supersonic on the deck, but the Crusader was the only one I did it in, so I can't speak for other aircraft."

Reconnaissance pilots like to boast about being "Unarmed, Unescorted, and Unafraid!" Typically, such missions during the Cuba crisis did have fighter protection, but their escorts stopped as the photo aircraft went feet dry. It was the intention of Pentagon mission planners to intimidate, but not to panic the jittery Cubans and Russians – already anticipating a US air attack at any moment – into an escalation that would lead to general war. Thus, the photo jets went in alone.

In October 1962, RF-8As did not have Electronic Counter Measures (ECM) gear to ascertain whether they were being "painted" (detected or targeted) by enemy radar. This vulnerability was addressed post-crisis through the provision of a pod containing electronic equipment that could be attached to a fuselage pylon. Starting in 1965, surviving RF-8As were re-manufactured by Vought as RF-8Gs, and this variant included an ECM antenna mounted on the vertical tail. The RF-8G also boasted a more powerful engine in the form of the J57-P-420, which could push it past Mach 1.8 into Mach 2 territory, ventral stabilizing fins, Doppler radar (for flying in poor weather), infrared scanners, underwing hard points for varied external stores such as ECM pods, beefed-up fuselage structure, auxiliary fuel tanks, relocated camera stations for improved photography, and more.[2]

While the RF-8G was heavier than the A-model, the J57-P-420 engine more than compensated for it. For example, the jet could climb from sea level at a gross weight of 28,000lb to 35,000ft in just 92 seconds.

The only VFP-62 detachment (Det 42, which was part of CVW-1 embarked aboard USS *Franklin D. Roosevelt* [CVA-42] in 1966–67) sent to the Vietnam War even mounted a Sidewinder missile under the wing of one of its RF-8Gs, and the detachment electricians wired a switch in the cockpit to fire it. Fortunately for everyone, the detachment was not given permission to fly its jets operationally in this configuration by the air group commander.

Lt Cdr Tad Riley describes a primitive ECM experiment during the Cuban Missile Crisis:

On one flight a civilian came out to my airplane after I had strapped in and gave me a small battery-powered Motorola tape recorder (2 x 3 x 6in approximately) that I stuffed under my torso harness and plugged into the jet's radios. It had a wire antenna that was to be taped to the inside of the canopy after it was closed – masking tape was provided. This was the extent of our ECM capability.

I was told that if I heard a "whoop whoop" sound, that was the indication that a Russian SAM radar was searching. If this was followed by a higher frequency rapid "beep, beep, beep," that meant it had "locked on" and I should dive for the deck. I heard the "whoop whoop" once, but no "beep, beep, beep." I don't think their SAMs were much of a threat to us because they were limited when targeting low-level high-speed aircraft. We were inside their non-lethal range.

FIGHTER PROTECTION OFFSHORE

In October 1962 VF-62 "Boomerangs" was equipped with F-8B Crusader fighters and deployed to Key West to provide protection for all US Navy surveillance aircraft involved in the crisis, including P-2 Neptunes and P-3 Orions taking pictures of Soviet ships entering Cuban waters. Capt Ron Knott was serving with the unit at this time, and he recalls:

> Somehow the MiG pilots knew when we were in hot pursuit of them and they headed back to Cuba as fast as possible. We never got a shot at a MiG, although we chased many away from the fleet. We were like a big brother coming to the aid of the surveillance aircraft. If a MiG harassed them, we took over the fight since they had no weapons with which to defend themselves.[3]

In his book *Supersonic Cowboys*, Ron describes one such incident that could have had profound consequences:

> Lt Howie "Kickstand" Bullman and Lt(jg) Jim "Diamond" Brady of VF-62 were on minute alert at NAS Boca Chica, Key West, when they got a call to scramble to intercept some threatening MiGs. They were airborne in two-and-a-half minutes from the alarm. They made a section takeoff in afterburner, accelerating and climbing to 25,000ft. They continued to accelerate to supersonic speed, while taking [intercept] vectors from "Brown Stone," the ground control radar station that was charged with the task of guiding such intercepts over the Florida Straits.
>
> About 63 miles from Key West, and perhaps six minutes from takeoff, both Lt Bullman and Lt(jg) Brady found two MiG-17s using their APG-94 radar systems. "Brown Stone" confirmed the targets and Lt Bullman acknowledged taking over the intercept by calling "Judy" over the radio. This was the code word for assuming control of the intercept in the cockpit.
>
> The MiG-17s never saw Lt Bullman or Lt(jg) Brady as they slid in behind and slightly below the rapidly departing communist jets as they headed south towards Santa Clara, Cuba. With his Sidewinders growling in his headset, indicating an infrared lock on the tail pipes of the MiGs, Lt Bullman requested permission to attack by firing a missile. There was what seemed like an interminable silence from "Brown Stone." Actually, the delay in responding was probably less than 20 seconds. The command

was to "Break off the intercept and return to base." Lt Bullman acknowledged the command and the section of F-8s headed back to Key West. Many hours were spent in debriefing the pilots by a host of military and civilian officials.

It was many years before both pilots came to understand why the attack had been called off. Negotiations between the White House and the Kremlin had reached a critical stage, and the destruction of two Russian-built (and probably flown) aircraft would have perhaps led to the outbreak of hostilities between the nations. No one can ever know for sure what would have happened had Lt Bullman not requested instructions from "Brown Stone." The rules of engagement in place at the time would have allowed the two F-8 pilots to fire on any aircraft engaged in a hostile or threatening act against any elements of the Armed Forces of the United States. Lt Bullman, through his cool-headed handling of the situation, may have prevented a chain of events from unfolding that could have been extremely unfortunate for both nations, as well as the entire world.[4]

VF-32 "Swordsmen" flew F-8Ds, which like the B-models assigned to VF-62 had a complement of missiles and 20mm cannon. VF-32 was tasked with escorting VFP-62's RF-8As to their feet dry position and then providing them with protection as they headed back to NAS Jacksonville. It is an interesting aside that US Navy "brass" decided to develop the successor to the Crusader, the F-4 Phantom II, without cannons because they considered them antiquated and unnecessary – it was believed that close-in dogfighting would never happen again following the introduction of advanced air intercept radar and both short- and medium-range air-to-air missiles with the F-4. The subsequent conflict in Vietnam proved this to be a serious mistake, and eventually USAF F-4Es were built from the late 1960s with an integral cannon in the nose. No US Navy Phantom IIs were ever fitted with cannon, however.

VF-32's Ken Walling tells of a Cuban Missile Crisis scramble that almost resulted in one Crusader shooting down another:

There was an alert called and the aircrews scrambled towards their aircraft. Lt(jg) James Miller taxied out to the runway, ready to take off. His Crusader was armed with four AIM-9 Sidewinder heat-seeking missiles.

It's now speculated that his aircraft had a malfunctioning missile launch switch or that he inadvertently hit the jettison switch with his foot while manning the cockpit. The consequence wasn't detected until his aircraft began to lift off the runway and the landing gear sensed weight off the wheels, thus engaging the rocket motors on the missiles. Suddenly, both sides of his cockpit glowed with a bright fire. Thinking that his aircraft had exploded, Miller pulled his Crusader up to gain as much altitude as possible before ejecting. Realizing that the aircraft was responding correctly, he caught a quick glimpse of his two Sidewinders in flight before him, headed down the runway.

Meanwhile, his section leader, Lt(jg) Gary Dillard, had the crap scared out of him as the two missiles roared by the side of his aircraft. The ill-fated mission was scrubbed and both pilots proceeded to the Officers' Club for a round of drinks.

Fortunately, the Sidewinders had not "locked-on" and the accident ended well. Fighter pilots never pass up an opportunity to relieve tensions by abusing one another. Capt Jerry Coffee remembers one such moment:

We "photo weenies" rode the fighter pilots for not being allowed to go feet dry over Cuba. They had to circle over the Straits of Florida waiting for us to come feet wet. We called them the "non-combatants." At one happy hour we presented the CO of VF-32, Cdr Ed Clayton, with a set of white coveralls that came complete with a big red cross and the words "Non-Combatant" across the back. He good-naturedly wore them during the whole party. [Cdr Clayton was killed in a night landing accident on March 19, 1963 while trying to land back aboard USS Saratoga (CVA-60) in F-8D BuNo 147920.]

The VF-32 guys were ready to go feet dry with weapons at a moment's notice. That was great comfort to us. We were always hoping a MiG would chase us out to sea for the "Swordsmen" to gobble up.

VFP-62's Capt Ed Feeks flew four missions over Cuba, and he is quick to give credit to the offshore fighter protection:

> In short, we "photo weenies" were most appreciative of the fighter guys who were there in spades. What a wonderful thought it was to know that they were waiting for us to exit from the beach. And when we did, they would say "that our tails were clear."

With tensions mounting over the trigger-happy Soviet commander of the SAM site that shot down and killed Maj Anderson, as well as the increase in AAA encountered by the low-level reconnaissance airplanes over targets, *Blue Moon* missions were becoming more and more risky. The Crusader's sleek design presented a rather small profile for the Cuban air defenses to aim at. The pilots took advantage of "ground clutter" to confuse radar, get to their target quickly, duck low again, and "run like hell" to the fighter escorts confined offshore.

It almost seemed like the Cubans were always caught off-guard, while simultaneously uncertain of "tugging at the tiger's tail." Cdr Kelt explains it this way:

> Usually our missions were flown between 0800 and 1000 hrs or 1500 and 1600 hrs to take advantage of shadows. [PIs use shadows to determine height of objects.] The Cubans loved baseball, and often would have five games going on at the time we made our pass. We sometimes heard the rumble of antiaircraft fire as we left the target area.

In the early 1960s, those of us who were lucky enough to witness a high-speed Crusader flyby from a carrier's flightdeck know how difficult it was to see its approach from a distance. A bit stealthy, it blended in well with the horizon, sea, and sky, even when you knew it was coming. The high-positioned knife-edged wings were nearly invisible from the front, and when you finally saw the jet, you could not help being mesmerized. The mind had nothing to compare it with – the long, sleek profile, with its prominent shark-like vertical tail, streaking momentarily abeam the ship, outracing the roar of its engine, gulping thousands of pounds of air each minute. Then, the airplane's ear-shattering sonic boom, followed by an abrupt, steep vertical climb, standing on the afterburner's translucent fiery plume, while performing a perfect eight-point roll. Still visible, the RF-8A clawed through the air with supersonic shock waves glowing above the wings. Then, it was gone.

Even after 50 years, the memory of it is still vivid – always producing goose bumps – evoking the pride we had in this most beautiful of man-made machines, and the aviators who flew them. The hapless Cuban antiaircraft gunners could be forgiven for missing their target, while most likely exclaiming in Spanish, "What the hell was that?"

The missile bases had a three-ringed defense configuration. The inner ring consisted of Cuban-manned antiaircraft artillery, but weren't effective. Further out, Soviet and Cuban MiG air bases were intended to defend against air attack. Finally, the outer ring was the surface-to-air missiles controlled by the Russians.

The MiG threat came from the Cuban Air Force, flying MiG-15s, MiG-17s and MiG-19s, but of more concern were the supersonic MiG-21s, crated and transported to Cuba by the Soviet Air Force. The MiG-21 had similar performance characteristics to the Crusader, if not better, and was flown only by the Soviet pilots. Lt Cdr Tad Riley's assessment of the aerial threat posed by the communist fighters was as follows:

Could the MiGs have shot us down? Of course they could, under the right conditions. They had guns and missiles, but at the speeds and altitudes we operated at, it wouldn't have been easy, unless they snuck up from the rear. If the truth were known, that's probably how most aerial kills are made, anyway.

The Russians didn't fire their SAMs at us because we weren't within their effective range. We were briefed that their SAMs didn't arm and track until they had traveled 1,500ft. We flew below 500ft and at about the same speed or more, so it is doubtful they could touch us – and they knew it. Those SAMs were designed to get high-altitude targets [the SAM's radar had inherent limitations under 3,000ft].

Soviet Air Force pilot Nikolay Pakhomov discusses the frustration of the constant low-level reconnaissance flights:

> The USAF airplanes appeared above our air base daily on a regular basis. [The Russians did not seem to distinguish between US Navy or USAF reconnaissance aircraft.] They were a pair of McDonnell RF–101 Voodoo aircraft, with the USAF identification – the leading jet was a two-seat "photographic," and it flew over our air base, increased their speed, and left off, leaving a black-smoky loop behind. And we were powerless to do anything.[5]

A frustrated Soviet pilot recalls, "Two RF–101s were on a reconnaissance mission. We requested permission to attack, but got the response, 'FORBIDDEN!' It didn't matter – we only had a training missile, and our 30mm guns were not loaded." Another complains, "The Americans made their flights over Santa Clara air base regularly, daily to be precise, at 1500 hrs. The AAA guns of the Cubans were nearby, and silent, our duty aircraft likewise. Why, after all, did we suffer all the tortures that resulted from preparations of our airplanes and our presence there?"[6]

A real danger to pilots and their aircraft was striking a bird (there was an abundance of buzzards over Cuba) while flying low and fast. Capt Ecker jokingly told Dino Brugioni that if the Cubans wanted to improve their defenses, they should have placed dead goats along the hillsides and let the vultures circle over them!

Lt Cdr (at the time) Newby Kelt was still dealing with a backache after his low-altitude ejection on October 16 but he had soon returned to flight duty. He was the flight leader on a *Blue Moon* mission that was to penetrate the western edge of Cuba near the Isle of Pines. Kelt and his wingman were flying at below 200ft at 500–520 knots, still over water, when he saw two very large birds off his starboard bow. Lt Cdr Kelt at first did not think that they were a threat, so he did not warn his wingman. Abruptly, one of the birds, perhaps sensing the jet's shockwave, turned directly towards the Crusaders.

As (now) Cdr Kelt remembers it, "We were closing in on the birds at tremendous speed, and before I could evade them, one crashed into the right-quarter [windshield] panel, with pieces of flesh and feathers (fortunately little glass) filling the cockpit." The flight of Crusaders were on radio silence, but Kelt contacted his wingman and told him to terminate the mission. The damage to Kelt's jet meant that his exit back to base would have to be at much lower speed and altitude, making him more vulnerable to MiGs. Fortunately, there were no communist jets around, and they landed safely. Today, Kelt reminisces, "It is a good thing the bird didn't go into the intake – for sure, I'd have lost the aircraft, at sea and in hostile territory."

Kelt would have another escape from death a few months later while aboard USS *Enterprise* (CVAN-65) as the officer in charge of VFP-62's Det 65. On April 16, 1963, during launch operations, his RF-8A (BuNo 146894) was on one of the angle-deck catapults when it was "downed" by a plane captain for an oil leak. He was directed to maneuver his aircraft forward to the elevator, where it could be taken down to the hangar deck for repairs.

Several A-4 Skyhawks were preparing for launch on the bow catapults at the time, and according to one observer, at least one of them was at 100 percent power. Suddenly, an exhaust blast from one of the Skyhawks caught Kelt's RF-8A broadside as the carrier was heading into the wind for launch operations. The A-4's blast caused his Crusader to slide on the slick deck surface, despite Kelt's efforts to control the jet using full brakes and nose gear steering. Aviation Mechanic Third Class Pete Wallace tried to stop the airplane's slide by putting a chock behind the wheel, but it was too late and the doomed jet tumbled over the side.

As his Crusader plummeted, 50 degrees nose down, towards the water some 80ft below the flightdeck, Cdr Kelt remembers seeing water approaching through his camera viewfinder (a 6in lens centered on his instrument panel, it was used on photo runs to center the target) just before he ejected from the ill-fated jet. With only seconds to spare, Kelt pulled the ejection handle and faced another low-altitude ejection without a full 'chute, but this time at sea – frequently a fatal situation. Because the airplane was falling vertically into the water, Kelt was ejected horizontally, and he hit the water face down.

Ejecting from an aircraft is always a hazardous event, especially so when the airplane is at zero altitude and zero speed (later, a so-called zero-zero ejection seat was developed). The ejection seat is powered by an explosive device that gives the pilot a "kick in the butt." This is necessary to propel him quickly so that he does not get hit by the vertical tail on his way out. The normal sequence is for the canopy to separate first, but if it does not, the pilot gets ejected through it, still attached to his seat. Under a more "normal" ejection, the pilot would separate from his seat automatically at a predetermined altitude, but there was no time for that in Kelt's situation. He hit the water still attached to his seat.

Kelt was fortunate that his ejection path was away from the carrier. There have been occasions where the pilot has ejected into the vessel, or, even worse, onto the flightdeck, hitting another jet preparing to launch. A frequent cause of pilot death following an ejection from the flightdeck is being sucked under the carrier and into its gigantic propellers. This author saw a pilot sink out of sight, still strapped into his Crusader. Witnessing that gives true meaning to the phrase "the price of freedom."

Once more Kelt had cheated death, for he was quickly rescued by the UH-25B Retriever plane-guard helicopter (from HU-2 Det 65) that was always stationed abreast of the ship during flight operations. After a few days in the sickbay recovering from the physical effects of his high-speed concussion with the water, Kelt was returned to flight status. An imposing, large man, he was lovingly chided by his shipmates, "Next time, please bring back the airplane!"

Flying a successful reconnaissance mission demands cool skill, rather than the frenetic aerial maneuvering associated with fighter-versus-fighter combat because the pilot must keep his photo-airplane perfectly level and precisely on course over foreign territory that is often prickling with SAMs or AAA.[7] In the final analysis, the Crusader's speed was its real defense. Later, in Vietnam, photo runs were often flown over targets at higher altitudes following heavy losses to AAA during low-altitude runs similar to those performed so successfully over Cuba. Capt Len Johnson, a VFP-63 pilot (who had had a tour with VFP-62 in 1967), flew many missions over North Vietnam. He describes his survival tactics:

The best defense against flak was to keep constantly moving (called jinking) around the sky – changing altitude and speed. Never descend below 3,000ft (the limit of AAA).

I didn't line up on any targets. Never fly in straight lines! I would fly in a zigzag path to my target and turn at the last minute to pass over it, going as fast as possible, which would be speeds in excess of 600 knots [approximately 700mph]. My favorite approach, again weather permitting, was to descend from high altitude, say 20,000ft, to pass over the target at supersonic speeds. Unfortunately, I still had to fly over the target at between 3,000 and 4,000ft, which the North Vietnamese gunners knew. They simply filled the sky with lead, and I had to fly through it.[8]

VFP-63 pilot Capt Will Gray sums up his feelings about the Crusader, particularly the photo-bird:

If you have to go to war, the Crusader was right for the job. Fast, maneuverable, easy on the fuel and a bit stealthy – its heart was the J57 engine, which was reliable and forgiving. The Crusader was hard to land aboard ship and very difficult to max perform in air combat, but for flat-out running in the world of the photo pilot, it was a real sweetheart. With the droops up in a descent, followed by a good shove from the hard-lighting afterburner, the airspeed spun up toward 700 knots indicated like a video game, only this was real.

Only a fighter pilot knows what it feels like to be running at such speeds. You can feel the power.[9]

Finally, in Cuba, the RF-8A and RF-101C pilots benefited from Khrushchev's and Kennedy's restraint. With the exception of the Soviet SAM commander who shot down Maj Anderson (thus violating Khrushchev's orders), the MiGs' presence tended to threaten and harass the invading jets, rather than pursue them and shoot them down. Likewise, President Kennedy kept fighters away from Cuba in an effort to de-escalate the tension and avoid all-out war. In the end, we were all lucky!

CHAPTER 12

NIGHT PHOTO MISSIONS OVER GITMO
NOVEMBER 5, 1962

Two attack carriers were in the naval armada enforcing the quarantine of Cuba, namely USS *Independence* (CVA-62) and the first nuclear-powered carrier, USS *Enterprise* (CVAN-65). The carrier task force remained poised to support the quarantine, and any military escalation of the crisis. VFP-62 had detachments on both carriers, with Det 62 being part of CVG-7 aboard CVA-62 and Det 65 part of CVG-6 embarked in CVAN-65.

Only two over-land reconnaissance missions originated from an aircraft carrier during the crisis, however, and they were flown by Lt (now Capt) Jim Curry from *Enterprise*. Both were night photo missions over the Guantanamo Naval Base. The primary mission of carrier-based VFP-62 aircraft was to fly peripheral photography of Cuba.

The RF-8A had a night photo capability and VFP-62 perfected a technique called night forward photography. Although the RF-8A was originally configured to do vertical night photography only, Cdr Koch and his photo-technicians modified it so that the jet could also capture a pilot's eye view of the target – a forward-oblique night photograph. This writer remembers his *Forrestal* detachment (Det 59) in mid-1962 testing the beefed-up support brackets for the nose (Bay 1) camera station that housed the new KA-45/46 cameras – the latter were larger and heavier than the as-delivered forward-shooting cameras. Typical of VFP-62's ingenuity, the brackets were handcrafted in the home workshop of Lt(jg) Cecil Ogles, an officer in the photo department. Carrier landings and launches stressed the cameras and brackets, sometimes causing cracks in the metal which could ultimately cause the loss of an aircraft.

Det 59 pilot Lt(jg) Ron Datka flew night photography over *Forrestal* and its destroyer escorts to assess the new system's capabilities. There were problems, with the most serious being mysterious streaks on the negatives caused by static electricity. The photo gurus back at the squadron soon found the source of the problem and fixed it. The untold story is that the marvelous cameras (KA-45/46) that gave VFP-62 the edge over all other military squadrons were still in a research and development phase a few months before the crisis began. Some very remarkable and talented men ensured the unit's success with this new equipment.

The RF-8A used two types of photographic flares – the M-123A-1 cartridge, rated at an intensity of 260 million candlepower, and the M-112 with 110 million candlepower – to illuminate the target. The flares were shot out of the airplane from a compartment at the rear of the cockpit and a light detector (photocell) synchronized the opening of the camera shutter with each burst of light. There is a photograph in the plates section showing results of a night flash exposure from an RF-8. It graphically illustrates that in a combat environment the aircraft dropping the flares would have been easily spotted by AAA gunners looking to shoot it down.

As mentioned previously, Secretary McNamara and Gen Taylor lobbied hard for night surveillance. They thought, correctly, that the Soviets were doing a lot of their construction work, and moving equipment around, after dark, and night photography was the only way to document it. Additionally, because of the exploding flares, they felt that there was an additional psychological benefit to the flights. President Kennedy deftly gave tentative approval for these missions, but withheld final approval for a later time. It never came. Without doubt, the president was fearful that the exploding flares would be misinterpreted by the Soviet or Cuban defenders, thus provoking a miscalculated response.

However, the Marines at Guantanamo heard noises at night on the other side of the perimeter fence and requested a night photo mission to investigate. It is undocumented if authority for these missions was given by the president. Capt Curry explains what happened:

On November 5, 1962, I launched from CVAN-65 at about 2100 hrs and lined up on the western perimeter fence before commencing my run over the fence line. The Marines positioned a jeep with lights on at the northern end as a reference point.

I flew along that fence line, followed by the fence line along the northern boundary from west to east, and then the eastern boundary from north to south. I landed at the airfield there, and the base photomates got the film from the aircraft and took it to their photo lab. Unfortunately, they put it into the hypo first and ruined the photos. [Hypo is the last of three solutions used in the development process.]

When I began the run over the western fence, I was very close to the BOQ (Bachelor Officers' Quarters). Men in the BOQ heard the explosions from the photo flares and saw the bright lights. They thought the war had started, and that the base was being attacked with mortars.

After the film had been removed from my aircraft, I went to the BOQ to bed down overnight, before returning to the *Enterprise* the next day. When I got to the small bar at the BOQ, there was still a lot of excitement and talk about the photo flares, and the fear they generated.

During 2002–03, in some exchanges of e-mails by Crusader pilots, a Marine aviator wrote to me about the impact of the Gitmo overflights. He was a captain during the Cuban crisis and the officer in charge of a Marine detachment of F-8s that had been sent from Beaufort, South Carolina, to Guantanamo Bay. He was in the BOQ the night I flew the first night photo mission around the fence line. He later served in Vietnam for several tours, flying both tactical aircraft and helicopters – he used the latter to rescue Marines and soldiers that had been wounded in combat.

Although he had many harrowing experiences in Vietnam, he told me that the night of the RF-8A photo mission was the most frightening he had ever experienced in his life. Indeed, it had been more horrific than anything he had endured in Vietnam.

The US Navy had established a naval base at Guantanamo in 1898. When the Cuban Missile Crisis erupted, the base was lightly defended by three Marine rifle companies and some Seebees manning 8mm mortars from perimeter positions. Additionally, a small number of on-base fighter aircraft flown in from *Independence* and *Enterprise* provided air support. Immediately after President Kennedy's address on October 22, USAF C-135 jet transports airlifted Marine reinforcements into Guantanamo. The Marines improved their defenses with tanks and antitank vehicles. To reinforce the base, thousands of landmines were placed along the base perimeter. Additionally, a Marine antiaircraft Hawk missile battalion was deployed.

The Marines, including inspecting generals, were typically gung-ho, satisfied that they were now ready for an attack. They were unaware, however, that Soviet FKR cruise missiles with 12 kiloton nuclear warheads (not known to exist until Michael Dobbs' research for his book) were deployed against the base.

As so often happens, word does not get passed down and the Marines were not notified about the night photo run. An eyewitness account from the ground comes from (then) 2Lt Tom Boardman, attached to the First Marine Regiment:

When Lt Curry flew the first photo-recon mission over Guantanamo Bay Naval Base, several thousand unsuspecting Marines were positioned along the base perimeter prepared to defend it against attack by Cuban ground forces. Most of the Marine brigade members were resting or asleep at the time.

Suddenly, the night erupted with a series of brilliant flashes and loud reports suggesting incoming artillery. Startled Marines were instantly awake with feelings ranging from bewilderment to fright. As the Marines watched the flashes and heard the noise of continuing explosions of magnesium photo flares ejected by Lt Curry's aircraft, men clutched their rifles and strained to hear small arms fire – trying to locate the point of attack. Machine guns were cocked, hand grenades were placed at the ready, and crew-served weapons were manned. The Marines were as confused as they were alert.

The intruding airplane disappeared and the night became quiet again, but the Marines were more awake than ever and, it would be hours before exhaustion replaced the adrenalin rush and allowed them to sleep. A readiness drill compliments of VFP-62.

Reconnaissance photographs taken by Lt Curry showed groups of isolated Cuban soldiers on the other side of the fence, leaning on shovels and looking up at the streaking Crusader. From the photographs, it appeared that the Cuban positions were defensive only, and did not point to an imminent attack on the base. No matter, the shock of that night surely remains in the permanent memories of the Marine eyewitnesses and, no doubt, is the source of reunion laughs and is a favorite among exaggerated stories told to grandchildren.

Capt Curry concludes:

I think Tom Boardman's story is an outstanding account of that evening. What I appreciate most about the accounting of this recce flight is that until I read this, I never knew that there was any useful information gleaned from the photography I obtained.

Night photography for the RF-8A would have been a challenge in Cuba. It would have been difficult to find the target, and once there, the Crusader pilot would have been more vulnerable to AAA. In addition, the response of the Gitmo Marines would have been the same for the Cubans and Russians, potentially causing an over-reaction that could have escalated the stand-off into general war. The Cuban Missile Crisis awakened the military to the need for an improved night photo capability. By the Vietnam War, better technology did indeed exist.

CHAPTER 13

VERIFYING THE REMOVAL OF MISSILES
NOVEMBER 1962

On November 1, President Kennedy was surrounded by skeptics who were concerned that the treacherous Soviet leader would not meet his commitments. With the October 29 surveillance results not providing any comfort and his agreement not to fly reconnaissance while U Thant was meeting with Castro on October 30–31, JFK was apprehensive as well. Responding to a reporter's concern that ground inspection was being thwarted by a disgruntled Castro, the president responded, "The camera, I think, is going to be our best inspector."[1]

He was also keeping his military options on the table. Despite his assurances to Khrushchev, archival evidence shows that ExComm and the JCS were still finalising attack and invasion plans. Putting such discussions into perspective is difficult because it is clear from so much documentation that the president had no interest in pursuing an invasion of Cuba. The best answer for why such a meeting took place is that it follows usual contingency planning during a dangerous time, and with the record of Soviet duplicity still hanging in the air, it was the prudent thing to do.

In the Afterword of Robert Kennedy's *Thirteen Days*, written by Richard E. Neustadt and Graham T. Allison, these analysts of crisis management offer the insight that in the first days of the crisis, the president was looking for a "clean-surgical" air strike, and he quickly learned from the military that this was not possible.

It is also known that the OPLANs went through more analysis and revision during the crisis as a result of new low-level photography being available that allowed the missile locations to be pinpointed. Such imagery also helped to refine the various attack folders that were created.

Yet the president waffled on the invasion issue, and gave guidance to the Army chief of staff, warning that "he wanted forces to be of such size that an operation against Cuba can be executed swiftly, [and he] is willing to take a chance about degrading capability for a Berlin contingency [troops reserved for Soviet hostile action against Berlin]."[2] Additionally, on November 7, he cautioned that planning should be adequate, "lest there be mistaken optimism 'that one Yankee could always lick ten gringos.' "[3]

At the 1000 hrs ExComm meeting on November 1, Secretary Rusk voiced concern and hesitation. "The most important question to be decided is whether we should make low-level flights over Cuba today." He also advised that if a reconnaissance airplane was lost, there should be no retaliation that day.[4] Secretary McNamara said he thought, "We ought to fly low-level. The Russians have not so far complied with their agreement to withdraw the missiles and the American public needs to be reassured that we know what is going on in Cuba," and concluded, "we need more information on the Il–28 bombers in Cuba. The flights should be authorized today because [Soviet First Deputy] Anastas I. Mikoyan would be arriving in Cuba tomorrow."[5] The president authorized six low-level sorties over the Il–28 base and several MRBM sites. Like McNamara, he also directed that if an airplane was shot down there would be no military reprisals that day. U-2 missions were ruled out because of weather conditions.

The reason for flying over the Il–28 base was to make clear to the communists that they were considered offensive weapons too, and to reinforce the demand that they had to be removed by the Soviets.[6] Again, RF–8As and RF–101s were being used as instruments of American diplomacy.

On November 2 Fidel Castro met with Mikoyan and evidenced his bitterness over the US–Soviet agreement by announcing he refused to allow ground inspection by the UN. On October 28, Fidel sent a letter to U Thant that listed five conditions that had to be met before he would consider any decision on ground inspections. The United States had to:

- move out of the Guantanamo Naval Base;
- end its economic blockade;
- quit aiding "subversive activities";
- abandon "piratical attacks";
- stop the "violation" of Cuba's air and sea space and territorial waters.[7]

The Soviets supported his proposal.

In an effort to appease the communist objections to US reconnaissance flights, the Canadian government offered to provide Canadian pilots and RF-101s to satisfy the American need to monitor the fulfillment of commitments. The president dismissed the offer.

With Castro's rejection of UN ground inspection and the inability of the organization to conduct aerial reconnaissance, the president realized the United States would have to continue its reconnaissance flights during the period of dismantling and withdrawal of the offensive weapons. The American government could not take the chance that some offensive weapons would be left behind. Essentially, the task of the PIs would be to count the crated missiles and related equipment making their way to ships heading out of Cuba (the Soviets reported, and it was confirmed by US intelligence, that there were 42 nuclear missiles shipped to Cuba).

Meanwhile, photo-reconnaissance, particularly low-level flights, remained controversial, with Castro asserting that the overflights threatened his national integrity and sovereignty. During an interview many years after the conflict, Tad Szulc recounts how Castro remained forceful about his right to protect Cuban airspace:

He [Castro] was just as vehement in saying that he was determined to destroy any American airplane his AAA could reach, regardless of the consequences. For him, it was again a matter of principle and sovereignty, and he had ordered that American aircraft that appeared over Cuba a few days after the crisis was settled be fired upon – even if it reopened the confrontation. Castro was aware when he spoke to me that Kennedy had resolved to bomb Cuba if a second American aircraft was shot down after the loss of the U-2.[8] [Actually, the president was more nuanced regarding retaliation for another shoot-down.]

Although no IRBM missiles per se had been found in Cuba, photography from the October 29 missions showed that work on some MRBM and IRBM sites was still being continued. Analysts made the assessment that if IRBMs existed in Cuba they were in an undiscovered facility, although they believed it was unlikely that any IRBMs had reached Cuba before the institution of the quarantine (this was confirmed after the crisis). By this time, three or four Il-28 bombers had been assembled, with an additional 23 or 24 aircraft still in crates at San Julian in western Cuba.[9] So, it was a mixed and confusing environment, and still a dangerous one for the photo airplanes to operate in. ExComm and the president struggled with the need for photo intelligence and the development of a response to a possible reconnaissance airplane being shot down, thus reigniting the crisis.

Finally, photography from the six reconnaissance sorties of November 1 produced good news – all known MRBM sites were partially or totally dismantled, launch pads had been bulldozed, and missile and launch equipment had been removed to unknown locations. Construction on IRBM sites had stopped, and all work carried out had been partially destroyed.[10] The next day the president issued a statement:

My fellow citizens, I want to take this opportunity to report on the conclusions which the Government has reached on the basis of yesterday's aerial photographs which will be made available tomorrow, as well as other indications, namely, that the Soviet missile bases in Cuba are being dismantled, their missiles and related equipment are being crated and the fixed installations at these sites are being destroyed.

The United States intends to follow closely the completion of this work through a variety of means, including aerial surveillance, until

This photo, taken either by Capt Ecker or Lt Bruce Wilhelmy on October 23, was most likely the exhibit presented to the Security Council on October 25, when Ambassador Stevenson said, "You can clearly see one of the pairs of launch pads with a concrete building from which launching operations for three pads are controlled." *(NPIC photograph)*

This VFP-62 photograph taken on October 23 shows the PI's marked up points of interest, revealing the wealth of intelligence that can be obtained from one photograph. This would be the type of image most likely shown at the UN Security Council on October 25 when the photographic evidence was presented by Ambassador Adlai Stevenson. *(Capt William B. Ecker collection)*

This photograph of an ExComm meeting at the White House in October 1962 shows Secretary of State Dean Rusk to the left and Secretary of Defense Robert McNamara to the right of the president. Attorney General (and brother) Robert Kennedy is sat directly opposite the president. *(JFK Library and Museum)*

A trusted and influential adviser, Secretary of Defense Robert McNamara confers informally with President Kennedy outside the Oval Office in the West Wing of the White House during an ExComm meeting. *(JFK Library and Museum)*

Above: The president's younger brother and most trusted adviser, Robert Kennedy, and the president are shown here in an intimate discussion at the White House in early October 1962. *(JFK Library and Museum)*

Right: A note written by the president on October 28, 1962 while preparing a message for Khrushchev accepting his proposal for the withdrawal of Soviet missiles from Cuba. "Fall out shelter Virginia" refers to his home at Middleburg, VA. *(JFK Library and Museum)*

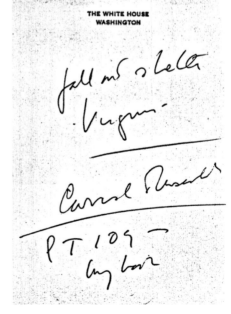

Senate photograph of President John F. Kennedy. *(JFK Library and Museum)*

President Kennedy had a tendency to scribble notes and doodles during meetings, often repetitiously writing words, such as here, "dangerous" and "Cuba." *(JFK Library and Museum)*

"PLAYBOYS"

VMCJ-2's nickname was "The Playboys" and the *Playboy* bunny was its logo. This bunny logo showed up on the tails of the unit's aircraft in the mid-to-late 1950s, and they remained until 1992, when the post-Tailhook high command ordered their removal when unfavorable attention was drawn to them. *(vfp62.com)*

VMCJ-2 RF-8A BuNo 144614, complete with the unit's *Playboy* bunny emblem on the tail. This aircraft survived almost three decades of service to be retired to the Aerospace Maintenance and Regeneration Center at Davis-Monthan AFB, in Arizona, in January 1987. *(Col Wayne Whitten USMC (ret.))*

This is an extremely detailed VFP-62 photograph of a San Cristobal missile site, showing five SS-4 MRBMs, a missile ready tent, and support vehicles. *(Dino A. Brugioni photo provided for this book)*

Cdr William B. Ecker (left) and VMCJ-2 pilot Capt (later Lt Gen) John I. Hudson shake hands after a flight to Homestead AFB for a USAF press briefing staged on December 1, 1962. Note the "Castro and Dead Chicken" stencilling on the RF-8A behind them. Each dead chicken denoted a completed mission over Cuba. *(Cdr. Peter Mersky collection)*

This photo of the San Cristobal No 1 MRBM launching site demonstrates the superior detail provided by low-level photography produced either by VFP-62 or VMCJ-2 on October 25, 1962. Erectors, missile transporters, shelter tents, and other ground equipment are easily identified. *(Dino A. Brugioni collection at National Security Archives, George Washington University)*

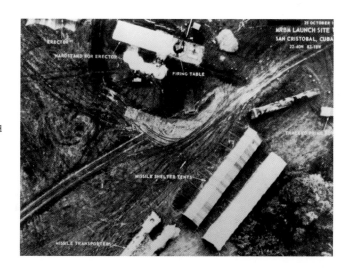

This photograph, taken on October 27, 1962, shows Cuban ground defenses, including 57mm AAA, aimed at low-flying reconnaissance aircraft. *(Dino A. Brugioni collection at National Security Archives, George Washington University)*

A VFP-62 crewman "chalking up another dead chicken" on the fuselage of the RF-8A. Each new chicken represented the completion of another low-level mission over Cuba. *(Cdr Peter Mersky collection)*

Lt Jerry Coffee (left), R Adm Joseph Carson, and Lt Cdr Art Day debrief their completed mission. *(vfp62.com collection)*

VFP-62 groundcrew (the "Rotten Cotton Ball" detachment) at NAS Boca Chica, in Key West, Florida. Vinnie Zabicki (standing, seventh from right) and Richard Flake (standing, tenth from right) contributed to this book. PHC Frank Wolle (left front, with his thumb raised) contributed greatly to the implementation of the KA-45 camera in the RF-8A. *(Vinnie Zabicki collection)*

A good view of Maj John Glenn's *Project Bullet* F8U-1P (BuNo 144608), showing its camera bay windows. In the nose cone is the small window for the viewfinder that helped the pilot align the jet with the target. Under the intake is the "gun-camera" bay 1 bubble, while on the port side can be seen both oblique and vertical windows for bays 2 and 3. On the starboard side is the bay 4 vertical window, while the small square window just aft of bay 1 is the scanner window, which automatically fed altitude and speed parameters to the camera systems. *(Cdr Peter Mersky collection)*

The camera system's viewfinder can be seen above Maj Glenn's right hand. He set a new transcontinental speed record of 3 hours, 23 minutes and 8.4 seconds on July 16, 1957, averaging an impressive 723mph throughout this period in his stock F8U-1P. *(Cdr Peter Mersky collection)*

The backup F8U-1 Crusader is refueled from an AJ Savage tanker during the early stages of *Project Bullet*. Maj Glenn holds off to port in his F8U-1P, waiting his turn to refuel. *(Cdr Peter Mersky collection)*

The RF-8A had four camera bays, and this photograph of a VFP-62 jet shows the window configuration for the bay 1 forward-pointing camera, the vertical windows for bays 2 (port side), 3 and 4 and the oblique windows for bays 2 (starboard) and 4. *(Art Scarborough PHC, collection)*

The Vought RF-8A Crusader is a beauty to behold from any angle. Note the distinctive VFP-62 squadron film stripes on the wings and tail of this machine, BuNo 146895. Starboard oblique camera bays 2 and 4 are shown. This photograph was taken by a wingman using the port oblique 9in format camera. *(vfp62.com collection)*

In a freak accident on April 16, 1963, Lt Cdr Newby Kelt's RF-8A (BuNo 146894) was blown over the side of USS *Enterprise* (CVAN-65) during launch operations by the exhaust blast from an A-4 Skyhawk. The tip of the doomed RF-8A's tail is just visible at the edge of the flightdeck. In this photo, Lt Cdr Kelt has ejected and is still attached to his ejection seat, with the drogue chute trailing. *(Cdr Newby Kelt collection)*

The drogue chute can be seen through the splash from the RF-8A hitting the water next to the carrier. *(Cdr Newby Kelt collection)*

Lt Cdr Kelt floats next to his sinking RF-8A, waiting to be rescued by the plane-guard helicopter. After being rescued, he remained in the sickbay for a number of days whilst recovering from his injuries. Kelt was eventually returned to flight status. *(Cdr Newby Kelt collection)*

Lt Cdr Kelt recovering in the sickbay, with shipmates giving him support. He suffered secondary glaucoma as a result of hitting the water face down, hence the eye pads. The officer on the right playing the guitar is Lt Jim Curry (others remain unidentified). *(Cdr Newby Kelt collection)*

An RF-8A practices night photography over NAS Mayport, Florida. The sequence of flares being ejected and exploding from the aircraft shows the Crusader ahead of each explosion. The flares were ejected from a compartment behind the cockpit, and they could produce either 110 or 260 million candlepower. At the peak of illumination, the camera would take its picture. *(vfp62.com)*

A night photo of USS *Forrestal* (CVA-59) shot by VFP-62 in 1962 using its then new KA-45 forward-firing camera. This image was taken as part of the carrier testing program for the new camera, which gave a pilot's eye view of the target. *(Kenneth V. Jack collection)*

This early November 1962 low-level photograph reveals 17 missile erectors at north Mariel port, waiting their return shipment to the USSR. *(Dino A. Brugioni collection at National Security Archives, George Washington University)*

On November 5, 1962, a low-level reconnaissance mission captured a convoy of Soviet trucks driving onto the dock at north Mariel port to begin the loading process. *(Dino A. Brugioni collection at National Security Archives, George Washington University)*

During the November 6, 1962 mission, the RF-101C pilot succeeded in capturing the shadow (see lower right corner) of his jet while taking a photograph of Soviet personnel loading six missile transporters onto a ship moored in Casilda port. *(Dino A. Brugioni collection at National Security Archives, George Washington University)*

This October 29, 1962 photo of the San Cristobal site No 2 provided hope to ExComm that the crisis was coming to an end. The low-level forward-firing picture shows that missile erectors and transporters have been removed. PIs would have compared this photo to a previous day's photos to see the changes. *(Dino A. Brugioni collection at National Security Archives, George Washington University)*

THE WHITE HOUSE

WASHINGTON

26 January 1963

Dear Commander Ecker:

My Naval Aide has delivered to me the excellent photograph taken by your squadron on the first low-level aerial reconnaissance flight over Cuba last October. I appreciate your thoughtfulness in presenting it to me, and ask that you convey my gratitude to your officers and men. You will be interested to know that it is now hanging in my outer office.

I would also like to take this opportunity to re-affirm my thanks for your hard work during those weeks. As I said at our meeting in Boca Chica, the reconnaissance flights which enabled us to determine with precision the offensive build-up in Cuba contributed directly to the security of the United States in the most important and significant way.

With all best wishes.

Sincerely,

Commander W. B. Ecker, U.S. Navy
Commanding Officer
Light Photographic Squadron Sixty-two
Fleet Post Office
New York, New York

To the Officers and Men of VFP-62
With Best Wishes,

Left and above: This letter and photograph were received by Capt Ecker on January 26, 1963. The photo was taken on November 26, 1962 at the presentation of the Navy Unit Commendation to VFP-62. In the background are the pilots and RF-8As that performed missions over Cuba, along with the "Rotten Cotton Ball" enlisted groundcrew that was detached to NAS Boca Chica in Key West, Florida. *(Kenneth V. Jack collection)*

On November 13, 1962 the six pilots who flew the first *Blue Moon* missions on October 23 1962 received their DFCs from RAdm Joseph M. Carson. These Naval Aviators are (from left to right) Lt Cdr James A. Kauflin, Lt Cdr Tad T. Riley, Cdr William B. Ecker, Lt Gerald L. Coffee, Lt Christopher B. Wilhelmy, and Lt(jg) John J. Hewitt. *(Capt William B. Ecker collection)*

On November 29, 1962 Adm Robert L. Dennison, commander in chief Atlantic, presented ten additional DFCs to VFP-62 and VMCJ-2 pilots. The recipients were Capt Frederick A. Carolan (USMC), Lt(jg) Robert W. Chance (USN), Capt Richard C. Conway (USMC), Lt Arthur R. Day (USN), Lt Edmond M. Feeks (USN), Lt(jg) Terry V. Hallcom (USN), Capt John I. Hudson (USMC), Lt Cdr William N. Kelt (USN), Capt Edgar A. Love (USMC), and Lt(jg) William L. Taylor (USN). *(Capt William B. Ecker collection)*

President Kennedy presents the Navy Unit Commendation to Cdr Ecker at NAS Key West. Standing behind the latter are the officers of VFP-62 and VMCJ-2, as well as the enlisted groundcrew detachment of Operation *Blue Moon*. *(Capt William B. Ecker collection)*

Capt Ecker receives the Navy Unit Commendation for VFP-62 presented by President Kennedy. Cdr Robert Koch is to the right of the president. *(Capt William B. Ecker collection)*

Kevin Costner, who helped produce *Thirteen Days*, as well as playing a major acting part in the film, gives a hug to Mrs William B. Ecker (Kit) at the premier of the movie on December 19, 2000. *(William B. Ecker collection)*

Two detailed mock-ups of the RF-8 cockpit allowed the creators of *Thirteen Days* to film action-filled interior shots during the animated/live film sequence depicting the first mission over Cuba. On the left, Christopher Lawford, playing the part of Cdr Ecker, sits in the cockpit. Note the film camera directly in front of him. *(Mike McDougall)*

Cdr Ecker returns to NAS Jacksonville after a last VFP-62 mission over Cuba on July 5, 1963. The mission was ordered to allay CIA concerns for intelligence not being obtained by U-2s. Note the Navy Unit Commendation ribbon decal proudly worn on the Crusader's nose cone. *(Cdr Peter Mersky collection)*

Having shut down the engine of his RF-8A and unstrapped himself, Cdr Ecker climbs out of the cockpit following the July 5, 1963 Cuba mission. Two of the camera bay doors have already been opened, ready for film removal. *(Cdr Peter Mersky collection)*

End of an era. VFP-62 was disestablished on January 1, 1968. This photo shows only two RF-8As remaining in the squadron hangar. *(Arthur Scarborough PHC collection)*

RF-8A BuNo 146871 GA 910 of VFP-62, NAS Key West, Florida, late November 1962

VFP-62's CO, Cdr William Ecker, flew this aircraft on a number of his missions over Cuba during the crisis. The Navy Unit Commendation ribbon painted on the nose of the Crusader dates this scheme as late November 1962, VFP-62 having been personally presented with the award (the first issued during peacetime) by President John F Kennedy during the latter's visit to Key West on the 26th of that month. Like many of the Cuban Missile Crisis RF-8As, this aircraft was later remanufactured as a G-model and saw extensive action in Vietnam with the VFP-63 det aboard USS *Oriskany* (CVA-34) in 1966. It was finally lost in an operational accident whilst flying with VFP-63 on December 2, 1976.

RF-8A BuNo 146886 GA 906 of VFP-62, NAS Key West, Florida, November 1962

Bearing the name "W. F FOARD" on its starboard canopy rail, this aircraft also boasts various unofficial unit insignia, including a blue-and-gold knight's helmet, a sword and shield, and a small Playboy rabbit (a nod to the Marines of VMCJ-2) just below the number "9" in the nose modex. BuNo 146886 was later upgraded into an RF-8G and shot down by AAA over North Vietnam on May 22, 1968 while serving with VFP-63's det aboard USS *Bon Homme Richard* (CVA-31). Its pilot on this occasion, Lt(jg) E. F. Miller, was captured and became a PoW.

RF-8A BuNo 146863 CY 11 of VMCJ-2 (Gitmo Det), NAF Guantanamo, Cuba, October 1962

BuNo 146863 was one of a small number of RF-8As used by the Marine Corps to overfly Cuba from the US Navy's forward base on the island itself. Note the unit's famous Playboy Bunny emblem below the wing leading edge. This aircraft was upgraded to RF-8G specification several years later, and subsequently survived many years of service with VFP-63 until being finally retired (as PP 646) to the "desert boneyard" at Davis-Monthan AFB, in Arizona, on December 15, 1980 – it is still in storage there today.

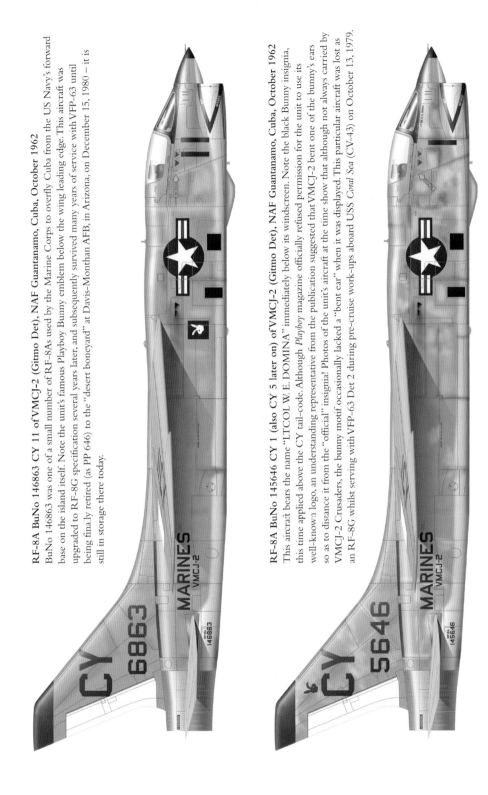

RF-8A BuNo 145646 CY 1 (also CY 5 later on) of VMCJ-2 (Gitmo Det), NAF Guantanamo, Cuba, October 1962

This aircraft bears the name "LTCOL W. E. DOMINA" immediately below its windscreen. Note the black Bunny insignia, this time applied above the CY tail-code. Although *Playboy* magazine officially refused permission for the unit to use its well-known logo, an understanding representative from the publication suggested that VMCJ-2 bent one of the bunny's ears so as to distance it from the "official" insignia! Photos of the unit's aircraft at the time show that although not always carried by VMCJ-2 Crusaders, the bunny motif occasionally lacked a "bent ear" when it was displayed. This particular aircraft was lost as an RF-8G whilst serving with VFP-63 Det 2 during pre-cruise work-ups aboard USS *Coral Sea* (CV-43) on October 13, 1979.

such time as an equally satisfactory international means of verification is effected.

Despite this progress, military tensions remained high, and the JCS lobbied for a strong response to another airplane being shot down. The following account provided by Lt Cdr Tad Riley illustrates this danger very well:

I flew three missions in November – on the 5th, 9th, and 12th. On November 5, Marine Capt Fred Carolan was my wingman. By this time, the US Navy and USAF were flying alternate days. This mission was to track the progress of the removal of missiles.

The missiles were mounted on a kind of low-boy trailer, towed by a tractor, and the whole rig was probably 80–90ft long. The Cuban highways were narrow – one to two lane blacktops, with lots of curves. This really limited their road speeds because they had trouble making the turns. As I remember, they were only able to make about 15 miles a day, and had to bivouac beside the road at night. Therefore, it wasn't hard to keep track of their progress. At least, these were the conditions in my central area of Cuba.

The missiles were from the Sagua la Grande and Remedios sites, and they were being transported, as I recall, to the port of Cientfuego on the south coast. From there, they were to be loaded aboard ships.

It was during the November 5 mission that Fred and I were jumped by a couple of MiG-21s. We were at about 1,000ft, just under a scattered-to-broken overcast. The MiGs came down through a hole and were making a run on us before Fred spotted them. We hit burner, broke into them, hit the deck, and headed for the north coast and home at about Mach 1.2 [approximately 900mph]. It was very turbulent and the airplane was a little "squirrelly." I couldn't read my instruments because things were rattling around so much, so I slowed to about Mach 0.99. [Later, ventral fins, under the rear fuselage, were added to improve stability at high speeds.] The RF-8A could go supersonic in level flight at any altitude, without diving. At low altitudes, fuel consumption was very high.

The No 2 MiG didn't stay with us in the turn, and I never saw it again. The MiG flight leader got sucked behind us and stayed a couple of hundred feet higher, while he chased us 20–30 miles, but apparently couldn't gain any ground. We were low enough that Fred, who was behind me, said he had no trouble keeping me in sight because I was leaving a rooster tail of dust every time I went over a plowed field – the sonic shockwave blew it up in an explosion of dust. I don't know if the jets were armed or not. I was later told that the lead airplane had been flown by a Russian instructor who was checking out a Cuban student pilot in the MiG-21.

The following account by Soviet pilot Col Dmitry Bobrov, included in Sergey Isaev's book *Pages of History of the 32nd Guards Air Fighter Regiment*, describes the chase of two reconnaissance airplanes. Note, the description references the American jets as USAF F-101 Voodoos, but this is almost certainly an identification error as these machines were, without doubt, Riley's and Carolan's RF-8As. Additionally, the date given for this encounter, November 4, is also in error. In a CNO report, the date of November 5 is confirmed. Bobrov's account of the event is presented as written:

On November 4, 1962, our squadron carried out training flights. After the task for interception of a training target was accomplished, I approached the air base, decreasing the height before the landing. At this moment, I received a radio command from Lt Col Perovsky, Flights [sic] Control Officer at that day: "Do you see two Americans approaching the base on the landing course at the height of 200m?" Having looked around, I have seen a "foe" at the range of about 1,500m, and answered, "Affirmative!" Perovsky gave an order "Attack! Frighten them!" he added.

I increased speed, closer to the two F-101 Wodoo [sic RF-101 Voodoo] fighters and turned at a distance of 500–700m just above the air base that would allow launching missiles. [Bobrov seems to have identified these, not as reconnaissance airplanes but as fighters, which were prohibited from overflying Cuba by US rules of engagement.] The American pilots found out [sic] pursuit behind them, boosted, and started carrying out vigorous, with black smokes [sic], anti-missile maneuvers (turn away to the left, to the right), and at maximum speed went to the sea, to Florida. My task has been executed, and later scouts stopped passing the space above our air base.

For the sake of justice, I should say that sortie was carried out with a training missile suspended, but the radar-tracking site was on and the F-101s consequently could find out the pursuit.

Many years have passed, and now I can easily tell about that event, but how I got the order to attack the American fighters, through detection and raprochments [sic], I felt an enormous pressure and responsibility, though I knew that it was a game since my airplane carried training missiles, and my 30mm gun was not charged.[11]

A CNO report confirmed Riley's account:

Two recon aircraft were pursued by MiG-21s. Flight 16 reported that it was jumped eight miles west of Santa Clara [the MiG air base in central Cuba, west of Remedios Sagua la Grande, which was Riley's target]. The MiGs stayed with them for five minutes. The high Combat Air Patrol [fighter protection off-shore] observed the action, but could take no action until after the incident was closed.

On November 6, a U-2 flight was terminated because the pilot detected surface-to-air radar guidance activity. Because of the danger of possible missile attacks on high-level recon flights, there is now a heavier reliance on low-level sorties, which could operate at altitudes low enough to render SAM defenses ineffective. Reconnaissance continued, with no sign of defensive action or harassment.[12]

And, finally, the MiG-21 incident caught the attention of the president, and the following communication was sent to Ambassadors Stevenson and McCloy, the UN negotiating team, with a warning to Soviet Ambassador Vasily Kuznetsov:

You should report to Kuznetsov that today [November 5] one of our low-level flights was harassed by MiGs, apparently manned by Soviets. No damage was done, and it is not clear that the MiGs fired, but the episode provides good basis for you to drive home our view of critical importance of unimpeded surveillance unless and until better arrangements can be made [ground inspection of the removal of offensive weapons]. You should remind Kuznetsov that surveillance must and will continue, and that further interference will be sure to bring prompt reaction, including armed action if necessary.[13]

The media were printing unsubstantiated rumors that not all the missiles were being removed and that some were being hidden in caves. At the November 6 ExComm meeting, the JCS requested ten low-level missions: four over the port of Havana, two over the Il–28 bases, two over the port of Isabella and two over Guantanamo and Santiago. McNamara recommended that the president turn down the request for sorties over Havana, as ships were being monitored as they left port. The president agreed and approved all the other reconnaissance requests. He again raised concern about what the US response should be if reconnaissance airplanes were shot at or shot down. He ordered that recommendations for setting a policy be given at the next meeting.[14]

November 6 was also midterm elections in the United States, and all eyes were on how the president's Cuban policies would affect the election results. The next day the *New York Times* reported, "Americans said OK to President Kennedy yesterday. Although Mr Kennedy didn't get quite what he wanted in the House and state capitals, his Democrats made quite a good showing for a midterm election."[15]

That day's ExComm meeting started with an intelligence briefing, and the good news that 90 percent of the missile erectors had been moved to Cuban ports. With that, the president authorized five U–2 and twelve low-level missions, some to photograph the cave areas. Cuba has lots of caves, and low-level photography was the best way to check them out. PIs started from the premise that caves seldom have roads leading to their mouths. From this they would proceed with their analysis.

Nature works in irregular curves, patterns, and textures. When a PI sees a straight line, a plane, or smooth texture, he knows it is man-made. When he sees a mound of earth, he traces it to its source. Reviewing photo coverage from previous photo runs of the same area provides clues if anything has changed.[16]

Gen Taylor presented the JCS's recommendations in the event an airplane was shot down. First, there would be an attempt to find out whether the shoot-down was an isolated incident or the first in a series of actions that constituted a deliberate attempt to destroy an American airplane. Then the choice would be whether to hit the offending source. If it could be determined it was a deliberate action, an air attack would destroy Il-28 bombers and SAM sites. President Kennedy then asked "at what point we would give up low-level missions — it appears we are running out of targets?"[17]

On November 8, the *Times* gave the president an encouraging assessment of the midterm election: "Tuesday's election demonstrated national support for President Kennedy's Cuban policies, warded off a Republican threat to his legislative strength and gave Democrats a remarkable midterm victory."[18]

The following day Lt Cdr Riley performed yet another *Blue Moon* mission over Cuba, as he describes here:

On November 9 Lt Bill Taylor was my wingman. We were checking the various missile sites in our area to see if they had continued to dismantle them — they had. We also made a run down the main runway at Santa Clara jet base, and were later told that one of our cameras caught a MiG taking off under us. I never saw that picture.

The last mission I flew was on November 12, and it consisted of four airplanes flown by Lt Cdr Newby Kelt, Lt Chance, Marine Capt Conway, and myself. We were to map the area just north of the Gitmo Naval Base to see what was happening there. We flew down [to Gitmo] the night before, briefed, and were ready to go early the next morning.

The order to launch was to be delivered via the operation officer's phone. He confided in me that all his phone calls were routed to him from Miami through the Havana exchange. I thought that was a strange way to run a war!

At a time when terrain-avoidance gear was not available, the pilot had to "keep his head out of the cockpit," always being aware of mountain ridges, antennae, other aircraft, or birds. As fighter pilot Capt Ron Knott commented in his book *Supersonic Cowboys*, "Flying high speed and low altitude is fun because the world seems to be rolling by below you. It is very dangerous because just a slightly wrong input on the flight controls can put you in the dirt, and as we commonly say, this could be 'church' [a pilot euphemism for death]."[19]

Lt Cdr Riley continues with his own account of his November 12 flight, and what pilots call a "pucker moment":

We flew solo – two from the east and two from the west – spaced out to get 100 percent coverage as we crossed simultaneously. At that time, Cuba didn't have much in the way of TV or radio towers or high-tension power lines, so at the altitude that I flew there wasn't much risk of hitting anything. I came from the west and had to let down through a cloud deck, which concealed the mountains in the area. I was a little premature in estimating that I had cleared the mountains. I started down through the clouds, and my low-level warning light came on. It had been set at 100ft! Before I even had time to react, I broke out right over an extensive installation of antiaircraft guns and missiles that were trying to track me. I only had a momentary glimpse of men running to man their guns. I was too close for the SAMs to be effective; I don't know if any of them fired at me.

We didn't land at Gitmo but proceeded back to JAX. That night when I was home in bed, I received a phone call from someone who called me by name and observed that I must have had a pretty exciting day. I never knew who made that call, but he made enough comments to show that he knew where I'd been.

On November 10 the public was made aware of the missiles' progress out of Cuba:

United States warships have begun intercepting homebound Soviet cargo vessels to verify the removal of Soviet missiles from Cuba. The Pentagon announced yesterday that five freighters had submitted to inspection on the high seas, with a display of cordiality – waving, smiles, and gift-exchanges. Under the unusual procedure, Soviet sailors pulled canvas tarpaulins off their open-deck cargoes, which were observed and photographed by the Navy vessels alongside the freighters. No boardings were indicated.[20]

United States and Soviet negotiations at the UN droned on for much of November, with the removal of the Il-28 bombers being the source of contention. The old argument of what was an "offensive" or "defensive" weapon (whether a weapon is offensive depends on which end of the barrel of a gun you are on) bogged down negotiations for weeks. The American negotiators insisted the bombers were a threat to the southeastern United States and the Soviets contended they were intended for coastal defense, obsolete (they were too slow and could be shot down easily), and no threat to a modern defense system. The Americans countered that they could carry atomic bombs and, therefore, could not be considered obsolete, nor defensive weapons.

It was obvious to everyone that the Soviet negotiators were using the Il-28s as bargaining chips for the discontinuation of reconnaissance flights. It seemed to work, as this whole dispute caused President Kennedy to severely limit low-level reconnaissance by mid-month – a political, not military, decision. As a result, *Blue Moon* missions were solely focused on fulfilling intelligence needs not being met by the U-2, and there was no longer any harassment of communist forces on the ground via low-level supersonic flybys. On November 15, the final *Blue Moon* missions were flown for 1962. One final mission would be flown in June 1963 (see Chapter 16).

The Cuban Missile Crisis was finally drawing to an end. On November 21 President Kennedy announced the lifting of the quarantine as a result of Khrushchev's promise to remove all Il-28 bombers within 30 days. *Blue Moon* sorties were canceled on a day-to-day basis. On

November 28, *Blue Moon* missions were placed on a 12-hour alert, and from December 2 through 5, *Blue Moon* missions were not to be resumed without JCS approval, and only if U-2s were unable to satisfy intelligence needs. Finally, on December 6, Director McCone reported to ExComm "that all Il-28 bombers had been located at Cuban ports or on ships leaving Cuba."[21] Later that month, in a television interview, President Kennedy gave credit to low-level reconnaissance aircraft for their role in the removal of the Il-28s:

> If we had to act on Wednesday [October 16] in the first 24 hours, I don't think we probably would have chosen as prudently as we finally did – a quarantine against the use of offensive weapons. In addition, that had much more power than we first thought it did, because I think the Soviet Union was very reluctant to have us stop ships which carried with them a good deal of their highly secret and sensitive material. One of the reasons I think that the Soviet Union withdrew the Il-28s was because we were carrying on very intensive low-level photography. Now, no one would have guessed, probably, that that would have been such a harassment.[22]

The crisis that brought the world to the brink of thermonuclear destruction ended with only one combat casualty – Maj Rudolph Anderson. The USAF also lost fourteen men due to accidents – four in an RB-47 crash at Kindley AFB, Bermuda; six in a C-135 transport crash at Guantanamo; and four in a second RB-47 crash at Florida's MacDill AFB.

On December 21, James B. Donovan obtained President Castro's signature on an agreement for the release of 1,113 Bay of Pigs prisoners, some suffering from severe malnutrition and disease. Cuba would receive $53 million in pharmaceuticals, medical supplies, and foodstuffs in return. While US government involvement in the agreement was not publicly announced, the CIA provided letters of credit for the transaction ($20 million to Pfizer and $17 million to Merck from covert activities funds).

Transportation companies, truckers, airlines, and shipping firms "donated" their services and the Internal Revenue Service provided legal tax write-offs for the companies. The United States provided $10 million in powdered skim milk from its surplus stocks.

Additionally, Castro agreed to future negotiations with Donovan to grant 24 American citizens clemency or amnesty.[23] Those negotiations would continue into 1963.

In Miami, the Cuban community welcomed home the Bay of Pigs prisoners on Christmas Eve after 20 months in Castro's prisons.

In later years, a number of conferences have shed new light on the depth of the crisis. Robert McNamara learned information he never knew:

– Although intelligence never found evidence of nuclear weapons on the island, Soviet nuclear missile warheads had, indeed, been delivered to Cuba and were to be targeted on US cities.

– At the time, the CIA reported 10,000 Soviet troops in Cuba. At the Moscow conference in 1989, participants learned that there were in fact 43,000 Soviet troops on the island, along with 270,000 well-armed Cuban troops. Both forces, in the words of their commanders, were determined to "fight to the death," and estimated they would have suffered 100,000 casualties.

– At the Havana conference in 1992 it was revealed that at the height of the crisis, Soviet forces in Cuba possessed a total of 162 nuclear warheads, including at least 90 tactical warheads. Also, it was reported that on October 26, the warheads were moved from their storage sites to positions closer to their delivery vehicles in anticipation of a US invasion. Clearly, there was a high risk that, in the face of a US attack – which, as I have said, many in the US government, military and civilian alike, were prepared to recommend to President Kennedy – the Soviet forces in Cuba would have decided to use their nuclear weapons, rather than lose them.

– Although a US invasion force would not have been equipped with tactical nuclear weapons, no one should believe that, had American troops been attacked with nuclear weapons, the United States would have refrained from a nuclear response.[24]

CHAPTER 14

MEDALS AND COMMENDATIONS

November and December 1962 was also a time for a nation's gratitude to the military units that had helped to bring about the peaceful resolution of the most dangerous confrontation of the Cold War. Capt Ecker writes about the awarding of Distinguished Flying Crosses (DFCs) to the reconnaissance pilots:

> Late October and early November passed quickly because we were so busy flying missions to confirm the dismantling of the missile sites. Time flew by so fast that it is hard to remember all that took place. However, certain great events began to take place about mid-month.
>
> On November 13, 1962, at about 1000 hrs, the six of us who flew the first *Blue Moon* missions on October 23 were summoned to the office of COMFAIRJAX (Commander Fleet Air Jacksonville), Rear Adm Joseph "Kit" Carson. In a secret ceremony, each of us was awarded the DFC, the sixth highest decoration of the nation. Because of the classified nature of all our missions, the citation was short and simple. It read as follows:
>
> > The President of the United States takes pleasure in presenting the DISTINGUISHED FLYING CROSS to COMMANDER WILLIAM B. ECKER UNITED STATES NAVY for services set forth in the following CITATION:
> >
> > "For extraordinary achievement while participating in aerial flights on assigned missions during the year 1962. His devotion to duty was in keeping with the highest traditions of the United States Naval Service."

The following letter accompanied the DFC ceremony:

Jacksonville, Florida, November 13, 1962. Today, six pilots from Light Photographic Squadron 62, of NAS Cecil Field, Florida, were awarded the nation's sixth highest award – the Distinguished Flying Cross – for "extraordinary achievement in aerial flight." Their achievement was the first low-level photographic flights over Cuba, on October 23, 1962. At that time the six pilots, in three two-airplane formations, covered the island, and their photographs ended up as a determining factor in the course of action taken by the United States in the Cuban crisis.

The six pilots, Cdr William B. Ecker, Commanding Officer of VFP-62; Lt Cdr James A. Kauflin; Lt Cdr Tad T. Riley; Lt Gerald L. Coffee, Lt Christopher B. Wilhelmy, and Lt John James Hewitt, Jr, were commended by RAdm Joseph M. Carson and awarded the Distinguished Flying Cross in the name of the President of the United States. RADM Carson is Commander Fleet Air, Jacksonville/Commander, Naval Air Bases, Sixth Naval District.

After this presentation, I began a campaign to make sure that proper recognition was given wherever deserved throughout the squadron. This, incidentally, was never done by the CNO. This effort took the form of additional DFCs for the other mission pilots, individual awards for the photographic and maintenance personnel, and an overall unit commendation for the squadron as a whole.

I recommended VFP-62's Chief Photo Officer, Cdr Bob Koch, for the Legion of Merit (LOM) and a number of others for Navy Commendation Medals (NCMs). As is usual for the US Navy, all the recommendations were downgraded. Bob's LOM was reduced to an NCM and all of the NCM recommendations became Letters of Commendation. Later in my career, I was twice recommended for the LOM, and in each case it came through as a Meritorious Service Medal (MSM). There was no MSM in 1962, but Bob later got his LOM while working for the Under Secretary of the Air Force in the Pentagon.

Bob was first spotted by the Air Force under secretary in late 1962. Sometime in mid-November a USAF Constellation transport aircraft arrived at NAS Jacksonville. Although this aircraft can carry 100–150 passengers, only Mr Joseph Charyk, Under Secretary of the Air Force, his wife, and about a dozen senior USAF officers deplaned. The US Navy's reception group consisted of Adm and Mrs Carson, Cdr and Mrs Koch, my wife Kit, and myself.

As already stated many times, the US Navy had outperformed the "boys in blue." The USAF in general and the secretary in particular wanted to see how such a small unit as VFP-62 had accomplished the job. After an informal luncheon at Adm Carson's quarters for the four couples, Bob and I took the secretary on a personal tour of our facilities, and explained our procedures to him. While we were at lunch, Jerry Pulley conducted a similar, but more technical and detailed tour for the rest of the USAF entourage.

Secretary Charyk was so impressed by Bob's input into the operation that later, when Bob had reported to OPNAV for duty, he had him assigned to his personal staff and incorporated as his US Navy liaison officer.

On November 14, 1962, the big brass had a get-together at the Little White House at Key West. The Little White House was President Truman's hideaway, like FDR's and Eisenhower's Camp David (which was also Roosevelt's Shangri-La). Truman would go down there and play poker with his buddies in order to get away from the rigors of Washington, D.C. I almost did not make it because after long hours and a lack of sleep, I was physically run down and had contracted pneumonia, albeit walking pneumonia, and had been grounded by the flight surgeon. He said my lungs sounded like Rice Krispies whenever he listened to my breathing. I was going to let Jim Kauflin, the most senior of the mission pilots, represent me, but at the last minute we all decided that as CO, I should attend in order to stand up for the squadron.

So, we borrowed a two-seater jet fighter trainer, colloquially known as the "Twogar," a play on the word "Cougar" which was the name of the straight fighter version, and I had another of my pilots fly us to Key West.

It was at this meeting that I asked Adm Dennison, who was CINCLANT, for the additional DFCs and the Navy Unit

Commendation (NUC). About halfway through the social event, I momentarily backed him into a corner and stated my requests. He concurred, and eventually both were granted.

November 26, 1962, was to be one of the most memorable red-letter days of my life! President John F. Kennedy flew down to Boca Chica, and with thousands of troops lined up behind me, and with the "RCB Det" and some of our aircraft in the front rank, the president presented me with the NUC for the squadron. This was the first NUC ever presented in peacetime, and the first ever to be presented personally by the president. [See Appendices for the president's remarks and for a list of squadron recipients of the NUC.]

Here are the words that accompanied the presentation:

The Secretary of the Navy takes pleasure in commending LIGHT PHOTOGRAPHIC SQUADRON SIXTY-TWO (VFP-62) for service set forth in the following CITATION:

"For extraordinary achievement in the planning and executing of aerial reconnaissance during the period 15 October to 26 November 1962 on missions in support of operations of the utmost importance to the security of the United States. The successful completion of these flights in the face of adverse circumstances was in keeping with the highest traditions of the United States Naval Service.

"All personnel attached to and serving with Light Photographic Squadron SIXTY-TWO (VFP-62) during the above period, or any part thereof, are hereby authorized to wear the Navy Unit Commendation Ribbon."

Looking back to the meeting with JFK, I remember thinking it was strange how his complexion was so dark reddish-brown. I learned later that this was the result of Addison's Disease. Also, his back brace was very evident in both his posture and his walk.

After further congratulations and handshakes from President Kennedy, Adm Dennison, and Gen Taylor, they walked off, and immediately Adm Anderson, Gen Wheeler (the Army chief of staff), and Gen David Shoup (commandant of the Marine Corps) came forth and each in turn shook my hand and offered their personal congratulations.

All the service chiefs had accompanied the president to Key West. The reader will notice that one of the chiefs normally associated with this group was conspicuous by his absence. Gen Curtis LeMay, the USAF chief of staff, remained seated in his open-topped convertible about 30 or so yards away and pouted. He refused to congratulate the US Navy in general and me in particular. Acting poorly was typical of LeMay when things did not go his way.

The president was to have re-awarded the first six DFCs and then to have awarded the additional ten, but between running late on his schedule and urgent happenings in Washington, D.C., this part of the ceremony was canceled.

On November 29, 1962, Adm Robert L. Dennison flew down from Norfolk to Cecil Field and personally awarded the delayed DFCs to the other ten *Blue Moon* pilots:

Capt Frederick A. Carolan, USMC

Lt(jg) Robert W. Chance, USN

Capt Richard C. Conway, USMC

Lt Arthur R. Day, USN

Lt Edmond M. Feeks, USN

Lt(jg) Terry V. Hallcom, USN

Capt John I. Hudson, USMC

Lt Cdr William N. Kelt, USN

Capt Edger A. Love, USMC

Lt(jg) William L. Taylor, USN

After the ceremony was over and I met Gen Richard Mangrum, I expressed how proud I was of "my" Marines, and he informed me in no uncertain terms that they were "his" Marines.

Besides Adm Dennison, the other flag officers attending were Vice Adm Frank O'Bierne (COMNAVAIRLANT), Maj Gen A. F. Binney (Deputy Commanding General of the Fleet Marine Force, Atlantic), Maj Gen R. C. Mangrum (Commanding General of the 2nd Marine Air Wing), and our old friend RAdm Carson.

The following is a press release from the CNO on January 24, 1963. This was as close as we ever got to kudos from George [Anderson]:

"Although it is difficult to single out the performance of any naval unit engaged in the recent Cuban quarantine operations for special mention, I think the accomplishments of Light Photographic Squadron SIXTY-TWO (VFP-62) are especially noteworthy.

"Some months ago, purely as a result of VFP-62 initiative, a highly improved forward-firing photographic reconnaissance capability was developed using the new KA-46 camera in the F8U-1P aircraft. When the Cuban crisis arose, this type of photography was the most suitable to gather the intelligence required.

"VFP-62 performed the first flights over Cuba and brought back the first conclusive proof of the offensive buildup.

"US Navy forward-firing photo equipment was very shortly adapted to the USAF surveillance aircraft.

"As President Kennedy stated, VFP-62 contributed as much to the security of the United States as any unit in our history. For this outstanding accomplishment, Light Photographic Squadron SIXTY-TWO was awarded the Navy Unit Commendation."

Finally, the following cable from Adm Robert L. Dennison (CINCLANTFLT) was sent to Commander Ecker for VFP-62:

I am exceptionally pleased with the professional manner you and your squadron executed Operation *Blue Moon*. The accomplishment of this very difficult and unique mission demonstrated outstanding competence in your squadron's primary mission. It pointed out to the highest authorities the readiness of VFP-62 and the US Navy to immediately respond to any assigned mission.

FAPL ROLE

As noted previously in this volume, as part of an early assessment of VFP-62's readiness to perform *Blue Moon* missions by high-ranking US Navy officials, the FAPL at NAS Jacksonville had been inspected. Following this visit, they had determined that special film processing equipment had to be obtained from Kodak and installed in a matter of days. The Lab's critical role is described by Capt Ecker:

> I've mentioned the fact that the FAPL located at NAS Jacksonville belonged to VFP-62. The officer in charge was Lt Cdr Jerry Pulley, who, 15 years earlier, had been the White House photographer for President Truman. Indeed, he was the person who took their daughter Margaret's wedding pictures. With VFP-62, it was his job to develop the film, give it a cursory analysis, have it annotated as required and get it couriered to Washington, D.C.
>
> Jerry and his people worked around the clock at times. These unheralded people did a magnificent job, processing more than 160,000 pictures without losing a single original negative. One of the first questions that Secretary Charyk's entourage asked Jerry, when they toured our operation, was "How many people do you supervise?" (The USAF always employs lots of people and lots of supervisors!) Jerry said that he thought for a minute and then replied, "I guess you would say that I supervise ONE person – that man over there, Chief Barney Gault." They could not imagine how such a small group, in such a small lab, could possibly do such a big job.
>
> A while back, I mentioned the "chiefs." The chiefs are the chief petty officers (CPOs) of the US Navy. Like the men (I guess that in today's Navy I'd better include the female chiefs) of equal rating in other branches of the service, these non-commissioned officers are the backbone of any unit or ship. I had about 50 CPOs in the squadron, although not all were on the scene at all times because of the deployed detachments on the carriers. It was because of professionals like this that my squadron command was so successful.
>
> On 26 January 1963, I received a personal letter from the president, plus an autographed picture [see plates section].

The USAF reconnaissance pilots also received DFCs for their photo missions. Capt Ecker tells how the USAF tended to manage public relations better than the US Navy:

The USAF counterpart to my squadron was the 29th Tactical Reconnaissance Squadron of the 363rd Tactical Reconnaissance Wing, based at Shaw AFB, South Carolina, and flying RF-101C Voodoo aircraft. Just as the US Navy staged out of Key West, the USAF staged out of MacDill AFB, which is just on the south side of the city of Tampa. The 29th was commanded by Lt Col Joseph O'Grady. In a series of press conferences we had, one would have thought that Joe was right there from the start – telling the press how tough it was in spite of his own admission, "We got started late."

I remember one specific incident, on December 1, 1962, when the US Navy CHINFO (Chief of Information) ordered Marine Capt John Hudson, one of the Marines temporarily assigned to my squadron, and me to fly to Homestead AFB – about 30 miles south of Miami – where we were interviewed by newsmen. From the start, the whole environment was pro-Air Force. Even though we were there, the press conference took place at an Air Force base and the press was, therefore, left with the impression that low-level reconnaissance over Cuba was an all Air Force show. Here are some excerpts from the resulting article, datelined Homestead AFB, December 1 (UPI):

> "... an Air Force pilot said today he saw puffs ... four or five, or maybe ten. Anyway, there were several antiaircraft shells bursting around his jet as he streaked over Cuba ... 'I was leaving the target, so I just continued on my way,' said O'Grady. He called the antiaircraft fire 'token' ... the rugged-looking Air Force officer didn't seem upset at the recollection of being a target for Cuban or Russian guns."

I mentioned before that I was pretty unhappy with the way the CNO let LeMay steal the scene from us. LeMay even arranged to have some of his pilots invited to the White House to meet with the president. The final straw was when Joe O'Grady appeared in *Life* magazine in a four-page article titled "Glassy Stare That Found The Evidence." The nose-section picture of the RF-101 is accompanied by the words:

> "As O'Grady flew this plane low over Cuban military installations time and again, this camera took rapid-sequence pictures through a window in the cowl. Similar cameras recorded the views on either

side. Sister RF-101s, plus the high-flying U-2s, brought back evidence which made the difference between what did happen and what might have happened."

This article was run in the December 7, 1962 issue – ironically, 21 years after another sneak-attack on the US Navy!

Down through the years I've talked with other retired Naval Aviators, who are contemporaries of mine, and they all confirm that they personally, and the US Navy in general, were in a continuous battle with Curtis LeMay, who spent most of his time trying to either scuttle or take over Naval Aviation. I'm pleased to say that he never accomplished this goal.

The Cuban Missile Crisis gradually wound down from about Christmas time on.

Capt Ecker's discontent with the press coverage that the USAF received reflects the troubled attitude that plagued Naval Aviators for decades. To be fair, however, it is also true that the USAF astutely took advantage of the very controlled news environment cultivated by the Kennedy administration. By early November the president had not met with the press for more than seven weeks. The press was hungry for details of the military operations. Unlike World War II or Korea, no embedded reporters were allowed on naval vessels enforcing the quarantine. Col O'Grady took the initiative and wrote his own press releases, including an article, "Over Cuba: Flak at 11 o'clock," for *TIME*, where he provided the most detailed account of how it feels to fly – and be shot at – over Castro's Cuba.

The previously mentioned news conference at Homestead AFB was heavily covered by the news media, where the "dark, rugged" O'Grady took center stage as he recounted some of his article's high points. "The Voodoo nosed over and I went down on the deck," O'Grady told reporters. "I trimmed the aircraft to allow the cameras to pass over the airfield and missile site at the best possible direction and altitude for the photography that was desired." At the same news conference, Cdr Ecker and Marine Capt Hudson were muted in their comments, with Ecker only saying, "The skyline of Havana was the first thing I saw. It was quite a thrill, and I think I enjoyed the sensation. The inner excitement was about the same as when I was fighting in the Pacific – it was a job that had to be done." Capt Hudson contributed, "Naturally, there was a bit of apprehension. The navigational duties of high-speed low-level flying kept me busy and I didn't have much time to think of much else."[1]

Unlike the USAF, the US Navy took the classified nature of its role seriously to the extent that those of us who were on carrier detachments never received any information about the home squadron's central role during the crisis. Except for those detached to Key West, the rest of us did not learn about the details of the missions until mid-1963, when the squadron issued a newsletter with photos and minimal information. In researching this book, the author encountered concerns from some who wondered if the details of the photo missions were still classified – almost 50 years after the event.

Capt Ecker describes his last words to the squadron:

I remained as commanding officer of VFP-62 until September 1963, and my parting remarks were as follows:

"VFP-62 was assigned the low-level photographic reconnaissance task during the history-making 'Cuban Missile Crisis' of 1962. Because of your long and untiring efforts, the United States was able to establish the national policy which prevented the offensive missile build-up in Cuba.

"The squadron's achievements are reflected in the DFCs awarded to some of our pilots and the Navy Unit Commendation which the squadron received as a whole. Our Navy Unit Commendation was the first ever given in peacetime, and the first ever presented personally by the President of the United States. Again, to all hands, let me say very sincerely, 'Thank you,' and I'm very, very proud of each and every man in 'Fightin' Photo.'"

CHAPTER 15

THIRTEEN DAYS – THE MOVIE

When Hollywood made the docudrama of the Cuban Missile Crisis in 2000, they chose the title well. *Thirteen Days* was also the title of Robert Kennedy's posthumous book, and the number of critical days of the crisis. Director Roger Donaldson and writers David Self and Ernest R. May provide a thrilling movie that dramatizes pivotal events – some with Hollywood flair and a small amount of misrepresentation.

Along with Bruce Greenwood playing JFK, superstar Kevin Costner played the role of Presidential Political Advisor Kenny O'Donnell (Robert Kennedy's roommate at Harvard and JFK's campaign manager) in a position of influence and responsibility that he did not have during the crisis. This artistic license is not a serious flaw, as it provided a means to tell the personal agonizing process that the president went through, as he maneuvered around the largely hawkish advice he was getting from his brainy advisors and military leaders in ExComm. To its credit, the movie is largely factual, except as will be described later. The screenplay documents well the tension within the US government, and the deft manner in which John F. Kennedy steered the crisis toward a peaceful resolution. It also does a reasonably good job of portraying VFP-62's first low-level photo mission on October 23. Capt Ecker tells about his involvement with the movie:

> In 1986, two actions occurred which stimulated me to commit my
> untold story to paper, and to correct history's inaccurate account of

"who" really did "what" in the low-altitude reconnaissance missions of the Cuban Missile Crisis of 1962.

Firstly, in August 1986, I was contacted by ABC-TV in New York and told that they were programming a new series called "*Our World*". The theme for the program for October 2, 1986 would be the "Cuban Missile Crisis," or "Three Weeks in October 1962." They asked me if I would appear. I agreed, and was one of the parties featured in the program. Secondly, as ABC was interviewing and filming me at my home in Virginia, one of my nieces (Rosemary) called to say that she was at the Air and Space Museum of the Smithsonian Institution, and that I was pictured there – featured in one of the exhibits, Gallery 110! Well, I guess that's where all "old fossils" end up! [It is the co-author's opinion that these incidents heightened Capt Ecker's sense that there was historical importance to his and VFP-62's involvement in the missile crisis. It was in 1986 that he wrote his memoir that motivated this book.]

In 1999 I was contacted by a Hollywood producer, and was told that because I was the pilot that flew the first low-level mission over the missile sites, I would be portrayed in the film *Thirteen Days*. When I read the first script, I was not happy with the way that I was presented. However, after a long while, and some serious editing, I signed off on it. On December 19, 2000, I was invited to be the Guest of Honor at the premier of the movie. Kit Ecker describes the affair:

"Upon arrival at Los Angeles airport, we were provided a limousine service to the Beverly Hilton Hotel and assigned a fabulous suite of rooms there. That night, Bill and I walked the red carpet at the Mann Village Theatre in Westwood, California, and faced a horde of reporters and their flashing cameras. In attendance were all the movie people involved with the production. Many accolades and speeches were given. Bill was asked to take a bow. He received a thunderous ovation – so much so, that I had to tug at his jacket to get him to sit down.

"Dinner and a reception followed the movie. We met Kevin Costner and his parents, among others. I even had my picture taken with Kevin – what a treat!

"The following day, we were invited to lunch with Kevin Costner and others. I understood that it was a 'men only' invitation at a bar for drinks and lunch, so I opted out and went shopping on Rodeo Drive. As it turned out, Bill went to the Costner home in Hollywood Hills and visited with the Costner family. I would have loved it, but I missed out on that one!"

The movie also had a Kennedy connection with Christopher Lawford, son of British-born actor Peter Lawford (who was married to President Kennedy's sister Patricia), cast to play the movie's Cdr Ecker, making him a nephew of the former president.

Scenes of Crusaders (Philippine Air Force F-8s mimicking RF-8As) on the flightline, ready for the first mission, were real enough – only someone familiar with Naval Aviation might detect the 20mm cannon and the absence of camera bay windows. The VFP-62 filmstrip insignias on the aircraft wings and tails were vivid and the cockpit view was the real thing. RAdm Paul T. Gillcrist, a former F-8 pilot, was a technical consultant for the movie, and here he describes how the flightline shot of VFP-62 Crusaders was filmed:

The two shooting locations in the Philippines were the former Clark Air Base, about two hours northwest of Manila, and Pagsanjan Lagunas, about the same driving time to the south. The scenes to be shot at Clark were to simulate flight operations at three bases in Florida – NASs Cecil Field and Key West and Homestead AFB. The scenes to be shot at Pagsanjan were to simulate a Russian medium-range ballistic missile site in Cuba. The portions of the film to be shot at Clark dealt with reconnaissance flights out of the Florida NASs, and strike preparation were shot at Homestead.

To set the historical record straight, in 1977 the Philippine Air Force (PAF) bought 26 F-8H Crusaders from the United States. The PAF began flying its refurbished Crusaders in 1979 and finally put them out of commission in 1989. When the *Thirteen Days* preparation crew arrived at the Crusader storage facility at Basa, R.P. (halfway between Clark and Manila), they found only 12 fuselage hulks left, none flyable – the engines would not even run. This implied that the PAF had destroyed 14 of the airplanes in the ten years they were in service. The set production crew picked ten of the best hulks and transported them to Clark for the filming.

The airplanes, in their new US Navy markings (circa 1962, of course), looked authentic. They were not "taxi-able," so a triple tow-bar rig was configured allowing us to simulate taxiing while towing them with a tractor that remained off camera. Later, during the editing process, the cinematic magicians would electronically erase the tow bars and dub in afterburners, etc.[1]

The computer animations of the low-level flights were well done, but the scenes of AAA shooting up the wing of Capt Ecker's RF-8A deviated from reality. As was mentioned earlier in this book, there is no evidence that any US Navy airplane was ever hit by any Cuban or Soviet antiaircraft fire during the crisis. Also, there is no evidence that Kenny O'Donnell ever telephoned Cdr Ecker, or that O'Donnell, or anyone else, ever pressured Ecker to minimize reports of any groundfire or hide any hostile action from his superior officers, who (according to the movie) were looking for a reason, and justification, to attack Cuba. When Cdr Ecker met with the JCS on October 23, he truthfully described his flight over Cuba as a "piece of cake" because, first, he had successfully obtained the pictures he wanted of the Soviet missile base and, second, his airplane had not been hit by any antiaircraft fire. So, when Ecker told the JCS that the mission had gone very well, he was simply telling the truth.

This, after all, was a movie, not a documentary, and the shortcomings are not reason enough to diminish the overall high quality of the dramatization. The audience is entertained, and yet walks away with a sufficient appreciation of the Cuban crisis. For many, it would be the extent of their knowledge, and for others, it might even stir an interest to learn more and dig deeper into the ample selection of excellent books on the subject.

Serious criticism of *Thirteen Days* is not about what the movie did not get right, but what it left out. Phillip Brenner, in his article "Turning History on Its Head," points out that the movie only focused on the United States and left both Cuba and the Soviet Union out. According to Brenner, it failed to give a perspective of the adventurism of all three countries, and painted the United States as an innocent bystander in the affair. It said nothing of the lengthy American effort to overthrow Castro with clandestine operation *Mongoose*, supervised by Bobby Kennedy, while giving the president "plausible deniability." It also failed to make the audience aware of the Cubans' fear of an American invasion, legitimized by the failed Bay of Pigs debacle. Mr Brenner makes the strong point that "by narrowing the timeline to the 13 days of the crisis, the omission of Cuba and the Soviet Union from a film about the Cuban Missile Crisis is almost inevitable."[2]

He argues further that "the second traditional lesson that the movie reinforces is that the crisis was resolved because the United States forced the Soviet Union to back down."[3] Indeed, the film gives us a cinematic validation of Dean Rusk's famous quote, "We were eyeball to eyeball, and I think the other fellow just blinked." Brenner gives credit that the audience sees the president's grasp of the point, ignored by his advisors and the JCS, that there would be no winners in a nuclear war. Not seen was Khrushchev's restraint, and willingness to risk humiliation rather than Armageddon. No one would know that the shooting down of the U-2 was against his orders.[4] And, Thomas S. Blanton wrote critically, "This calibrated brinkmanship, where we hang tough, ratchet up the pressure and the other guy blinks, was tried in Vietnam [and failed]."[5]

Thirteen Days is being re-run on television as this book is being written, and as we approach the 50th anniversary of the Cuban Missile Crisis. Surely, new documentaries and books will arise and hopefully correct some of these omissions. With equal hope, perhaps the public will be motivated by the movie to learn more about these important missed lessons, and why the Cuban Missile Crisis periodically needs revisiting as a milestone in American foreign policy.

Movie critic Roger Ebert provides an eloquent, hopeful comprehension of what audiences of *Thirteen Days* should walk away with:

Suppose nobody blinked in 1962, and missiles had been fired. Today we would be missing most of the people of Cuba, Russia, and the US eastern seaboard, and there'd be a lot of poison in the air. That would be our victory. Yes, Khrushchev was reckless to put the missiles in Cuba, and Kennedy was right to want them out. But it is a good thing somebody blinked.[6]

CAPT ECKER VISITS CUBA FOR THE LAST TIME

Captain Ecker describes his participation in the last conference between Soviet, Cuban, and American officials, hosted by Cuba:

In October 2002 – the 40th anniversary of the Cuban Missile Crisis – I was contacted by Tom Blanton, Executive Director of the Gilman Library at the George Washington University. He had been referred to me by Peter Almond, one of the producers of *Thirteen Days* and my friend in Hollywood.

Mr Blanton invited me to participate in an international conference consisting of representatives from the United States, Russia, and Cuba. I was initially reluctant to participate. However, certain people in the Washington, D.C. area (who knew of the US Navy's role in the crisis) convinced me that I should participate. I eventually agreed, but I let it be known that I would: (1) not shake Castro's hand; (2) not have my picture taken with him; and (3) not embarrass the United States.

Whether by design or coincidence, certain things occured that prevented any of the above. For example, my wife and I were not informed of the time to report for our transportation to the state dinner at the Palace of the Revolution. By the time we arrived, the reception line with Castro had just ended – design or coincidence?

The conference in Cuba was interesting in a number of respects. It allowed me to meet some of the key advisors to President Kennedy – men like Robert McNamara, Ted Sorenson, and Arthur Schlesinger. I was also able to meet Christopher Lawford, the actor who played the role of Cdr William B. Ecker in the movie *Thirteen Days*. Finally, I was able to visit the old San Cristobal missile site along with the other conference participants. I believe that we were among the first Americans to ever visit the site. [See photos of the visit in the plates section.]

Kit Ecker adds her memories of the occasion:

> We stayed at a small hotel that obviously catered to tourists. For several days we attended the conference, which included former government officials and special invited guests. There was lively discussion among the participants. *The Miami Herald* of October 19, 2002 reported the following:
>
> > "If one thing came across loud and clear at the recent conference marking the 40th anniversary of the Cuban Missile Crisis, it is that Cuban President Fidel Castro has a very long memory, and still harbors a grudge against his former Soviet allies. Castro deeply resents the way Cuba was treated by the Soviets, both in the installation of the missiles and the manner of their withdrawal.
> >
> > "Apparently, he had little say about the former decision – and no say at all in the latter. In retrospect, said Castro at one point during the conference, Cuba would 'rather have been invaded by the Americans than accept the missiles' and the humiliation that resulted from their sudden withdrawal."
>
> On the day of our departure, we received a shopping bag of gifts from Fidel Castro. It included a bottle of excellent Cuban rum, a box of Cuban cigars, CDs by a famous Cuban singer, and a signed and dated modernistic print by a Cuban artist. Bill gave the rum to the desk clerk at the hotel, who was really thrilled to receive it.

From 1963 to 1974, Capt Ecker had various assignments and commands, starting with OPNAV in the Pentagon as the Head of Naval Photography and Reconnaissance, followed by Naval War College and Chief of the Navy Military Assistance Advisory Group in Copenhagen, Denmark. Next came a posting as Commanding Officer of Photographic Technical Training at NAS Pensacola, Florida. Capt Ecker's final years on active duty were again at the Pentagon, where he served as the Deputy Director of Navy Space and Reconnaissance Programs in OPNAV. While serving in this position, he was the sole US Navy liaison officer on the Space Shuttle program.

Capt William B. Ecker died from pneumonia on November 5, 2009 at the age of 85.

CHAPTER 16

"HOOLIGANS IN THE SKY"

It was clear that by November 1962, the relentless American reconnaissance overflights were getting under the skin of the Soviets and their Cuban hosts. The Kremlin's protestations at every diplomatic opportunity are best illustrated by Mr Anastas I. Mikoyan, First Deputy of the Council of Ministers of the USSR, when he met with President Kennedy on November 29, 1962, and complained "Low-altitude overflights are blatant hooliganism. High-altitude overflights are also hooliganism, but less blatant."[1]

American aerial surveillance had ruined their game plan. After all, the Soviets had accomplished an amazing engineering feat. In a few short months, they had secretly crated, transported, and erected highly complex weapon systems on a foreign tropical island thousands of miles from home. The unpredictable Khrushchev has been characterized as a "thug among thugs" as he advanced through the communist party ranks, having survived Joseph Stalin's purges and mass executions during the 1930s. Always the consummate survivor, his aggressive bullying personality led him to believe he could install the missiles before they were detected. He almost got away with it. Had his weapons of mass destruction become operational before they were detected, there would have been little that the United States could have done about it.

This book makes the assertion that aerial photographic intelligence played a crucial role in maintaining world peace in October 1962. Most books about the Cuban Missile Crisis acknowledge the early photography by the USAF and CIA U-2s, but they provide scant information, if any at all, on the contributions of low-level photography, a detail of no small importance. Certainly, credit has to be given to the U-2's discovery of the first missile sites on October 14, 1962, as well as photo coverage throughout the crisis that enabled intelligence agencies to pinpoint where all the sites were.

During the Cold War U-2s made huge contributions to the security of the United States, providing hard intelligence not obtainable by other means, but the deployment of the aircraft was always a balance between its valuable photos and its risks. The U-2's vulnerability to SAMs, problems with cloud cover, and their small-scale imagery presented mission planners and PIs with serious limitations. These shortcomings in the combat environment of Cuba forced a standdown of U-2 missions at critical moments, causing intelligence gaps that resulted in an increased importance being given to "Fightin' Photo's" capabilities.

The shoot-down of the CIA U-2 in May 1960 created a worldwide furor resulting in the canceling of the Paris four-party summit. This episode cast its dark shadow over the use of the airplane in the early months of the military build-up in Cuba. Again in Cuba, the U-2's vulnerability cost Maj Anderson his life on the twelfth day of the crisis, and could have lit the fuse of nuclear war.

For the U-2, resolution (details the PIs could see), while remarkable from the altitudes they flew, was measured in feet, while the resolution of the RF-8A was in inches. This compromise was necessary to allow the spyplane to fly at the extreme altitudes that enabled it to cover wide swaths of terrain – four U-2s could cover the entire island of Cuba in one day, giving analysts a macro-view of the build-up. While the photos these flights generated were essential for discovering points of interest, they were not detailed enough to allow PIs to fully assess how operational the missiles were, nor optimum for making up strike packages for an attack.

On the other hand, VFP-62 provided very precise intelligence for decision-makers to develop policy around. Because of its high altitude, the U-2 was less irritating to the Cubans. It did not disturb the ground that it flew over, and provided no visible evidence of Castro's weakness in his efforts to defend Cuban skies. On the other hand, Crusaders and Voodoos *were* provocations, and psychological reminders – "hooligans" in Mikoyan's words – that demonstrated, internally and externally, the Cuban government's inability to secure its own airspace; a fundamental responsibility of any government. The speedy low-flying jets provided a constant aggravation to the Cuban-Soviet ground forces, and a visible reminder that their defenses could not stop an American air attack.

This "hooliganism" became an effective pressure tactic and negotiating tool for the removal of all offensive weapons, and a guard against their reintroduction. The full value of this harassment was recognized by President Kennedy late in the crisis when he told a reporter that the Soviets and Cubans hated the intrusions so much that they would agree to remove their Il-28s in trade for their cessation. Khrushchev conceded to Kennedy's 30-day demand for removing the Il-28s in late November after weeks of Soviet negotiators proposing two to three months. The president ignored requests for low-level reconnaissance by halting *Blue Moon* missions in mid-November to provide the "carrot" that would break the deadlock.

And then there was the USAF's 363rd Tactical Reconnaissance Wing, flying the RF-101C Voodoo, which was not ready on day one, and had to rely on US Navy cameras to get useable photography thereafter. Of the 168 *Blue Moon* missions flown, from October 23 to November 16, the US Navy flew the early and most critical sorties – shouldering the entire burden until the USAF got its act together. While getting the lion's share of publicity during the crisis, little is available today in the public record to assess the USAF contribution. Even books favorable to the Voodoo give its Cuban Missile Crisis operations little space, compared to coverage of the jet's role in the Vietnam War. We will leave it to future authors to make their case.

Finally, the US Navy flotilla enforcing the blockade certainly helped to keep out any undelivered missiles, made a strong show of force and provided the valuable service of inspecting the crated missiles, warheads, and airplanes on their exit from Cuba. While their presence kept more war material from coming into Cuba, it could do nothing about what was already there. That job was left to diplomacy, backed up by the United States' superior conventional military power and nuclear advantage – fully recognized and feared by the Soviet leadership. Other books have amply documented their historic contributions.

How exactly did President Kennedy avert nuclear war, and how did VFP-62 and other low-level reconnaissance help him? These pages have pointed out that the president resisted, time and again, advice to attack or invade Cuba. He was able to do that after consultation with the daily photographic evidence and analysis that provided him with the operational status of the missiles, allowing him the opportunity to give Khrushchev time to think things over.

As a World War II veteran, Kennedy knew that conflicts can be started by uncontrolled events, such as the rogue Soviet colonel who most likely disobeyed orders and shot down Maj Anderson's U-2. Or the JCS who ignored the intelligence of Lt Jerry Coffee's October 25 mission, showing the presence of Soviet tactical nuclear-capable missiles ready to annihilate an American invasion force or Guantanamo Naval Base.

The historical records show that the military chiefs, particularly Gen Curtis LeMay, did not seem to distinguish between nuclear or conventional weapons. As Thomas S. Blanton, Executive Director of the National Security Archives suggested, "nukes were seen by many military folks as just big cannon."

And then there was the USAF U-2 pilot who selected the wrong star to navigate by and strayed over Soviet territory on October 27 – the most critical day of the crisis. Had the Soviets overreacted, or if the pursuing MiGs and USAF jets – carrying nuclear-tipped missiles – destroyed each other, World War III could have erupted over the incompetence of one Air Force pilot. An exasperated President Kennedy is frequently quoted as saying "There is always some son-of-a-bitch that doesn't get the word." Blanton summarizes the dangers of an accidental Armageddon:

The bottom line is that it wasn't luck that Kennedy and Khrushchev avoided pushing the [nuclear] button, because both were committed not to push it. But it sure was luck that nobody else pushed the multiple buttons that were scattered all over the Caribbean and quarantine line.[2]

When it comes to analyzing the Cuban Missile Crisis, the most important, and frequently asked, question is: How close to nuclear war did we actually come? At the 2002 three-day Havana conference on the 40th anniversary of the crisis, a former CIA analyst at the NPIC helps us understand the potential for war:

> The number of nuclear weapons that were on alert DEFCON 2, just short of war, on October 27 was something like 2,952 nukes on ICBMs, Polaris subs, and SAC bombers, all ready to go. Brugioni said it was "divine providence" that kept us from going over the brink.[3]

Reflecting on this question, President Kennedy thought the odds of war, according to Theodore Sorensen, "between one out of three and even [33 to 50 percent]." Arthur M. Schlesinger Jr, a White House advisor and historian, sums up the prevailing view. "I would say one lobe of the brain had to recognize the ghastly possibility, and another found it quite inconceivable."[4]

John F. Kennedy realized the path to peace was to prepare for war. He sustained the support of his military and civilian advisors by seeming at times to approve their militant advice, while at the same time pursuing a non-military resolution to the crisis. His approval for the build-up of an invasion force – the largest military mobilization since World War II – demonstrated his seriousness to deal with the removal of the missiles, but in the end he delayed recommendations to execute the invasion plan. He understood that a strong response was needed to counter Khrushchev's bold attempt to alter the balance of power in the world. As this book demonstrates, he often initially supported plans that had the potential for escalating the situation, but as Commander in Chief he withheld authority to execute them, to the frustration of his military commanders. The best example is, while there was a strong argument for night photography, he feared that exploding high-intensity flares could have been mistaken for an attack. He gave a preliminary supporting nod of approval, but withdrew it at the last moment.

As the archives give up more of their secrets, we see that during the Cuban crisis the president was not in lockstep with his military chiefs. In fact, as the movie *Thirteen Days* dramatizes, his relationship was turbulent with Gen LeMay, but he did not allow the crusty cigar-chewing general, accustomed to having his way, intimidate him. The bitter lessons he took from the failed Bay of Pigs invasion, where the military approved the invasion plan, even though the CIA had designed it, taught him to "never rely on experts or trust the military brass." Of course, history shows the invasion plan that was executed was not the plan the Pentagon approved – due in part to the president's meddling. Kennedy concluded that the JCS did not recognize the invasion plans' inherent flaws – the importance of air cover for the CEF, and the absurd premise that 1,400 rebels could defeat 25,000 Cuban defenders. They should have advised him to cancel it. To his credit, Kennedy did take responsibility for its failure.

Robert Kennedy wrote in *Thirteen Days*, "One member of the Joint Chiefs of Staff, for example, argued that we could use nuclear weapons on the basis that our adversaries would use theirs against us in attack. I thought, as I listened, of the many times that I had heard the military take positions which, if wrong, had the advantage that no one would be around at the end to know [they were wrong]."[5] "On that fateful Sunday morning [October 28] when the Russians answered they were withdrawing their missiles," the attorney general recollected, "it was suggested by one high military advisor [Gen LeMay] that we attack [on] Monday in any case. Another [Adm Anderson] felt that we had in some way been betrayed."[6]

Robert Kennedy's conclusion that the generals thought solely in terms of *military* outcomes, while ignoring diplomatic or political considerations, disturbed the president as well. "We had to remember," the president reminded his brother, "that they were trained to fight and to wage war – that was their life. Perhaps we would feel even more concerned if they were always opposed to using arms or military means – for if they would not be willing, who would be?"[7] The Bay of Pigs taught the president not to be "star struck" with his admirals and generals, and to use the military in the most effective way. Kennedy's genius was to recognize that he had to avoid backing Khrushchev against a wall and avoid humiliating him or the Soviet Union.

As a group, Kennedy's military commanders were often at odds with his approach to decision-making. In one instance, Gen Taylor criticized a JCS talking paper for a meeting with the president as "full of platitudes and condescending. We're saying, 'Now see here young man, here is what we want you to do.'"[8] And the military chiefs were frustrated with his willingness to trade Turkish missiles for Cuban ones, even though the Jupiter missiles were militarily obsolete due to the US deployment of the intercontinental ballistic missile (ICBM). Kennedy had actually given orders to the military to consider their removal before the crisis, but they had not been acted on – much to the chagrin of the State Department and the president.

As Chapter 14 demonstrates, President Kennedy had nothing but the highest respect for the military. However, the history of the Cuban Missile Crisis reminds us that the founding fathers were very wise to impose civilian control over the military.

The president's key decisions were firmly grounded in his concern for history (past and future), and he most likely decided – as early as October 21 – not to execute plans for an air attack against missile and air bases. As he explained, "An air strike would involve an action comparable to the Japanese attack on Pearl Harbor – [it] had all the disadvantages of Pearl Harbor. It would not insure the destruction of every strategic missile in Cuba, and would end up eventually in our having to invade. And finally, an air strike would increase the danger of worldwide nuclear war."[9]

In the early days of his presidency, he was viewed by some, including Nikita Khrushchev and Congressional Democrats and Republicans, as not being tough enough for the job. Much has been made of Kennedy's diffident first encounter with the Soviet leader in Vienna in 1960. However, in a memoir, Khrushchev paints a different picture:

If I had to compare the two American presidents with whom I dealt – Eisenhower and Kennedy – the comparison would not be in favor of

Eisenhower. Our people whose job it was to study Eisenhower closely
have told me that they considered him a mediocre military leader and a
weak president. He was a good man, but he wasn't very tough. There
was something soft about his character. As I discovered in Geneva [1955],
he was much too dependent on his advisors.[10]

But it is also true that the Bay of Pigs fiasco gave Khrushchev the false
impression that a man so brash as to order such a daring attack and fail at
executing it was perhaps incompetent and indecisive at the last moment.
And then for Kennedy to have taken the blame for the failure was
anathema to the Soviet style of leadership. For all of this, Khrushchev did
not realize that John F. Kennedy became strengthened by his mistakes and
grew into the responsibilities of Commander in Chief. For the Cuban
Missile Crisis, he firmly established himself at the top of the chain of
command – always in control of critical details and decisions – but, most
importantly, he realized that he could not micro-manage the conflict. As
brilliant and qualified as they were, had any of his advisors been president,
the outcome of the crisis might have been very different. When one reads
the Kennedy–Khrushchev letters that were exchanged during the crisis,
Kennedy is the one who was consistently tough-minded.

President Kennedy's use of photo intelligence as a means to gauge
how much time he had to work on a peaceful resolution was an
important strategic approach. In moments of national crisis, presidents
need the best information and advice. He gambled that Nikita
Khrushchev, like him, would recognize that neither of them was in full
control of their militaries, and that unanticipated events could spiral the
crisis out of control. Additionally, he used aerial photography as the major
hard evidence to solidify allies' – some skeptical of US claims – support
for the United States' objectives and strategies. There was a point in
November when mission planners were running out of targets to cover.
ExComm, following Kennedy's direction, continued the flights to protect
the *right* to do so.

Using the media effectively, President Kennedy provided details of
low-level missions to assure the American public that the administration

was taking aggressive action in Cuba. During the days of a government-imposed news blackout, reconnaissance photos helped to relax worldwide anxiety. It may be true that the USAF press releases, which caused Capt Ecker and other Naval Aviators angst, were in some way blessed or ignored by the White House.

In summary, reconnaissance overflights were a demonstration of military power and determination, with limited potential liabilities. This show of force highlighted the impossible military dilemma the Soviets faced. They were vastly outgunned by American nuclear and conventional military strength, over-extended halfway around the globe, and world opinion was not in their favor. A conventional war was out of the question and the only alternative, a nuclear one, was unacceptable.

INTELLIGENCE FAILURES

There were serious intelligence failures as well. During the crisis, PIs never found evidence of the location of nuclear warhead storage areas. Not until Michael Dobbs' research for *One Minute to Midnight* was published did we learn that low-level photographs had captured the actual storage locations at Bejucal and Managua. In an interview for this book, Dino Brugioni revealed that PIs were told to look for sites where there were security fences and gates surrounding potential nuclear storage facilities. Because security around the actual nuclear storage sites was so primitive, they were ignored. Dobbs writes, "The CIA's dismissal of Bejucal as a nuclear storage bunker – after it was earmarked as 'best candidate' – can best be explained as the tyranny of conventional wisdom."[11]

As often happens with intelligence failures, "connecting the dots" is subject to human shortcomings. And perhaps most disconcerting of all, intelligence only found 33 of the 42 missiles in Cuba, justifying President Kennedy's early rationale against an air attack.

Another failure of the CIA was its grossly underestimating the number of Soviet troops present in Cuba (10,000 versus an actual 43,000). The CIA's crude estimate was based on the number of ships arriving in Cuba. Gathering this kind of intelligence should have been accomplished by HUMINT, not aerial reconnaissance. On February 4, 1963, the president's Foreign Intelligence Advisory Board made an assessment of the intelligence agencies' performance during the Cuban Missile Crisis. The board concluded that human intelligence was lacking in Cuba. This shortcoming was actually recognized during the critical thirteen days of the crisis, and there was a plan to insert a team of CIA agents by submarine into Cuba, but this operation was abandoned.

The Advisory Board's postmortem of the crisis gave credit to "skillful photo interpreters," and the use of "intelligence previously obtained [by U-2s] concerning strategic missiles and defense installations within the Soviet Union."[12] However, the Board harshly condemned "the near-total intelligence community surprise experienced by the United States with respect to the introduction and deployment of Soviet strategic missiles in Cuba, which resulted in part from a malfunction of the analytic process by which intelligence indicators [e.g. reports of missiles in Cuba] are assessed and reported. This malfunction diminished the effectiveness of policy advisors, national intelligence estimators, and civilian and military officers having command responsibility." The Board allowed that "during September weather delayed some U-2 missions, and U-2 missions were suspended because of the loss of the Chinese Nationalist U-2 over China on September 8. These factors were responsible for the lack of intensification of the scheduled U-2 flights, and the delays should have been made known to the Special Group."[13]

Criticism was also leveled against "McNamara's denial of low-level photography on September 14 when the U-2 flights were delayed. There should have been an immediate re-examination of the proposal for low-level flights."[14]

The Advisory Board's analysis that the September 19 CIA Special National Intelligence Estimate's conclusion "that the establishment of Soviet medium- and intermediate-range ballistic missiles in Cuba would be inconsistent with Soviet practices to date, and with Soviet policy as the [intelligence] community assessed it," was blamed on:

- lack of adequate coverage of Cuba;
- the fact that a rigor of view was held that the Soviet Union would not assume the risks entailed in establishing nuclear striking forces on Cuban soil;
- lack of imaginative appraisal of the intelligence indicators [reports from refugees, clandestine agents, friendly foreign diplomats, Cuban pilot training, SAMs, and so forth] which, although limited in number, were disseminated by our intelligence agencies.[15]

John McCone defended his agency against the above charge pleading, "[It was] one of the difficulties of dealing with the imponderables of what the other fellow will or will not do." The DCI explained further, "About 3,500 agent and refugee reports were analyzed and only eight in retrospect were considered as reasonably valid."[16]

All of this is reminiscent of intelligence criticisms after the terrorist attack of September 11, 2001, when again the misinterpretation and resultant lack of communicating information across the intelligence community threatened us all. For sure, some of this was a result of President Kennedy's insistence on maintaining "the highest possible control of all information related to offensive weapons," on October 9.[17] The reader is reminded of VFP-62's lack of U-2 photos for its mission planning.

Finally, the Armed Services Preparedness Subcommittee of the Armed Services Committee (Senator John Stennis, Chairman) released a report to Congress on May 9, 1963 reporting its conclusions. "While the CIA and other intelligence agencies made mistakes in some areas, US intelligence 'performed creditably' in other areas." The report discounted the idea of an "intelligence gap" between September 5 and October 14, but expressed concern that all Soviet strategic bombers and missiles might not have been removed after the crisis, and that there was a minimum of 17,500 Soviet troops remaining in Cuba.[18]

Having acknowledged these intelligence failures, the Cuban Missile Crisis was unmistakably a triumph of Cold War intelligence. Photographic intelligence, often ignored by missile crisis historians, emerged from the beginning and continued throughout as a reliable means to assess the status of the military build-up and missile site construction effort. VFP-62's motto, "Eyes of the Fleet," could be rephrased "Eyes of the Nation." In a letter to the president defending intelligence successes during the crisis, the director of the CIA wrote, "Aerial photography was very effective and our best means of establishing hard intelligence."[19] In agreement was John J. McCloy when he told President Kennedy, "We can't think of giving up overflights, which everyone in the Hemisphere now knows have played such an important role in maintaining the security of the Hemisphere."[20]

And finally, it is difficult to acknowledge intelligence successes. As President Eisenhower said, licking his wounds after the May Day U-2 disaster, to bipartisan leaders of Congress, "There was no glory in espionage. If it's successful, it can't be told."[21]

A NEEDLESS CRISIS? A COUNTER-VIEW

Some wise man said, "History is an endless argument." Historically documented events are hard to distort, but the circumstances upon which they evolved and the outcomes they spawned can be challenged. In times of national crisis, there are always some who have different interpretations based on their pre-existing biases. That remains true with the Cuban Missile Crisis and President Kennedy's handling of it. Arthur M. Schlesinger Jr, Kennedy's resident historian and advisor (arguably a biased authority), outlines these criticisms, and makes a cogent defense against them in his book *Robert Kennedy and His Times*.

The critics' main points run like this. The Cuban Missile Crisis was a needless crisis that could have resulted in nuclear war, and should have been prevented by President Kennedy's willingness to confront Khrushchev privately and diplomatically, immediately after he learned about the missile build-up. This would have allowed him to convince the supposed malleable "thug among thugs" to remove his missiles, without the resultant US blockade that caused the humiliation of Khrushchev and the Soviet Union.

One of the modern-day critics agreeing with this scenario, Seymour M. Hersh, in his book *The Dark Side of Camelot*, exposes a multitude of Kennedy scandals, dalliances, unprincipled behaviors, betrayals and, as the book title suggests, "dark side" tactics. "The Kennedy brothers brought the world to the edge of war," Hersh argues, "in their attempts to turn the dispute into a political asset."[22] This echoes old accusations that the president was more concerned with Congressional elections, only weeks away, and his own 1964 re-election, than accidentally triggering World War III – a reckless roll of the nuclear dice so to speak.

Hersh and other critics who think like him also demean Robert Kennedy's secret meeting with Ambassador Dobrynin on October 27 to offer the trade of Turkish for Cuban missiles – a secret meeting and concession that most ExComm advisors knew nothing about. Hersh writes, "Anything was better, in Jack Kennedy's world, than being compelled to admit to his admirers in the government – and to the hard-nosed generals and admirals who ran the armed forces – that their heroic young president had compromised to avoid war."[23] In other words, Kennedy also "blinked" during the "eyeball to eyeball" moment.

The Cuban Missile Crisis does expose legitimate concerns not resolved to this day. The constitutional black hole that allows presidents to wage war without a congressional declaration of it seems to block the founding fathers' belief in checks and balances. "No man was entrusted with unlimited prerogatives; neither was the mob," Neustadt and Allison wrote; "presidents could not declare war, congressmen could not deploy troops."[24]

Congress, a typically "leaky" organization, could not be trusted with highly important national security secrets – a traditional concern of presidents. Thus, oversight and consultation were often ignored or reluctantly adhered to. To his credit, Kennedy did meet with congressional leaders, but they were largely informational courtesies and the participants not brought into the final decision-making. One exception was when JFK asked Senator William Fulbright's advice on the Bay of Pigs invasion. He advised against it, but the president ignored Fulbright.

There is also the necessarily secretive, insular, but necessary national intelligence apparatus that has a periodic tendency to bungle key indicators that end up threatening our national security. The CIA demonstrated frightening organizational incompetence during the lead-up and aftermath of the U-2 shoot-down over the Soviet Union and the Bay of Pigs debacle. Its botched assassination attempts against Castro, planned hokey amateurish covert *Mongoose* operations (reminiscent of the "gang who couldn't shoot straight"), and almost-too-late discovery of missiles in Cuba suggested a dangerous organization out of control. Presidents Eisenhower and Kennedy recognized this and suffered politically from erroneous CIA advice and assurances – both tried to bring it under control.

The questions still remain: what is the alternative and how does our government develop an effective and efficient intelligence organization that both respects national and international laws and, at the same time, protects us? Recent history suggests we still do not have the question resolved.

It is important to surface these historical controversies because they help us understand the present. This author believes that Schlesinger made a credible defense against these conspiracy theories and, more importantly, the declassified documentation from the CIA, White House, and State Department shows President Kennedy was an early – and sometimes solitary – advocate of diplomacy as the first means to resolve a national crisis. As Nitze maintained, "When starting down a path that might lead to nuclear war, any man with responsible regard for the lives of American citizens had to distinguish sharply between the consequences of war before and after those missiles became operational."[25]

THE AFTERMATH

In 1963, President Kennedy faced a suspicious public and Congress – they and his administration were concerned that the Soviets would try to reintroduce offensive weapons, and the presence of a large number of Soviet troops left behind perpetuated the anxiety that Cuba remained a communist satellite that continued to endanger the hemisphere. Nevertheless, the president's popularity rose to 74 percent. Not everyone was happy, however. New York Republican Senator Kenneth Keating, one of Kennedy's most persistent critics, charged that his administration had purposefully overestimated the extent of Soviet withdrawal from Cuba and downplayed the Soviet presence in Cuba [estimated by the CIA at 17,000].[26] The president was alerted to expect an investigation by the Senate Foreign Relations Committee. All of this criticism and suspicion brought recommendations to reveal more of the aerial reconnaissance pictures to demonstrate how extensive surveillance efforts continued to be.

The Administration was still faced with the dilemma of what to do about Castro. The long-term goal remained, as it had through two presidencies – to overthrow the regime and eliminate communism from Cuba and stop its expansion in the Western Hemisphere.

High-altitude surveillance would continue at a steady pace (an average of two U-2 sorties per day). Throughout 1963, MiG-21s regularly tried to harass U-2s by zoom climbing (going very fast at high altitude and pulling the aircraft into a steep climb to 60,000ft). U-2 pilots had orders to abort the mission if an aircraft came within 40 miles at altitudes in excess of 40,000ft. This concerned John McCone, who complained passionately to the president, "The intelligence community could not depend exclusively on high-level photography and still say with assurance that we know all there was to know about what was going on in Cuba."[27] At the same time, a new diplomatic metaphor was coined for photographic reconnaissance – "peaceful observation", which referred to keeping an eye (both U-2 and emerging satellite reconnaissance) on Cuban and Soviet military installations to assure the peace.

In February the president resisted requests for low-level missions because they were considered more intrusive, provocative, and threatening. As he told his advisors:

> There were two limitations on our use now of low-level reconnaissance
> missions: [first] he did not want to upset delicate negotiations by John

Donovan for the release of prisoners (CIA and US citizens) in Cuba, which he understood might be successfully concluded sometime in early March; and, [second] the continued evacuation of Soviet military forces – the Russians might misread low-level reconnaissance as an indication of our preparing for military action in Cuba and decide that their forces must remain to counter anticipated US actions.[28]

Thus, the delicate state of negotiations and other political concerns meant that all intelligence needs would not be met, as illustrated by Secretary McNamara's assessment:

The USIB (United States Intelligence Board) listed 21 targets in Cuba which they wish to cover with low-level missions involving 14 sorties. The risk of the loss of a low-level airplane is very low, but the risk of a strong Soviet and Cuban reaction is very high.[29]

A divide within the government was developing over the CIA's need for more intelligence and the secretary of defense's reluctance to support it. The CIA was still sensitive to criticism heaped upon it for its failures during the Bay of Pigs invasion, resentful of the extreme caution used through September (1962) in considering U-2 operations over Cuba, and mindful of Secretary McNamara's reluctance to use low-level surveillance when the intelligence community requested it. The president was made aware of these squabbles when McGeorge Bundy briefed him that McCone "was something between concerned and angry because many of Secretary McNamara's statements did not agree with some of his (McCone's) statements already on record."

Bundy appeared worried that this could result in the first big, internal, high-level personality clash of this administration. Bundy himself said that the difference in their views "was a simple reflection that McCone is afraid of the military situation in Cuba, while McNamara is not."[30] McNamara's views prevailed for the next several months because they reflected the president's own cautious approach to reconnaissance in 1963.

On May 21 Col Steakley presented to the president a plan for a low-level reconnaissance flight over Remedios. To support him, NPIC's Lundahl displayed the relative photography from high- and low-altitude reconnaissance runs from previous missions (for a comparison of resolution). Supporting this lobbying effort, the Director of the CIA complained "that U-2 photography gave no evidence of whether people were on a base. Only low-level photography could throw some light on that important question." It appears that the intelligence agencies were interested if there was any new activity at the dismantled missile sites. The president finally approved a mission to be flown after Castro departed the USSR on May 28.[31] Capt Ecker flew the mission, with Lt Cdr Burt Larkins as his wingman, on June 5. Capt Ecker picks up the story:

> I flew the last [VFP-62] flight over Cuba on June 5, 1963 in RF-8A BuNo 145607. I think looking back that somebody had screwed up again, and the US Navy needed another two missions to even up the score. Anyway, the target was Remedios and the flight was uneventful except that as we (Lt Cdr Burt Larkins was my wingman) reached the over-water turn point to go feet dry, there was a Russian tanker anchored at the exact spot. My first thought was, "How did they [mission planners] know?" I guess it was just coincidental! To this day I don't know what Washington was looking for. There were materials there but I never did find out why they wanted it photographed again.

The mission was not as frivolous as Capt Ecker thought it was, and there was no attempt to even up the USAF–US Navy score. The previously discussed CIA concerns were being addressed by the president, and often the purpose of the mission was not handed down to the pilots who flew them – even the commanding officer. His mission was noticed however, and the government of Cuba issued the following protest about "... the recent low-level flight over Cuban territory, for the purpose of espionage, of a US military airplane, which the US press has taken upon itself to reveal, and warns that Cuban gunners have orders to fire upon any foreign military airplane which flies at a low level over our territory."[32]

President Kennedy had calculated, correctly, that the Cubans would tolerate a rare low-level surveillance intrusion, but protest it for propagandistic effect.

In the meantime, groups within the administration continued to plan or support Cuban exiles' clandestine plots against Cuba, including placing explosive devices on Cuban ships, manipulating sugar prices to weaken the Castro regime, propaganda efforts (including a balloon release in Havana with 300,000–500,000 leaflets on May Day) and "show-off" low-level flights flaunting US freedom of action.[33] Today, those plots would be considered acts of terrorism. However, few were executed and almost all were abandoned – the real expertise for inciting a revolution existed in Havana, not Washington, D.C.

As the year progressed, Castro toned down his inflammatory appeals for violent revolution throughout Latin America, and the administration was starting to realize that time favored Castro, as Cubans and others became accustomed to the idea that he was there to stay. A CIA National Intelligence Estimate on June 14 presented a sober assessment. "It is unlikely that political opposition or economic difficulties will cause the regime to collapse. All our evidence points to the complete political predominance of Fidel."[34] The expectation that an internal upheaval would emerge to oust Castro in response to a US plot was central to the planning of the Bay of Pigs invasion and every other effort to change the government in Cuba. Each time, the Cuban populace rallied under the Cuban flag and stood with Castro. Cuban nationalism trumped discontent with the tyrannical communist government.

By mid-September back-channel sources revealed that Castro was unhappy with his dependence on the Soviet bloc, and that he would consider discussions with the United States for some kind of accommodation. Informal diplomatic explorations were made to facilitate a secret discussion (even Robert Kennedy was willing to explore a secret meeting).[35]

Dr Carlos Lechuga, Cuba's chief delegate to the UN, made a harsh anti-US speech on October 7. In response Ambassador Stevenson said,

"If Castro wanted peace with his neighbors, he need only do three things – stop being a Soviet stooge, stop trying to subvert other nations, and start carrying out the promises of his revolution regarding constitutional rights."[36]

Behind the scenes Dr Rene Vallejo Ortiz, Castro's aide and personal physician, proposed on October 31 that a Cuban airplane would fly to Mexico to pick up a US official and fly him to a secret airport near Varadero, Cuba, where Castro would talk to him alone.[37] This proposal was briefly considered by the Kennedys but declined. There seemed to be some receptiveness to these entreaties to improve relations with Cuba, and a series of other attempts were made, but all failed to materialize. Cold War fears of communism, politics, and the growing political power of the Cuban exile community dictated the US government's stance. Cuban–American unhappy relations seemed destined to remain frozen in time. The Kennedy brothers never seemed to accept William J. Fulbright's (the Democratic senator from Arkansas and chairman of the Senate Foreign Relations Committee) admonition "Cuba is a thorn in our side, not a dagger to our heart."

On November 12, John McCone reported that the Soviets continued to withdraw troops from Cuba, and those that remained were mainly manning the SAM sites. He also disclosed that about 25 agents (presumably Cubans working for the CIA) had been killed or captured over the last year due to the increased effectiveness of Castro's internal security forces.[38]

Tragically, on November 22, 1963, President Kennedy was assassinated in Dallas, Texas, and with him, any chance of appeasement with Cuba also died. In his memoir, Khrushchev expressed his respect for the president:

> As for President Kennedy, his death was a great loss. He was gifted with the ability to resolve international conflicts by negotiation, as the whole world learned during the so-called Cuban crisis. Regardless of his youth he was a real statesman. I believe that if Kennedy had lived, relations

between the Soviet Union and the United States would be much better than they are. Why do I say that? Because Kennedy would never let his country get bogged down in Vietnam.[39]

Castro also felt an equal anguish over Kennedy's death, despite being the repeated target of CIA assassination attempts. In Fidel's words, "I really felt a profound pain the day I received the news of his death – it shocked me, it hurt me, it saddened me to see Kennedy brought down."[40]

Unlike Kennedy, President Lyndon B. Johnson lacked a history of being tough with Cuba, and was facing the 1964 election campaign where a conciliatory stance on Cuba would not help his election. And conspiracy theories of Castro's involvement in Kennedy's assassination, as well as Lee Harvey Oswald's pro-Cuba exploits, made rapprochement with Cuba impossible. Ominously, the menacing dark cloud of Vietnam was forming on the not-too-distant horizon, and this would overwhelm the Johnson administration with a new Cold War problem, sweeping obsessions with Cuba aside.

Nikita Khrushchev never felt that the end result of the Cuban Missile Crisis was a failure for the Soviet Union. To the contrary, he felt that he had secured Cuba from "the open jaws of predatory American imperialism. And Cuba's existence would serve as an example and incentive for other Latin American countries wishing to choose the course of Socialism."[41] However, his adversaries in the Kremlin took advantage of the missile withdrawal as a national humiliation and ousted Khrushchev from office in October 1964 – he was sent home to meditate over his interesting and dangerous life – to write his memoirs, where he reflected on his fall from power.

Years later, just before his death, Khrushchev dated the beginning of his decline in power to the day that the Gary Powers U-2 was shot down. After May Day 1960, he was "never again" able to regain full control of his government. Khrushchev said that from that day on, he had to share power with those who believed that "only military force" enabled Moscow to deal with Washington.[42]

In September 1971 Nikita Khrushchev died and *Pravda* reported the news in a single sentence. In the twelve years after his burial, the national Soviet press mentioned Khrushchev only once.[43]

Today, the Cuban Missile Crisis remains a reminder of how easy it is for nations to repeat the near catastrophe of 1962, as Thomas Blanton points out:

There's way too much similarity. Robert McNamara talked at the Havana Conference [in October 2002] about his trips to India, trying to convince them not to go nuclear. He told Castro that he had told the Indians, "you got conventional superiority over Pakistan. If you go nuclear, they will too and then you can each blow up each other's cities, and for what?" The Indians and the Pakistanis have not had their Cuban Missile Crisis. They think they are exempt from those lessons, and the world is a much riskier place for it.[44]

Castro was the big winner in the Cuban Missile Crisis, having secured Kennedy's public agreement not to invade Cuba with little cost to him – and, with no obligations to fulfill. Szulc concludes, "A military consolation prize for the Cubans after the departure of the nuclear missiles was SAM batteries (enabling them to shoot down marauding U-2 spyplanes if they wished), to which the United States did not object because of their defensive character."[45] The Cuban–Soviet relationship did suffer, however, but its marriage of convenience continued. Cuba needed the Soviet Union for its economic survival and the Soviets needed Cuba for its political relevance in the communist world.

Five decades later, Fidel Castro has out-survived his communist benefactors and American adversaries. However, today, there is a glimmer of hope that someday soon Cuba and the United States will find a way to improve relations and drop their remnant Cold War fears, suspicion, and national paranoia. Should that happen, the 50th anniversary of the Cuban Missile Crisis would be an opportune time for a celebration. The Cold War would be truly over.

END OF AN ERA

After the Cuban Missile Crisis, VFP-62 continued to support carrier air groups of the Atlantic Fleet. In June 1966, it sent its only detachment (Det 42) to the Vietnam War aboard USS *Franklin D. Roosevelt* (CVA-42). In combat operations, the detachment lost Lt(jg) Norm Bundy (in RF-8G BuNo 144624) to unknown causes off the coast of Vietnam on September 6, 1966. In addition, Lt Norm Green earned a Silver Star and two DFCs (one for his skill flying his disabled RF-8G, which had sustained massive damage from North Vietnamese AAA, back to the carrier).

NAS Cecil Field was closed by the US Navy in July 1993 and taken over by the Jacksonville Aviation Authority and Florida's Duvall County. Today, it is a civilian aviation complex that also includes a retirement community, housed in former US Navy quarters.

The West Coast squadron, VFP-63, flew RF-8Gs over Vietnam until the war ended. Twenty RF-8Gs and nine photo pilots were lost in combat during the conflict.

The last operational US Crusader, RF-8G BuNo 146860, was retired in 1987 and is now an exhibit in the Udvar-Hazy National Air and Space Museum at Dulles airport, Virginia. RF-8A BuNo 145645, flown over Gitmo during the Cuban crisis, has been restored and is on exhibit at Battleship Park in Mobile, Alabama.

Capt Ecker has the final word:

Light Photographic Squadron 62 was disestablished in January 1968. On December 8, 1967, all tangible evidence of the existence of the squadron – awards, insignia, signs, plaques, and pictures – was placed into "coffins." After an evening of "mourning on the death" (disestablishment) of the squadron, a trail of approximately 100 persons escorted the "remains" to the grave site. The funeral began on the stroke of midnight, and with each of the mourners carrying a lighted torch (and with some carrying a pretty good load of other spirits as well), the procession wound its way to the "grave." The grave is located in the rear of the ORF (no longer called the Officers' Club but the Officers' Recreation Facility) at NAS Cecil Field. It was intended to be a time capsule, but as far as I knew, no opening date had been set.

Former VFP-62 Aviation Electronic Technician Second Class Greg Engler conducted a six-month search at the dismantled ORF at Cecil Field and located the time capsule in May 2011. After 43 years its contents were mostly ruined by water damage, but what could be salvaged was presented to squadron members at their reunion in Jacksonville, Florida, on September 18, 2011.

"Fightin' Photo" joins the long list of US Navy aviation squadrons that influenced historic events and will always be remembered for helping a grateful President Kennedy avert nuclear war.

ENDNOTES

ABBREVIATIONS OF SOURCES

CIADOCS

CIA Documents on the Cuban Missile Crisis 1962, Mary S. McAuliffe (ed.), Washington, D.C. – Central Intelligence Agency, 1992.

FRUS

Foreign Relations of the United States Series, 1961–1963, Volumes X and XI, Washington, D.C. These are available on the George Washington University website www.gwu.edu page: *National Security Archive.* An additional source can be found on the State Department website: www.state.gov

HOCUTT-NOTES

William T. "Bill" Hocutt, PHCS, USN (ret.), *Cuban Missile Crisis 1962.* This unpublished paper, which was a compilation of personal experiences during his service at the CINCLANT Atlantic Intelligence Center, as well as excerpts from other published works was put into digital format and distributed to chief petty officers as a reflection on the Cuban Missile Crisis.

JCSNOTES

Notes taken from transcripts of meetings of the Joint Chiefs of Staff, Oct–Nov 1962, dealing with the Cuban Missile Crisis. Typed in 1993.

JFKTAPES

John F. Kennedy, Presidential Library and Museum. Transcripts of tapes recorded in Cabinet Room. Also, major portions included in FRUS documents.

NSA

The National Security Archive at George Washington University (www.nsarchive.org).

CHAPTER 2: "EYES OF THE FLEET"

1   Dino A. Brugioni, *Eyeball to Eyeball: The Inside Story of the Cuban Missile Crisis* (New York, Random House, 1991), pg 11.

2   Michael R. Beschloss, *MAYDAY* (New York, Harper & Row, 1986), pg 71.

3   Ibid, pg 254.

4   Editorial Note: Joint Chiefs Briefing, 0730 hrs September 18, 1962, FRUS Vol. X, Document 142.

5   Memorandum of Conversation, FRUS, Document 121, April 18, 1961.

6   Telegram from Chief of Subsidiary Activities Division (Gray) to the Commander in Chief, Atlantic (Dennison), FRUS Vol. X, April 18, 1961, 1337 hrs, Document 122.

7   Jim Rasenberger, *Brilliant Disaster* (New York, Scribner, 2011), pg 275.

8   Memorandum from Presidential Special Assistant (Schlesinger) to President Kennedy, FRUS, Document 196, May 3, 1961.

9   Television interview, *After Two Years: A Conversation with the President*, JFK Presidential Library and Museum, December 17, 1962.

10   Paul B. Faye, "Oral History Interview – JFK No 1," November 11, 1970, JFK Library.

11   Ibid.

12   Ralph G. Martin, *A Hero for Our Times* (New York, MacMillan Publishing Co, 1983), pg 331.

13   Memorandum from the President's Assistant Council (Goodwin) to President Kennedy, FRUS, Documents 269 and 270 (Editorial Note), November 1, 1961.

14   Ibid.

CHAPTER 3: MILITARY BUILD-UP IN CUBA

1   Tad Szulc. *Fidel: A Critical Portrait* (New York, William Morrow and Company, Inc. 1986), pg 582.

2   Ibid.

3   Edward Crankshaw and Strobe Talbott, *Khrushchev Remembers* (Boston and Toronto, Little, Brown and Company, 1970), pg 496.

4   Sergey Isaev, *The Pages of the History of the 32nd Guards Fighter Regiment. Part I. 1941-1967* (Moscow, "Arbor" Publishers, 2006) in Russian.

5   Ibid.

6   HOCUTT-NOTES, 14.

7   Richard Lehman, Excerpt from Memorandum for Director of Central Intelligence, *CIA Handling of the Soviet Build-up in Cuba*, CIADOCS, Document 36, November 14, 1962, pg 102.

8   Memorandum, *U-2 Overflights of Cuba, 29 August through 14 October 1962*, CIADOCS, Document 45, February 27, 1963, pg 128.

9   Tim Weiner, *Legacy of Ashes* (New York, Doubleday, 2007), pgs 194–195.

10   Memorandum, *U-2 Overflights of Cuba*, pg 128.

11   John A. McCone, Memorandum, *Soviet MRBMs in* Cuba, CIADOCS, Document 4, October 31, 1962, pg 13.

12   Lyman B. Kirkpatrick, Memorandum for the Director, *Action Generated by DCI Cables from Nice Concerning Cuban Low-Level Photography and Offensive Weapons*, (no date), CIADOCS, Document 12, pg 39.

13   Ray S. Cline, Memorandum for Acting Director of Central Intelligence, *Recent Soviet Activities in Cuba*, CIADOCS, Document 11, September 3, 1962, pgs 35–36.

14   Weiner, pg 194.

15   President Kennedy's Statement on Soviet Military Shipments to Cuba, September 4, 1962.

16   HOCUTT-NOTES, pg 17.

17   Memorandum from Malinovsky and Zakharov Informing of Decision to Provide Il-28s and Luna Missiles and of the Pre-delegation of Launch Authority to Pliyev, NSA, September 8, 1962.

18   Memorandum, *U-2 Overflights of Cuba*, pg 131.

19   Ibid, pg 135.

20   Memorandum by Director Central Intelligence McCone, Meeting with the President, FRUS, Document 12, October 10, 1962.

21   Ibid.

22   Jeffrey G. Barlow, *Some Aspects of the US Participation in the Cuban Missile Crisis* (Naval Historical Center).

23   Memorandum, *U-2 Overflights of Cuba*, pg 137.

24   Editorial Note (Excerpts from Volume V), FRUS, Document 16.

25   President's Foreign Intelligence Advisory Board, *Memorandum for the President and Report*, James P. Killian Jr, Chairman, February 4, 1963, FRUS, Document 111, pg 10.

CHAPTER 4: CUBAN CRISIS BEGINS

1   CIA Memorandum, *Probable Soviet MRBM Sites in Cuba*, October 16, 1962, CIADOCS, Document 46, pg 140.

2 Arthur M. Schlesinger Jr, *Robert Kennedy and His Times* (Boston, Houghton Mifflin Company, 1978), pg 507.

3 Transcript of a Meeting at the White House, October 16, 1962, 1150 hrs, FRUS, Document 18.

4 Curtis A. Utz, *Cordon of Steel: The US Navy and the Cuban Missile Crisis* (Naval Historical Center, Department of the Navy, Washington, 1993).

5 Transcript of a Meeting at the White House, October 16, 1962, 1150 hrs, JFKTAPES, 2.

6 Robert F. Kennedy, *Thirteen Days – A Memoir of the Cuban Missile Crisis* (New York, W. W. Norton & Company, Inc, 1969), pgs 23–24.

7 Albert D. Wheelon, Memorandum for Chairman, United States Intelligence Board, *Evaluation of Offensive Missile Threat in Cuba*, October 17, 1962, CIADOCS, Document 58, pgs 176–177.

8 HOCUTT-NOTES, pgs 95–96.

9 Ibid.

10 "Eyes in the Sky," *Washington Post*, December 9, 1962, reproduced in HOCUTT-NOTES, pgs 95–96.

11 Brugioni, pgs 234–236.

12 Utz.

13 Brugioni, pgs 234–236.

14 Ibid, pgs 236–237.

15 Richard Helms, Memorandum for the Record, *Mongoose Meeting with the Attorney General*, October 16, 1962, FRUS, Document 19.

16 John McCone, Memorandum for File, October 19, 1962, CIADOCS, Document 60, pg 183.

17 Vincent Touze and John Hawkes, *Cuban Missile Crisis ExComm Transcripts – October 18, 1962*, Forum of American Scientists website: www.fas.org. Additional source: *Lundahl, Memorandum For Director of Central Intelligence, and Director, Defense Intelligence Agency "Additional Information – Mission 3102,"* CIADOCS, October 18, 1962, Document 59.

18 Joint Evaluation of Soviet Missile Threat in Cuba, October 18, 1962 (Excerpt), CIADOCS, Document 61, pgs 188–189.

19 Specifications can be found at: Federation of American Scientists (www.fas.org), Global Security (www.globalsecurity.org) and at www.russianspaceweb.com.

20 John McCone, Memorandum for File, October 19, 1962, CIADOCS, Document 60, pg 183.

21 Record of Meeting, October 19, 1962, FRUS, Document 31.

22 Ibid.

23   Brugioni, pgs 369–371.

24   HOCUTT-NOTES, pg 42.

25   *Joint Evaluation of Soviet Missile Threat in Cuba*, October 19, 1962
      (Excerpt), CIADOCS, Document 65, pg 207.

26   For more information, consult www.cia.gov or James Britt Donovan,
      Strangers on the Bridge: The Case of Colonel Abel (Atheneum House, Inc.,
      New York, 1964).

27   Utz.

28   Special National Intelligence Estimate, *Major Consequences of Certain
      Courses of Action on Cuba*, October 20, 1962, CIADOCS, Document 67,
      pgs 211–213.

29   JCSNOTES, October 22, 1962.

30   Ray Cline, DDI notes for DCI for NSC Briefing at 1500 hrs in Cabinet
      Room, October 22, 1962, CIADOCS, Document 79, pgs 271–273.

31   Briefing Paper, Washington, D.C., October 1, 1962, FRUS, Document 1.

32   Utz.

33   Ibid.

34   Letter from Chairman Khrushchev to President Kennedy, October 24,
      1962, FRUS, Document 61.

CHAPTER 5: EXECUTING THE MISSION

1   HOCUTT-NOTES, pgs 26–27.

2   Ibid, pgs 32–33.

3   Ibid, pgs 35, 37–38.

4   Ibid, pgs 46–47.

5   Brugioni, pgs 370–371.

6   VP Patrol Squadrons, whose primary mission was antisubmarine
     warfare, but they had hand-held cameras for shipping surveillance.
     VQ Squadrons (Electronic Counter Measures (ECM)) had monitoring
     equipment to pick up electronic emissions.

7   Capt Ron Knott, USN (ret.), *Supersonic Cowboys* (Plymouth, MN, River
     City Press Inc, 2009), pg 86.

8   On the comment about the Virgin Mary, in the Memorial Chapel at
     NAS Pensacola, the statue of Mary holds the baby Jesus in one arm and
     in her other hand, extended palm up, she holds a model of the latest US
     Navy fighter.

9   "Cloak & Dagger is Old Hat," *Washington Post*, December 9, 1962,
     excerpted form HOCUTT-NOTES, pg 93.

10   Memorandum for the File: Leadership Meeting, October 22, 1962, 1700 hrs, FRUS, Document 43.

11   Editorial Note, FRUS, Document 49.

12   Ibid.

13   Brugioni, pgs 373-74.

CHAPTER 6: PENTAGON BRIEFING

1   "Former Missile-Crisis Rivals Visit Cuba," *Sarasota Herald-Tribune* (The Associated Press), October 14, 2002.

2   Neil Sheehan, *A Fiery Peace in a Cold War* (New York, Random House, 2009), pg 455.

CHAPTER 7: THE USAF GETS ITS CHANCE

1   Michael Dobbs, *One Minute to Midnight*, (New York, Alfred A. Knopf, 2008), pg 361.

2   Robert F. Dorr, *Osprey Air Combat – McDonnell F-101 Voodoo* (London, Osprey Publishing Limited, 1987), pg 128.

3   Ibid, pg 71.

4   Ibid, pg 73.

5   Brugioni, pgs 443–444.

6   Ibid, pg 442.

7   Ibid, pg 444.

8   Dorr, pg 128.

9   Robert Kennedy, pg 68.

10   Ibid, pg 71.

11   Ibid, pg 72.

12   CNO Report: *The Naval Quarantine of Cuba, 1962* (Naval Historical Center, Washington, 1993).

13   Utz.

14   CNO Report.

15   Crankshaw and Talbott, pg 496.

16   HOCUTT-NOTES, 47, 51-52.

17   Supplement 5 to Joint Evaluation of Soviet Missile Threat in Cuba, October 24, 1962, CIADOCS, Document 89.

18   HOCUTT-NOTES, pg 47.

19   Peter Mersky, *Osprey Combat Aircraft 13 – RF-8 Crusader Units over Cuba and Vietnam* (Great Britain, Osprey Publishing, 1999), pg 11.

CHAPTER 8: SHOWDOWN AT THE UNITED NATIONS

1   Sherman Kent, *The Cuban Missile Crisis of 1962: Presenting the Photographic Evidence Abroad*, Studies in Intelligence, Spring NSA, 1972.

2   Ibid.

3   Ibid.

4   Ibid.

5   Ibid.

6   Ibid.

7   *Wikisource:* speeches, www.wikipedia.org.

8   Brugioni, pg 429.

CHAPTER 9: MARINES JOIN *BLUE MOON* MISSIONS

1   Col H. Wayne Whitten USMC (ret.), "Castro's Revenge," *Foundation*, Spring 2009, Vol. 30 No. 1, Naval Aviation Museum Foundation, Pensacola, Florida.

2   Col H. Wayne Whitten USMC (ret.), "USMC VFP-62 Cuban Missile Crisis Augmentation Detachment," Marine Corps Aviation Reconnaissance Association (www.mcara.us).

3   Ibid.

4   Conversation with author.

5   Col H. Wayne Whitten, USMC (ret.), *Countdown to 13 Days – VMCJ-2 vs Cuba 1960–1962*, unpublished, pg 14.

6   Ibid, pg 14.

CHAPTER 10: THE CRISIS MOUNTS

1   Memorandum for Files, Department of State, Executive Committee Meeting October 25, 1962, 1000 hrs, FRUS, Document 70.

2   Dobbs, pg 119.

3   Ibid, pg 119.

4   Summary Record of the Fifth Meeting of the Executive Meeting of the National Security Council, October 25, 1962, 1700 hrs, FRUS, Document 73.

5   Dobbs, pgs 137–138.

6   Supplement 6 to Joint Evaluation of Soviet Missile Threat in Cuba, October 26, 1962, CIA-DOCS, Document 94.

7   Memorandum for Files, Executive Committee Meeting, October 23, 1962, 1800 hrs, FRUS, Document 51.

8   Crankshaw and Talbott, pg 504.

9   Brugioni, pg 495.

10   Cholene Espinoza, OpEd article in *The New York Times*, May 6, 2010.

11   Richard D. Mahoney, *Sons & Brothers: The Days of Jack and Bobby Kennedy* (New York, Arcade Publishers, 1999), pg 211.

12   Memorandum of telephone conversation between President Kennedy and Prime Minister Macmillan, October 26, 1962, FRUS, Document 87.

13   HOCUTT-NOTES, pg 47.

14   Supplement 7 to Joint Evaluation of Soviet Missile Threat in Cuba, October 27, 1962, CIADOCS, Document 98.

15   Central Intelligence Agency Memorandum, *The Crisis USSR/Cuba,* October 27, 1962, CIADOCS, Document 99.

16   See Summary Record of the Eighth Meeting of the Executive Committee of the National Security Council, October 27, 1962, 1600 hrs, FRUS, Document 94.

17   Telegram from the Embassy in the Soviet Union to the Department of State, October 26, 1962, 1900 hrs, FRUS, Document 84.

18   Message From Chairman Khrushchev to President Kennedy, October 27, 1962, FRUS, Document 91.

19   FRUS, Document 94, Ibid.

20   JCSNOTES, October 27, 1962, 1940 hrs.

21   JFKTAPES, Cabinet Room, October 27, 1962, 1600 hrs.

22   Ibid.

23   Robert S. McNamara, *In Retrospect: The Tragedy and Lessons of Vietnam* (New York, Random House, 1995), pg 339.

24   Mahoney, pg 212.

25   JFKTAPES, October 27, 1962.

26   Dobbs, pg 65.

27   Szulc. *Fidel: A Critical Portrait* (New York, William Morrow and Company, Inc, 1986), pg 584.

28   JCSNOTES, October 27, 1962, 1830 hrs.

29   JFKTAPES, October 27, 1962.

30   Robert Kennedy, pg 73.

31   Szulc, pg 584.

32   JCSNOTES, October 27, 1962.

33   JCSNOTES, October 28, 1962, 0900 hrs. In fact, the JCS were willing to sustain more losses of U-2s before they would attack the SAM sites (see JCS meeting minutes October 23, 1962).

34   Dobrynin Cable to the USSR Foreign Ministry, October 27, 1962, George Washington University, The Cuban Missile Crisis, 1962: The 40th Anniversary, NSA.

35   Message from Chairman Khrushchev to President Kennedy, October 28, 1962, FRUS, Document 102.

36   Summary Record of the Tenth Meeting of the Executive Committee of the National Security Council, October 28, 1962, 1110 hrs, FRUS, Document 103.

37   JCSNOTES, October 28, 1962, 0900 hrs.

38   Telegram From the Department of State to the Embassy in the Soviet Union, October 28, 1962, FRUS, document 104.

39   Summary Record of the 11th Meeting of the Executive Committee of the National Security Council, October 29, 1000 hrs, FRUS, Document 108.

40   Summary Record of the 13th Meeting of the Executive Committee of the National Security Council, October 30, 1962, 1000 hrs, FRUS, Document 114.

41   Szulc, pg 585.

42   Ibid.

43   Arthur M. Schlesinger Jr, *Robert Kennedy and His Times* (Boston, Houghton Mifflin Company, 1978), pgs 524–525.

44   Memorandum of Telephone Conversation Between Secretary of State Rusk and the Permanent Representative of the United Nations (Stevenson), October 31, 1962, FRUS, Document 124.

CHAPTER 11: UNARMED, UNESCORTED, & UNAFRAID

1   Capt Ron Knott's recollection of the Crusader distributed by e-mail to the author.

2   Steve Ginter, *Navy Fighters 17 – Vought's F-8 Crusader Part Two: Navy and Marine RF-8 Photo-Recon Squadrons* (Simi Valley, California, Ginter Books, 1988).

3   Knott, *Supersonic Cowboys*, pg 194.

4   Ibid, pgs 195–197.

5   Isaev, *The Pages of the History of the 32nd Guards Fighter Regiment. Part I.* Chapter: "The 32nd Guards Air Fighter Regiment in Cuba (1962–63)."

6   Ibid.

7   HOCUTT-NOTES, pg 94.

8   Correspondence between Capt Johnson and the author.

9   Mersky, pgs 82–83.

CHAPTER 13: VERIFYING THE REMOVAL OF MISSILES

1   Memorandum From the President's Special Assistant for National
     Security Affairs Bundy to President Kennedy, January 4, 1963, FRUS,
     Document 261.

2   JCSNOTES, November 1, 1962, 1400 hrs meeting.

3   Ibid, November 7, 1962, 0900 hrs meeting.

4   Summary Record of the Sixteenth Meeting of the Executive
     Committee of the National Security Council, November 1, 1962, 1000
     hrs, FRUS, Record 130.

5   Ibid.

6   Ibid.

7   Telegram from the Mission to the United Nations to the Department of
     State, November 2, 1962, FRUS, Record 133

8   Szulc, pgs 583–584.

9   Memorandum, *Soviet Offensive Weapons in Cuba*, October 29, 1962,
     CIADOCS, Document 108, pg 351.

10   CNO Report, *The Naval Quarantine of Cuba, 1962,* Naval Historical
     Center.

11   Isaev, *The Pages of the History of the 32nd Guards Fighter Regiment. Part I.*
     Chapter: "The 32nd Guards Air Fighter Regiment in Cuba (1962–63)."

12   CNO Report, *The Naval Quarantine of Cuba.*

13   Telegram from the Department of State to the Mission to the United
     Nations, November 5, 1962, FRUS, Document 147.

14   Summary Record of the 21st Meeting of the Executive Committee
     of the National Security Council, November 6, 1962, FRUS,
     Document 154.

15   *New York Times* Chronology November 1962, John F. Kennedy
     Presidential Library and Museum archives.

16   HOCUTT-NOTES, pgs 95–96.

17   Summary Record of the 22nd Meeting of the Executive Committee of
     the National Security Council, November 7, 1962, FRUS, Document 158.

18   *New York Times* Chronology.

19   Knott, *Supersonic Cowboys*, pg 7.

20   *New York Times* Chronology.

21   Summary Record of the 33rd Meeting of the Executive Committee of the National Security Council, December 6, 1962, FRUS, Document 230.

22   Television interview, *After Two Years: A Conversation with the President*, December 17, 1962, JFK Library and Museum.

23   Circular Telegram to All Latin American Posts, December 22, 1962, FRUS, Document 255.

24   McNamara, pgs 339–341.

CHAPTER 14: MEDALS AND COMMENDATIONS

1   Dom Bonafede, "Spy Plane Pilot Says He Was Shot At Over Cuba," *The Calgary Herald*, December 5, 1962.

CHAPTER 15: *THIRTEEN DAYS* – THE MOVIE

1   RAdm Paul T. Gillcrist, "A Trip down Memory Lane," *THE HOOK*, Summer 2010, pgs 28–29,

2   Phillip Brenner, *Turning History on Its Head*, The Cuban Missile Crisis, 1962: The 40th Anniversary, NSA.

3   Ibid.

4   Ibid.

5   Thomas S. Blanton, NSA.

6   Roger Ebert, "Thirteen Days," *Chicago Sun-times*, January 2, 2001.

CHAPTER 16: "HOOLIGANS IN THE SKY"

1   Memorandum of Conversation, Washington, D.C., November 29, 1962, 1640–1955 hrs, FRUS, Document 218.

2   "The Cuban Missile Crisis 40 Years Later" (a conversation with Thomas S. Blanton during the three-day Havana Conference of the 40th anniversary of the crisis), *Washington Post*, October 16, 1962.

3   Ibid.

4   Schlesinger, pgs 528–529.

5   Robert Kennedy, pg 38.

6   Ibid. pg 91.

7   Ibid.

8   JCSNOTES, November 15, 1962, 1300 hrs.

9   Minutes of the 507th Meeting of the National Security Council, October 22, 1962, 1500 hrs, FRUS, Document 41.

10   Crankshaw and Talbott, pg 397.

11   Dobbs, pg 175.

12   President's Foreign Intelligence Advisory Board, "Memorandum for the President and Report," James P. Killian Jr, Chairman, February 4, 1963, FRUS, Document 111, pg 2.

13   Ibid. pg 6.

14   Ibid. pg 3.

15   Ibid. pg 5.

16   John McCone, Memorandum for the President, "Conclusions," February 28, 1963, CIADOCS, Document 112.

17   Foreign Intelligence Advisory Board, "Memorandum for the President and Report," pg 8.

18   Summary Record of the 509th National Security Council Meeting, quoting Congressional Quarterly Almanac, Vol. XIX, 1963, pg 216, March 13, 1963, FRUS, Document 292.

19   John McCone, Memorandum for the President.

20   Memorandum from the Assistant Secretary of State for International Organization Affairs (Cleveland) to Secretary of State Rusk, November 28, 1962, FRUS, Document 213.

21   Michael R. Beschloss, MAYDAY (New York, Harper & Row, 1986), pg 309.

22   Seymour M. Hersh, The Dark Side of Camelot (Boston and New York, Little & Brown, 1997), pg 369.

23   Ibid, pg 371.

24   Robert Kennedy, pgs 132–133.

25   Ibid, pgs 120–121.

26   Memorandum for the Record, January 7, 1963, FRUS, Document 262.

27   John McCone, Memorandum for the Record, April 25, 1963, FRUS, Document 324.

28   Summary Record of the 40th Meeting of the Executive Committee of the National Security Council, February 5, 1963, FRUS, Document 276.

29   Ibid.

30   Memorandum for the Board, February 6, 1963, FRUS, Document 278.

31   John McCone, Memorandum for the Record, May 21, 1963, FRUS, Document 341.

32 Telegram from Acting Secretary of State Ball and the president's Deputy Special Assistant for National Security Affairs (Kaysen) to the president's Special Assistant for National Security Affairs (Bundy) in Ireland, Washington, D.C. June 25, 1963, 1945 hrs, FRUS, Document 352.

33 Memorandum from Gordon Chase of the National Security Staff to the President's Special Assistant for National Security Affairs (Bundy), April 3, 1963, FRUS, Documents 306 and 337.

34 CIA National Intelligence Estimate (NIE 85-63), June 14, 1963, FRUS, Document 347.

35 Memorandum from William Attwood to Gordon Chase of the National Security Council Staff, November 8, 1963, FRUS, Document 374.

36 Ibid.

37 Ibid.

38 See Memorandum for the Record, November 12, 1963, FRUS, Documents 375 and 376.

39 Crankshaw and Talbott, pg 505.

40 Szulc, pg 561.

41 Crankshaw and Talbott, pg 505.

42 Beschloss, pg 325.

43 Ibid, pg 387.

44 "The Cuban Missile Crisis 40 Years Later," (a conversation with Thomas S. Blanton during the three-day Havana Conference of the 40th anniversary of the crisis) *Washington Post*, October 16, 1962, NSA.

45 Szulc, pg 589.

APPENDICES

All drawings on these pages are of an RF-8A

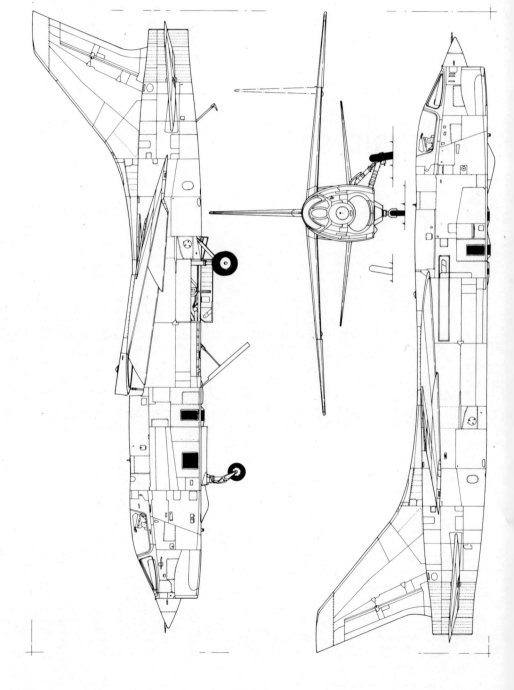

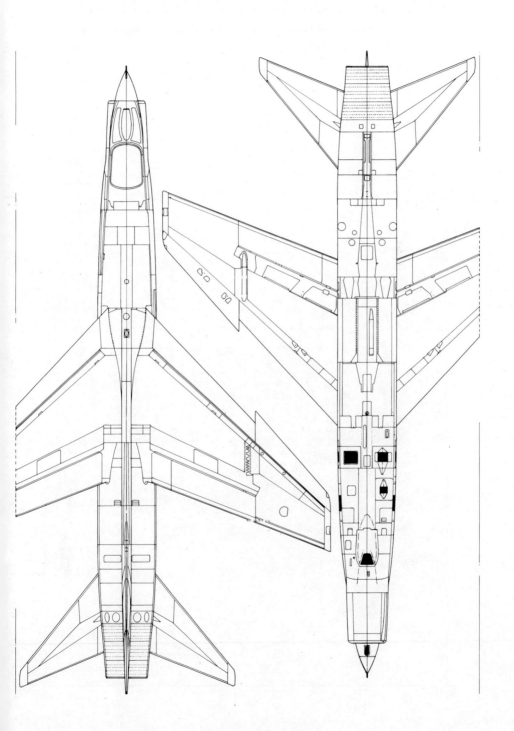

THE NUCLEAR UMBRELLA FACING PRESIDENT KENNEDY

The security threat and reach posed by Soviet medium- and intermediate-range ballistic missiles (MRBM/IRBM) in Cuba.

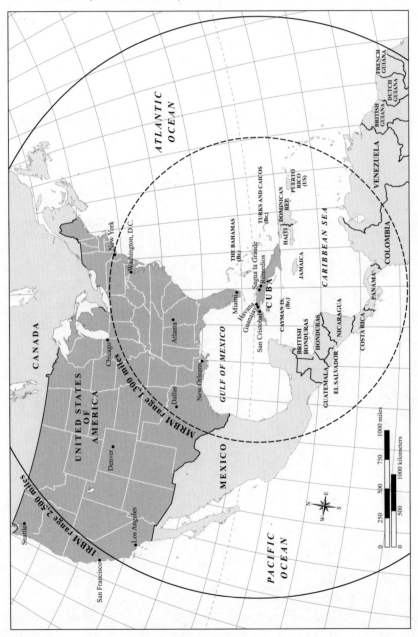

CUBA, OCTOBER 1962

Major Caribbean locations and proximities in play during the critical thirteen days in October 1962.

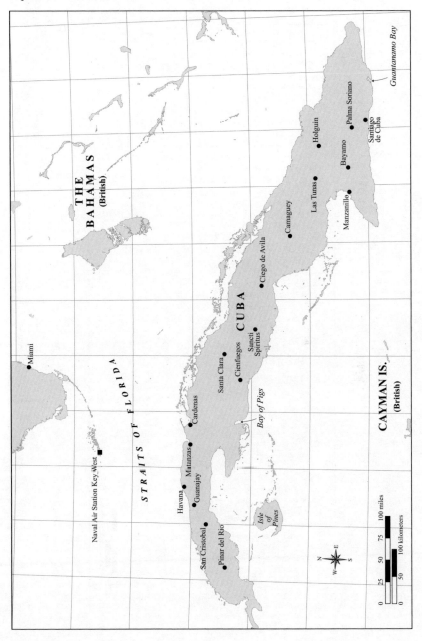

THE CUBAN MILITARY BUILD-UP

Key sites in Cuba that American photo intelligence aircraft monitored daily during the Cuban crisis.

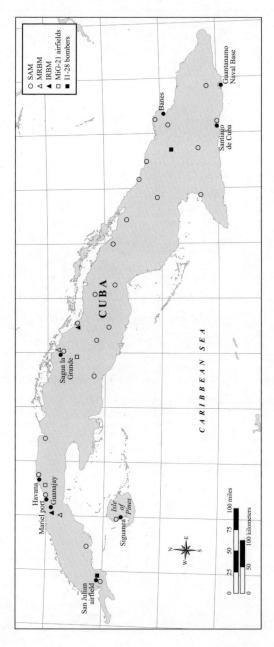

ADDRESS BY PRESIDENT JOHN F. KENNEDY
OCTOBER 22, 1962

Good evening, my fellow citizens. This Government, as promised, has maintained the closest surveillance of the Soviet military build-up on the island of Cuba. Within the past week unmistakable evidence has established the fact that a series of offensive missile sites is now in preparation on that imprisoned island. The purposes of these bases can be none other than to provide a nuclear strike capability against the Western Hemisphere

Upon receiving the first preliminary hard information of this nature last Tuesday morning (October 16 at 0900 hrs), I directed that our surveillance be stepped up. And having now confirmed and completed our evaluation of the evidence and our decision on a course of action, this Government feels obliged to report this new crisis to you in fullest detail.

The characteristics of these new missile sites indicate two distinct types of installations. Several of them include medium-range ballistic missiles capable of carrying a nuclear warhead for a distance of more than 1,000 nautical miles. Each of these missiles, in short, is capable of striking Washington, D.C., the Panama Canal, Cape Canaveral, Mexico City or any other city in the southeastern part of the United States, in Central America or in the Caribbean area. Additional sites not yet completed appear to be designed for intermediate-range ballistic missiles capable of traveling more than twice as far, and thus capable of striking most of the major cities in the Western Hemisphere, ranging as far north as Hudson Bay, Canada, and as far south as Lima, Peru. In addition, jet bombers, capable of carrying nuclear weapons, are now being uncrated and assembled in Cuba, while the necessary air bases are being prepared.

This urgent transformation of Cuba into an important strategic base by the presence of these large, long-range, and clearly offensive weapons of sudden mass destruction constitutes an explicit threat to the peace and security of all the Americas, in flagrant and deliberate defiance of the Rio Pact of 1947, the traditions of this nation and Hemisphere, the Joint Resolution of the 87th Congress, the Charter of the United Nations and my own public warnings to the Soviets on September 4 and 13.

This action also contradicts the repeated assurances of Soviet spokesmen, both publicly and privately delivered, that the arms build-up in Cuba would retain its original defensive character, and that the Soviet Union had no need or desire to station strategic missiles on the territory of any other nation.

The size of this undertaking makes clear that it has been planned for some months. Yet only last month, after I had made clear the distinction between any introduction of ground-to-ground missiles and the existence of defensive antiaircraft missiles, the Soviet Government publicly stated on September 11 that, and I quote, "The armaments and military equipment sent to Cuba are designed exclusively for defensive purposes," and, I quote the Soviet Government, "There is no need for the Soviet Government to shift its weapons for a retaliatory blow to any other country, for instance Cuba," and that, and I quote the Government, "The Soviet Union has so powerful rockets to carry these nuclear warheads that there is no need to search for sites for them beyond the boundaries of the Soviet Union." That statement was false.

Only last Thursday, as evidence of this rapid offensive build-up was already in my hand, Soviet Foreign Minister Gromyko told me in my office that he was instructed to make it clear once again, as he said his Government had already done, that Soviet assistance to Cuba, and I quote, "pursued solely the purpose of contributing to the defense capabilities of Cuba," that, and I quote him, "training by Soviet specialists of Cuban nationals in handling defensive armaments was by no means offensive," and that "if it were otherwise," Mr Gromyko went on, "the Soviet Government would never become involved in rendering such assistance." That statement also was false.

Neither the United States of America nor the world community of nations can tolerate deliberate deception and offensive threats on the part of any nation, large or small. We no longer live in a world where only the actual firing of weapons represents a sufficient challenge to a nation's security to constitute maximum peril. Nuclear weapons are so destructive and ballistic missiles are so swift that any substantially increased possibility of their use or any sudden change in their deployment may well be regarded as a definite threat to peace.

For many years both the Soviet Union and the United States, recognizing this fact, have deployed strategic nuclear weapons with great care, never upsetting the precarious status quo which insured that these weapons would not be used in the absence of some vital challenge. Our own strategic missiles have never been transferred to the territory of any other nation under a cloak of secrecy and deception, and our history, unlike that of the Soviets since the end of World War II, demonstrates that we have no desire to dominate or conquer any other nation or impose our system upon its people. Nevertheless, American citizens have become adjusted to living daily on the bull's eye of Soviet missiles located inside the USSR or in submarines.

In that sense missiles in Cuba add to an already clear and present danger – although it should be noted the nations of Latin America have never previously been subjected to a potential nuclear threat.

But this secret, swift and extraordinary build-up of Communist missiles in an area well known to have a special and historical relationship to the United States and the nations of the Western Hemisphere, in violation of Soviet assurances, and in defiance of American and hemispheric policy – this sudden, clandestine decision to station strategic weapons for the first time outside of Soviet soil – is a deliberately provocative and unjustified change in the status quo which cannot be accepted by this country if our courage and our commitments are ever to be trusted again by either friend or foe.

The 1930s taught us a clear lesson – aggressive conduct, if allowed to grow unchecked and unchallenged, ultimately leads to war. This nation is opposed to war. We are also true to our word. Our unswerving objective, therefore, must be to prevent the use of these missiles against this or any other country, and to secure their withdrawal or elimination from the Western Hemisphere.

Our policy has been one of patience and restraint, as befits a peaceful and powerful nation, which leads a worldwide alliance. We have been determined not to be diverted from our central concerns by mere irritants and fanatics. But now further action is required – and it is underway; and these actions may only be the beginning. We will not prematurely or unnecessarily risk the costs of worldwide nuclear war in which even the fruits of victory would be ashes in our mouth – but neither will we shrink from that risk at any time it must be faced.

Acting, therefore, in the defense of our own security and of the entire Western Hemisphere, and under the authority entrusted to me by the Constitution as endorsed by the resolution of the Congress, I have directed that the following initial steps be taken immediately:

First: To halt this offensive build-up, a strict quarantine on all offensive military equipment under shipment to Cuba is being initiated. All ships of any kind bound for Cuba from whatever nation or port will, if found to contain cargoes of offensive weapons, be turned back. This quarantine will be extended, if needed, to other types of cargo and carriers. We are not at this time, however, denying the necessities of life as the Soviets attempted to do in their Berlin blockade of 1948.

Second: I have directed the continued and increased close surveillance of Cuba and its military build-up. The Foreign Ministers of the Organization of American States in their communique of October 3 rejected secrecy on such matters in this Hemisphere. Should these offensive military preparations continue, thus increasing the threat to the Hemisphere, further action will be justified. I have directed the Armed Forces to prepare for any eventualities, and I trust that in the interests of both the Cuban people and the Soviet technicians at the sites, the hazards to all concerned of continuing this threat will be recognized.

Third: It shall be the policy of this nation to regard any nuclear missile launched from Cuba against any nation in the Western Hemisphere as an attack by the Soviet Union on the United States, requiring a full retaliatory response upon the Soviet Union.

Fourth: As a necessary military precaution I have reinforced our base at Guantanamo, evacuated today the dependents of our personnel there, and ordered additional military units to be on a standby alert basis.

Fifth: We are calling tonight for an immediate meeting of the Organ of Consultation, under the Organization of American States, to consider this threat to hemispheric security and to invoke articles six and eight of the Rio Treaty in support of all necessary action. The United

Nations Charter allows for regional security arrangements, and the nations of this Hemisphere decided long ago against the military presence of outside powers. Our other allies around the world have also been alerted.

Sixth: Under the Charter of the United Nations, we are asking tonight that an emergency meeting of the Security Council be convoked without delay to take action against this latest Soviet threat to world peace. Our resolution will call for the prompt dismantling and withdrawal of all offensive weapons in Cuba, under the supervision of United Nations observers, before the quarantine can be lifted.

Seventh, and finally: I call upon Chairman Khrushchev to halt and eliminate this clandestine, reckless and provocative threat to world peace, and to stable relations between our two nations. I call upon him further to abandon this course of world domination and to join in an historic effort to end the perilous arms race and transform the history of man. He has an opportunity now to move the world back from the abyss of destruction by returning to his Government's own words that it had no need to station missiles outside its own territory, and withdrawing these weapons from Cuba by refraining from any action which will widen or deepen the present crisis, and then by participating in a search for peaceful and permanent solutions.

This nation is prepared to present its case against the Soviet threat to peace, and our own proposals for a peaceful world, at any time and in any forum in the Organization of American States, in the United Nations, or in any other meeting that could be useful, without limiting our freedom of action against this latest Soviet threat to world peace. Our resolution will call for the prompt dismantling and withdrawal of all offensive weapons in Cuba, under the supervision of United Nations observers, before the quarantine can be lifted.

We have in the past made strenuous efforts to limit the spread of nuclear weapons. We have proposed the elimination of all arms and military bases in a fair and effective disarmament treaty. We are prepared to discuss new proposals for the removal of tensions on both sides – including the possibilities of a genuinely independent Cuba, free to determine its own destiny. We have no wish to war with the Soviet Union, for we are a peaceful people who desire to live in peace with all other peoples.

But it is difficult to settle or even discuss these problems in an atmosphere of intimidation. That is why this latest Soviet threat – or any other threat which is made either independently or in response to our actions this week – must and will be met with determination. Any hostile move anywhere in the world against the safety and freedom of peoples to whom we are committed – including in particular the brave people of West Berlin – will be met by whatever action is needed.

Finally, I want to say a few words to the captive people of Cuba, to whom this speech is being directly carried by special radio facilities. I speak to you as a friend, as one who knows of your deep attachment to your fatherland, as one who shares your aspirations for liberty and justice for all. And I have watched and the American people have watched with deep sorrow how your nationalist revolution was betrayed and how your fatherland fell under foreign domination. Now your leaders are no longer Cuban leaders inspired by Cuban ideals. They are puppets and agents of an international conspiracy which has turned Cuba against your friends and neighbors in the Americas, and turned it into the first Latin American country to become a target for nuclear war, the first Latin American country to have these weapons on its soil.

These new weapons are not in your interest. They contribute nothing to your peace and well being. They can only undermine it. But this country has no wish to cause you to suffer or to impose any system upon you. We know that your lives and land are being used as pawns by those who deny you freedom.

Many times in the past Cuban people have risen to throw out tyrants who destroyed their liberty. And I have no doubt that most Cubans today look forward to the time when they will be truly free – free from foreign domination, free to choose their own leaders, free to select their own system, free to own their own land, free to speak and write and worship without fear or degradation. And then shall Cuba be welcomed back to the society of free nations and to the associations of this Hemisphere.

My fellow citizens, let no one doubt that this is a difficult and dangerous effort on which we have set out. No one can foresee precisely what course it will take or what costs or casualties will be incurred. Many months of sacrifice and self-discipline lie ahead – months in which both our patience and our will will be tested, months in which many threats and denunciations will keep us aware of our dangers. But the greatest danger of all would be to do nothing.

The path we have chosen for the present is full of hazards, as all paths are, but it is the one most consistent with our character and courage as a nation and our commitments around the world. The cost of freedom is always high – but Americans have always paid it. And one path we shall never choose, and that is the path of surrender or submission.

Our goal is not the victory of might but the vindication of right – not peace at the expense of freedom, but both peace and freedom, here in this Hemisphere and, we hope, around the world. God willing, that goal will be achieved.

PRESIDENT KENNEDY'S REMARKS IN KEY WEST UPON PRESENTING UNIT CITATIONS AT THE BOCA CHICA NAVAL AIR STATION ON NOVEMBER 26, 1962

Adm Dennison and members of the United States Navy and the Marine Corps.

I want to express in presenting this commendation to you two units the great appreciation of the people of the United States to all of you. I think that the American people should realize what an extraordinary burden they have carried in the last 17 years in the maintenance of freedom.

I pointed out this morning that there are over a million Americans who are serving outside of their country, and I suppose that really, since the beginning of recorded history, there have been great periods where soldiers or sailors or airmen of a country have served outside of their country in the camps in other nations, but I know of no period in the history of the world or any nation that has done so in the defense of freedom and not made its object subjugation.

The United States has carried this load now for 17 years, in rebuilding Europe, in the defense of freedom in recent days in the Caribbean, in the defense of freedom in Vietnam, Berlin, all around the globe. The 180 million people of the United States, with their will and determination, and with you gentlemen as the point of the spear, have carried a load unprecedented in history. So no American need express any sense of inadequacy. As they look back on our history, and look ahead on the days to come, the title of being a citizen of the United States, I think, is one we should all bear with the greatest pride and distinction, because upon it and upon our will and upon all of you depends the freedom of the United States and the freedom of a great many dozens of countries which stretch all the way around the earth.

We express particular thanks to you for your work of the last five weeks. The reconnaissance flights which enabled us to determine with precision the offensive build-up in Cuba contributed directly to the security of the United States in the most important and significant way.

The days that we have recently passed through have been among the most dangerous since the end of World War II. We have no assurance that in other times we may not pass through other dangerous days, but it gives all of us – and I'm sure I am speaking on behalf of members of the Joint Chiefs of Staff, as well as the members of the Congress who are here, as well as the people of the United States – the greatest satisfaction to come today and see the First Armored Division, representing the Army divisions which have been prepared, the Navy, the Marines and the Air Force, all working together in the greatest causes – the defense of the United States.

We thank you all.

(Note: The president spoke following an inspection tour of the naval air station. The units receiving commendations were the Navy Light Photographic Squadron 62 and the Marine Composite Squadron VMCJ-2.

The President's opening words "Adm Dennison" referred to Adm Robert L. Dennison, Commander in Chief Atlantic, and Commander in Chief of the Atlantic Fleet.)

VFP-62 RECIPIENTS OF THE NAVY UNIT COMMENDATION

OFFICERS

Ecker, W. B. Cdr

Koch, R. A., Cdr

Love, H. H. Jr., Lt Cdr

Parks, W. W., Lt Cdr

Larkins, B. J., Lt Cdr

McCall, J. M., Lt Cdr

Kelt, W. N., Lt Cdr

Smith, G. E. Lt Cdr

Foard, W. F., Lt

Dechant, J. A., Lt

Ream, R. L., Lt

Jordan, W. T., Lt

Lee, B. C., Lt

Coffee, G. L., Lt

Orgill, D.V., Lt

Taylor, W. L., Lt(jg)

Hewitt, J. J., Jr., Lt(jg)

Browne, W. L., R., Lt(jg)

Hamlin, R. B., Lt(jg)

Rogers, R. O., Lt(jg)

Kortge, B. W., Lt(jg)

Miklovis, A. S., Lt(jg)

Bee, F. A., Lt(jg)

Richardson, J. R., Lt(jg)

Starliper, C. H., Lt(jg)

Hallcom, T.V. Lt(jg)

Miller, T. L., Lt(jg)

Satterlee, T. M., Ens

Coulthard, R. O., Cdr

Kauflin, J. A., Lt Cdr

Liberato, F. A., Lt Cdr

Pulley, G. P., Lt Cdr

Riley, T. T., Lt Cdr

Day, A. R., Lt Cdr

Feeks, E. M., Lt Cdr

Holmes, H. C., III, Lt

Kalvin, N. H., Lt

Thomas, R. K., Lt

Gallion, L. B., Lt

Cook, T. L. P., Lt

Cool, D. L., Lt

Wilhelmy, C. B., Lt

Curry, J. D., Lt

Chance, R. W., Lt(jg)

Datka, R., Lt(jg)

Battenburg, J. A., Lt(jg)

Larson, T.V., Lt(jg)

Ogles, H. C., Lt(jg)

Cox. M. M., Lt(jg)

Gaughran, G. J., Lt(jg)

Hamilton, W. C., Lt(jg)

Baucom, J. M. Lt(jg)

Mann, H. W., Lt(jg)

Lingley, J. R., Jr., Lt(jg)

Linn, J. E., Lt(jg)

Pulver, W. D., Ens

ENLISTED

Admave, R. K., ADJ3

Aiken, J. L., AMH1

Alexander, A. W., PH3

Allen, V. R., ADJAN

Anderson, E. L., AMS3

Andino-Ba'ez, G., PH3

Baker, R. H., Jr, PT1

Ballard, R. B., AMS2

Barbee, G. W., AT3

Barnett, J. R., PT2

Bartholomew, D. H., PH1

Baumhoff, C. L., PH1

Bender, R. E., AMH3

Benton, D., AMH2

Birdyshaw, W. C., II, PH3

Bofto, D. J. W., PH1

Booth, T.P., AN

Boucher, G. A., AK2

Bousquet, W. E., ADJ3

Bowman, R. R., AN

Boyer, C. P., ADJCA

Breedlove, J. J., AE2

Brousseau, R. R., AMH2

Brown, C.A., ADJ1

Brown, W. A., PHAA

Buell, W. C., PH2

Burnes, E. R., AMS2

Cantu, G. L., AMS3

Caprio, F. A., AOCA

Carpenter, I. W., AA

Carr, H. A., Jr, AA

Carter, T. G., ADJ3

Channer, C. M., AMHCA

Ahern, W. P., AN

Akins, P. H., AME1

Alexander, J. P., PH3

Amberson, D. M., YN3

Andes, C. G., AMH3

Baker, H. F., ADJ1

Baker, W., SD3

Banfield, L. L., AE3

Barcus, T. D., AE2

Bartelmes, R. J., ATN3

Bauman, F., AMS3

Beck, C. R., AMSC

Bennett, T. J., ADJ3

Billotti, J. A., AN

Blake, V. D., AMS3

Bolton, T. L., Jr, AMS3

Boring, C. L., PH3

Boucher, R. L., AA

Bowlds, H.V., AA

Bowns, R. E., AE3

Bray, R. L., AN

Bridges, W. P., PH2

Brower, T. M., AMHAN

Brown, J. L., PH3

Bruce, R. W., AN

Burkemo, R. T., AN

Caldwell, J. R., AMHCA

Cappeta, A., AE2

Carlson, M. D., AN

Carpenter, J. E., AK2

Carroll, A. L., ATR3

Cates, J. W., ATCA

Chapman, M. L., AN

Chase, B. D., AMH3

Cheeseman, D. L., ATN3

Chevalier, M. L., AN

Chillton, R. W., ATAN

Christian, D. W., AMH3

Christian, T. F., ADJ3

Clark, B. R., AN

Clark, E. C., AT1

Clarke, C. R., PH3

Clayton, I. E., Jr, PH1

Clemons, J. P., SN

Collier, C., Jr, AN

Conklin, R. J., AN

Connelly, M., AE3

Cooper, J. H., PH2

Copas, S. R., PR3

Coviello, J. P., AN

Coville, R. L., AE3

Craft, R. H., PH3

Crain, E. B., Jr, PH2

Crawford, D. W., AK2

Crawford, E. E., AK1

Crocker, A. E., PH3

Croll, L. A., AN

Cromoll, R. H., PHC

Crowe, R. P., PH2

Crumley, D. H., PN3

Cruz, E. F., DK2

Cummings, L. J., AA

Cunningham, J. C., ATN3

D'allessio, P., AN

Dailey, W. R., III, AO3

Damschroder, J. A., AN

Datu, R. I., TN

Davis, J. R., ADJ3

Davis, L. D., PH3

De Jesus, J. J., AA

Deering, C. A., AMH2

Dement, H. H., PH2

Dennee, F. A., PH1

Dent, K. W., PR2

Dewolfe, M. L., ATN3

Diamond, J. A., AECA

Diaz, E. A., AE3

Dickerson, R. L., AMS2

Diquarto, I. J., ADR3

Domingo, A., AME3

Dougherty, J. J., AN

Dowling, A. M., AE3

Draxler, C. F., Jr, ADJ3

Duff, C. W., AMH1

Dummond, N. R., Jr, AK1

Easterling, C. F., AA

Eccleston, J. M., AT1

Echavarria, I., PH3

Eidson, J. R., ADJ3

Ellis, J. F., AE2

Emmelkamp, R. L., AN

Engeman, J. J., AN

Everette, T. F., Jr, PNSN

Fair, M. F., SA

Fanton, W. J., PH3

Farri, R. M., ADJAN

Farris, J. E., AN

Faulkenberry, M. M., AE1

Fedele, L. P., AEC

Ferguson, T. J., AE1

Ferrell, J. A., AA

Fessenden, P. P., AE1

Fischer, J. R., AO2

Flake, R. M., AMS2

Folsom, D. W., AA

Forrest, B. B., AE1

Forshee, A. R., PR3

Foster, G. R., AMH1

Freeman, J. E., ATCA

Fullerton, I. R., PHC

Funderberg, J. H., HMCA

Gaudreau, R. A., PHCA

Gay, D. C., Jr, AN

George, L. F., AT2

Geske, J. C., AA

Gilbert, S. W., AA

Goldsmith, H., AMH2

Graham, C. R., AT2

Grantham, D. F., PH2

Green, W., CS2

Gregory, E. P., Jr, AN

Greiner, E. A., Jr, AN

Gromer, J. H., AK3

Hafele, J. F., SA

Hale, R. E., Jr, PH3

Handspike, B., Jr, AA

Hanner, N. L., AE2

Harper, E. L., PH1

Harvey, W. J., ADJ2

Hatcher, D. W., AN

Haynes, K. G., TN

Hazelwood, R. C., PRCA

Helton, C. H., PH2

Henry, B. J., AN

Higgens, J. C., Jr, AMH3

Finley, R. C., PHCA

Fisher, C. H., AA

Folsom, D. G., AMH2

Ford, P. E., AN

Forrest, L. L., Jr, AE2

Forshey, A. E., AMS2

Frazier, A. H., AA

Fuerstenberg, L. E., AA

Fulton, J. L., AE1

Garling, R. L., AMH1

Gault., O. H., PHCS

Gehring, H., AN

Gerrans, D. L. AA

Gilbert, M. W., ADJCA

Glass, H. J., PTAN

Gozdur, S., ADJ

Grant, V., BMCA

Green, R. M., PTAN

Greenwood, L. J., AN

Gregory, R. L., AE1

Grissom, J. T., Jr, AECS

Gundersen, L. F., SN

Haggard, R. J., ADJAN

Halley, W. E., SN

Haney, J. L., AE3

Hargiss, V. F., PHAN

Hartsell, J. S., AK3

Hassinger, J. P., AMHCA

Haugh, W. F., PHCA

Haywood, H. G., ADJ2

Hearn, W. G., AMS3

Hendrick, C. E., CS3

Hertzog, B. L., AEAA

Highsmith, F., AN

Hile, W. R., PT3

Hill, J. O., PHCM

Hodge, J. W., AO2

Holmes, J. R., PH3

Hostetler, E. P., PH2

Houle, P. G., ATRAN

Howard, T. W., PR3

Hoyer, A., SN3

Iverson, G. M., SN

Jackson, S. L., ADJ2

Jeannotte, T. K., PC3

Jenkins, C. E., AN

Jeter, W. E., AE1

Johnson, C. H., AMH1

Johnson, W. F., ADJ3

Jones, C. W., PH2

Jones, D. L., AN

Jordan, L. B., ADJ2

Jusko, D. A., PTAN

Karobeinick, J., AMSCA

Kelly, K. G., SN (YN3)

Kennedy, A. T., AA

Kenyon, C. D., ADJ2

Kerr, W. J., ADJ2

Kertesz, T. S., AN

Kimbell, D. L., AO2

Kirby, J. V., AE3

Kitchens, L. L., AA

Krajewski, T., PH3

Kristoff, A. S., ABFAA

Kuykendall, B. L., PH2

Ladsinski, R. D., AN

Lambert, D. L., ADJ3

Lawson, T. L., PH3

Hill, J. E., AE2

Hires, J. W., ADJ1

Hohman, J. G., Jr, AA

Horton, J. E., PH3

Houle P. G., ATRAN

Houlne, E. L., CS2

Howell, K. C., Jr, ATRAA

Huff, O., PHC

Jack, K.V., PH2

Jaeger, D. L., AA

Jeffrey, R. E., AE2

Jenkins, R. D., AA

Johnson, B. A., PH3

Johnson, D.V., AN

Jones, B. G., ADJ3

Jones, C., PT3

Jones, M. P. S., AK2

Jorgensen, R. P., PH3

Kale, T. D., ATR3

Kelley, J. W., AN

Kennard, W. E., PNSN

Kent, F. R., ADJ2

Kerns, K. C., AK2

Kerrigan, W. P., ADR2

Keyser, M., L., AE2

King, F. G., AMH3

Kissa, P., PTAN

Knutson, M. O., AA

Kress, L. P., PTAN

Kunz, A. C., PH3

La Grant, J. R., Jr, AN

Lahr, B. W., AN

Lane, F. J., ADJC

Lee, P. R., AA

Leeson, W. L., ADJ3

Leouses, G. J., AA

Little, D. R., AN

Lowis, K. McC, ADJ1

Lyle, K., AO1

Lynch, J. W., ADJ3

Macon, C., AMH2

Maloney, J. A., ADJ2

Maracz, P. J., ATR3

Mark, J. Q., PH2

Martin, C. A., AMS2

Martin, O. D., SD1

Martin, T. T., AA

Mc Bride, D. D., AA

Mc Cord. W. J., AMH1

Mc Creary, A. W., Jr, AMH1

Mc Daniel, J. E., AT2

Mc Henry, C. L., AMS2

Mc Kenzie, R. R., ATCS

Mc Nanara, T. A., AMH2

Menhennett, J. R., PH1

Meyer, J. A., AMH2

Miele, R. B., AMH3

Milton, R. W., PH2

Moore, B. F., PH2

Moore, J. R., ADJCA

Morden, E. L., PH3

Morin, T. R., AA

Morris, E., AMH1

Morrison, G. S., AE1

Mott, H. T., Jr, AMS2

Naipavel, N. J., AMH2

Newbury, R. M., ATRAN

Newman, E. C., PHC

Lemons, P. W., ATN2

Lewellyn, W. G., ATN3

Loudon, R. L., AMS3

Lutton, R. I., III, AO3

Lyles, R. L., PH3

Machak, S. J., AMSCA

Maire, P. F., AECS

Maloney, R. E., AA

Marbut, M. D., PHCA

Marshall, S. A., AN

Martin, C. W., AA

Martin, R. E., AA

May, W. E., AA

Mc Cann, A. R., AMECA

Mc Coy, G. W., Jr, PH3

Mc Cune, F. D., AMS1

Mc Guire, J. D., ADJ3

Mc Kenney, C., Jr, AA

Mc Mahan, G. F., AE1

Means, M. W., PRAN

Merritt, R. H., ADJ2

Meyer, R, D., ADJAN

Miller, R. G., PHAN

Monson, A. J., PRAA

Moore, C. L., ADJ2

Moore, S. J., AE2

Morgan, F., PH1

Morris, B. W., AMH1

Morris, P. G., ATCA

Morrow, B. E., PR2

Mullaney, J. M., PHCA

Neal, W. T., ADJC

Newby, W. T., PH2

Newsome, R. O., AN

Nichols, A. L., PH1

Norman, C. E., ADJ3

Nunnally, D. F., AE1

Oaks, F. S., AMS2

Olson, G. O., ATR3

Orsulak, J. J., PH1

Overcash, J. L., ADJ3

Page, H. R., Jr, AMH1

Parenteau, W. C., PH2

Parker, J. W., PH2

Patterson, R. W., AMS3

Pelt, H. E., AN

Penland, C. A., Jr, AMH3

Pierce, D. L., YN3

Pierce, R. H., ADJ1

Pool, C. E., AN

Porter, T. L., AMS2

Powers, J. W., AE2

Pye, J. M., ADJ1

Ragsdale, J. A., PNS

Reed, J. E., ADJ3

Reese, R. J., PHC

Reimer, I. J., AN

Renaud, E. R., AA

Rhoades, J. F., PH2

Rideaux, L., AMH3

Rippard, W. H., IV, PNSN

Roberts, L. G., ADJ2

Robinson, W. L., Jr, ATN2

Roebuck, R. G., AMHAN

Rogers, J. C. AA

Rossman, J. A., ADJ3

Routt, J. M., ADJ3

Rushing, A. D., AA

Nickless, G. R., AMH1

Nuckles, B., L., AN

O'conner, R. W., ATCA

Oaks, J. M., AMS2

Orr, H. Dew., ADJ2

Osburn, O. R., PHCA

Pace, J. R., ADJ1

Painter, J. W., AMS1

Parker, D. C., SN

Parker, P. W., PH3

Peiffer, J. G., PH3

Pendelton, D. L., AO3

Pickering, R. L., AT2

Pierce, L. F., PH3

Plott, J. R., III, PR2

Poplin, W. M., AMS3

Powell, L., ADJ3

Powers, L.E., AKCS

Rafferty, C. G., AMS3

Ramos, J. A., AN

Reed, M. T., Jr, ADJ2

Reid, D.E., SN

Renaldo, B. J., YN1

Rettenmeyer, J. M., AE3

Richardson, D. E., AO2

Riggs, N. G., PHAN

Roberts, G. L., AMHAN

Robertson, D. W., AMHCA

Roebuck, J. W., AN

Roen, A. N., PH3

Rooney, C. T., AMH2

Roth, G. R., ATR3

Rowman, R. W., ADJCA

Russell, B. G., PH1

Salyers, R. H. ADJ2

Sanchez, R., AN

Sasser, J., AT2

Scarbarough, A. W., PHCA

Schmidt, R. E., PRCA

Schubert, W. A., ADJCA

Schwarzenback, M. C., AMH1

Sees, J. A., PH3

Shaffer, W. N., AN

Shea, J. G., PHCA

Shepard, L. H., ADRC

Siebken, R. A., AN

Sims, J. C., Jr, AMH2

Smith, J. E., AKCM

Smith, M. O., AKCS

Smith, R. D., ADJ2

Smith, R. R., PH3

Snarr, C. M., Jr, AMS3

Solomon, J. H., AA

Sorrel, R. F., ADJ1

Spahn, J. N. PTCM

Spillane, R. M., PH1

Stacy, D. J., ADJ3

Steele, V. B., ADJ1

Stinnett, K. W., AN

Stull, T. R., AKAN

Suiter, R. A., AN

Sweet, D. A., ADJ1

Sypher, C. A., AN

Tanner, R. H., AN

Teska, B. J., AA

Thomas, A. D., YN3

Thomas, C. H., ADRCA

Thompson, J. D., AE2

Sampson, J. W., AMH3

Sapoch, W. E., AT3

Saulny, D. C., AA

Schendel, A. R., AMH2

Schoch, W. M., ADJC

Schwartz, F. G., ADJ2

Scofield, J. H., YN3

Self, S. N., AA

Shatto, J. W., ADJ2

Shepard, D. W., PH1

Sides, W. D., AN

Simmons, R. L., AN

Slaugher, D. W., PH3

Smith, J. H., AE3

Smith, P. M., ADJ2

Smith, R. F., AN

Smith, W. G., ADJ3

Snell, C. H., PH2

Sones, E. T., ADJ1

Sousa, D. A., AN

Spencer, D. B., AN

Spooner, E. H., AEC

Starkey, J. A., PN2

Stillson, T. H., SN

Strohl, R. M., AME3

Sudro, W. C., AN

Swartzfager, E. W., PR2

Syboda, D. J., BM1

Talley, J. G., ADJ1

Tassi, A. J., AN

Thaggard, R. S., AN

Thomas, B. W., AMS2

Thompson, E. M., PHCA

Thompson, K. G., AMS3

Thompson, L. H., ADCS

Torbert, C. S., SN

Triplett, J. M., AA

Trudeau, L. C., Jr, AMS3

Tucker, J. E., AMS3

Van Boskerck, L. C., PR1

Vearil, R. F., ATC

Verbinski, R. M., AE2

Voyles, B. M., AA

Walker, J. H., AA

Wallace, P. D., ADJ3

Warden, S. G., CS1

Washington, J. F., TN

Watkins, D. A., AN

Watson, R. O., AT1

Weaver, R. L., AMH1

Wells, J. D., AE2

Westerberg, W. J., ADJAN

Wilbanks, V. J., PH1

Williams, P. E., ADJ3

Willis, J. A., AA

Wilson, J. M., AE2

Witte, C. A., ADJ3

Wolle, F. R., PHC

Wood, W. F., AA

Wright, R. A., AN

Young, R. F., Jr, AT2

Zilcosky, T. G., AA

Todd, C. A., Jr, PT2

Trenoskie, J. M., AME2

Trollinger, C. L., ADJ2

Tucker, G. O., AA

Tyner, W. F., AE3

Van Patten, J. S., AMH2

Velez, J., PN3

Vigen, R. A., ADJ2

Wagner, R. T., AN

Wallace, B. E., AEAN

Ward, W. D., ADR3

Warner, T. J., AE3

Wate, C. R., AA

Watson, E., ADJAN

Weaver, J. A., AMH2

Weber, D. C., PH3

Wenker, V. N., PHAA

White, J. C., PH2

Williams, J. A., PH2

Williams, P. G., ADJ3

Wilson, J. J., AE3

Wilson, W. W., AN

Wittenauer, R. A., ADJ3

Wood, M. A., PH1

Woodward, C., ADJ2

Wyman, R. A., AE3

Zabicki, V. P., ADJAN

Zoeller, T. R., AA

INDEX

ABC-TV "*Our World*" series 214

Abel, Col Rudolf 78

Acheson, Dean 64, 65, 75, 167

Allison, Graham T. 189, 233

Almond, Peter 218

Anderson, Adm George W. 70, 71, 85, 108, 117, 120–121, 164, 206–208, 226

Anderson, Maj Rudolf 145, 154, 155, 168, 177, 200, 222, 224

Armed Services Preparedness Subcommittee 231

Atlantic Intelligence Agency (AIC) 54, 58, 88, 89, 121

Ball, George 64, 151, 152

Banes, Cuba 59

Barrow, Lt Cdr John 44

Batista, President Fulgencio 41, 158

Battleship Park, Mobile, Al. 242

Bay of Pigs invasion (1961) 42–49, 125, 226–227, 228, 233; casualties 48; failure of 47, 48; negotiations to release prisoners 78; photographic reconnaissance 43–46; prisoners released 200, 201

Beech SNB-5P 34

Bejucal, Cuba 229

Binney, Maj Gen A. F. 207

bird strikes 179–180

Bissell, Richard 42–43

Blandy, USS 85

Blanton, Thomas S. 217, 218, 224–225, 241

Boardman, 2Lt Tom 186–187

Bobrov, Col Dmitry 194–195

Boeing: B-47 200; C-135 186, 200

Boroughs, Cdr 92–93

Bottomley, Capt Sid 111

Brady, Lt(jg) Jim "Diamond" 174–175

Brenner, Phillip 216–217

Brilliant Disaster 46

British reaction to Cuban Missile Crisis 123, 124

Brugioni, Dino A. 69–71, 96–97, 112, 117, 121, 130, 179, 225, 229

Bullman, Lt Howie "Kickstand" 174–175

Bundy, McGeorge 55, 63, 65, 144, 150, 152, 163–164, 236

Bundy, Lt(jg) Norm 242

Cabot, USS 26

Calabazar de Sagua, Cuba 137–138

cameras: Chicago Aerial Industries Inc. KA-45/KA-46 5-inch 37–38, 70, 71, 96–97, 99–100, 113, 117, 183–184, 208; Fairchild CAX-12 70mm 37

Canadian government 191

Carlisi, Ens Russ 28

Carolan, Capt Frederick A. 134, 193–195, 207

Carroll, Gen Joseph 154

Carson, RAdm Joseph F. "Kit" 104–105, 203, 204, 205, 207

Carter, Lt Gen Marshall 56, 57, 59, 69

Castro, President Fidel: agrees arms deal with USSR 51–52; agrees to release Bay of Pigs prisoners 200–201; anguish over Kennedy's death 240; assassination plots 41; assesses Kennedy as weakened and indecisive 50; attempts to undermine regime of 41, 42, 50 *see also* Operation *Mongoose*; and Bay of Pigs invasion 43, 47, 48; becomes Cuban leader 41; bitterness over US–Soviet agreement 189, 190, 219; first trip to UN 158–159; furious with Soviet ally's agreement to withdraw 166; gifts to 2002 conference attendees 219; impatience with reconnaissance airplanes 153; meets with Mikoyan 190; negotiations to release Bay of Pigs prisoners 78; orders return of U-2 pilot's body to US 168; refuses on-site inspectors verifying missile site removal 166; right to protect Cuban airspace 191–192; rumor on $10,000 dollar reward 131; sets conditions to be met before deciding on ground inspections 190–191; and shooting down of U-2 155; tones down appeals for revolution 238; visit to antiaircraft artillery battery 167; as winner in Crisis 241

Castro, Raul 41

Chance, Lt(jg) Robert W. 197, 207

Charyk, Joseph 105, 205, 209

Chicago Aerial Industries Inc. KA-45/KA-46 5-inch cameras 37–38, 70, 71, 96–97, 99–100, 113, 117, 183–184, 208

China, relations with Soviet Union 143–144

CIA (Central Intelligence Agency)
assessment of Soviet weapons in Cuba 81, 84
and Bay of Pigs invasion 125
and Cuban trade agreement 201
failures 201, 229–231, 232, 234, 236
National Intelligence Estimate (NIE) 59, 81, 230–231, 238
National Photographic Interpretation Center (NPIC) 38, 62, 71, 105, 106, 110, 111, 142; photo interpreters (PIs) 62, 66, 67, 68–69, 73, 142–143
operations to remove Castro 41, 42, 48, 50
see also Bay of Pigs invasion; Operation *Mongoose*
report on world sentiment towards US position 147
reputation plummets 47
surveillance of Cuban imports by sea 54, 60
U-2 flights over Cuba 55, 56, 57, 58, 59, 60, 88, 144, 145, 221–223
and U-2 spyplane 38, 39–41, 42–43

Cientfuego, Cuba 193

Clayton, Cdr Ed 176

Coffee, Capt Gerald L. "Jerry" 97, 118, 119, 140–141, 142, 154, 176, 204, 224

Cold War (1945–91) 38, 40, 222, 239, 241

Collier Trophy 170

commendations 204, 205–208, 212

communists, spying on 38–41

Convair F-102 Delta Dagger 148

Conway, Lt Col Richard C. "Dick" 133–134, 197, 207

Copp, DeWitt S. 129
Cordon of Steel 70, 79–80
Costner, Kevin 213, 214, 215
Coulthard, Cdr Bob 79
Crowe, Photomate 2nd Class Richard 105
Cuba: aid given in return for release of prisoners
200–201; arms deal with USSR 52, 52–53; Bay of
Pigs invasion 42–49, 125, 226–227, 228, 233; cave
areas 196; CIA surveillance of imports by sea 54,
60; continuing relationship with Soviet Union 241;
early VFP-62 missions over 49–50; first US Navy
reconnaissance mission over 97–101, 102–104,
109–110; Khrushchev seals relationship with 51;
later plots against 238; military build-up in 51–62;
missile bases defense configuration 178; MRBM
sites discovered by US in 62, 64, 66–67; revolution
in 41; rumors of Soviet missiles in 54–55; SAC
reconnaissance flight over 61–62; SAM sites
discovered by US in 57, 59, 60; Soviet Air Force
move to 53–62; Soviet troops in 229–230, 231;
U-2 flights over *see* Lockheed U-2: flights over
Cuba; US operational plans against 61–62; US
sanctions against 41
Cuban Air Force 42, 45–46, 178
Cuban Expeditionary Force (CEF) 42, 43, 45–46, 47,
48, 226
Cuban Missile Crisis *see also* Operation *Blue Moon*
aftermath 234–243
beginning of 63–85; CIA assessment of Soviet
weapons in Cuba 81, 84; evacuation of
GITMO dependents 82–83; evaluation of
missile threat 74; Kennedy addresses US and
world about 82, 83, 84, 85, 123; Kennedy
discusses air strike against missile sites 65–66;
Kennedy weighs up options 66; low-level
photography missions delayed 74–75; missile
sites discovered in 62, 64, 66–67, 73; naval
"quarantine" (blockade) 82, 85, 105, 119–121,
223–224; threat posed by weapons in Cuba 84;
VFP-62 prepares for reconnaissance flights
71, 80
carrier-launched photo missions 183
casualties 200
crisis mounts 139–168; 48-hour deadline
145–146; "Black Saturday" 147–162;
DEFCON 2 state of alert 139; "Golden
Sunday" 162–168; Kennedy's proposal to
Khrushchev 161–162; Khrushchev offer
following Kennedy's proposals 162–164, 165;
proposals from Khrushchev 148–151, 154, 155;
retaliation to U-2 shoot-down considered 161,
162; surveillance to continue despite defenses
153; U-2 shot down 154–155, 177; US attack
and invasion plans 152–153, 189–190
Crusader vs Crusader shoot-down scare 175–176
direct line between USA and USSR as an outcome
150
ECM experiment 173
ExComm meeting October 24: 119, 120
fighter protection offshore 173–182
Havana conferences: 1992 201; 2002 109–110, 146,
218–219, 225, 241
Kennedy creates environment for 47, 48
MiG-17s intercepted 174–175

MiG-21 encounter with photo mission aircraft
193–196
movie (*Thirteen Days*) 112–113, 213–218, 226
as needless crisis? 232–234
nuclear war averted 224–226
public advised of removal of missiles from Cuba
198–199
reconnaissance aircraft fired on after agreement
167, 177
reconnaissance missions to monitor missile removal
164–165, 166, 167
Robert Kennedy favors action 75
showdown at United Nations 125–130
Soviet pilots' view of low-level reconnaissance flights
179
terms agreed between US and USSR 164–166, 167
troops on island 201, 229–230, 231
USAF participation 115–116, 117–119, 120
verifying removal of missiles 189–201
VFP-62's execution of mission *see* Operation *Blue
Moon*: VFP-62's execution of mission
world reaction to first VFP-62 photos 123–125
Curry, Capt Jim 183, 185, 186
Curtiss: R-5C Commando 31; SB2C Helldiver 30
Custer, Lt Cdr George 105–106

Dankworth, Capt Edwin "Ed" 146
Dark Side of Camelot, The 233
Datka, Lt(jg) Ron 184
Davison, John "Lightnin'" 171
Day, Lt Cdr Arthur R. "Art" 122, 160, 207
de Gaulle, President Charles 125
DeChant, Lt John 71
Defense Intelligence Agency (DIA) 58, 151
Demmler, Lt Cdr Charles F. 169, 170
Dennison, Adm Robert L. 46, 61, 85, 88, 115, 167,
205–207, 208
Desoto County, USS 82, 83
Dietz, Capt Willard D. 70
Dillard, Lt(jg) Gary 176
Dillon, Douglas 64, 75
Dobbs, Michael 115, 130, 140–141, 142–143, 153,
186, 229
Dobrynin, Ambassador Anatoly 57, 161, 233
Doctor's Inlet, Fl. 61
Donaldson, Roger 213
Donovan, James B. "John" 78, 200, 201, 235–236
Dorr, Robert F. 115, 116, 117–118
Douglas: B-26 Invader 42, 43, 125; EF-10B Skyknight
133; RA-3 Skywarrior 157–158
"doves" 64, 65, 163–164
Dubinsky, Ens Morrie 27
Dulles, Allen 40, 43, 56
Duxbury Bay, USS 82–83

Eastman Kodak high-speed film processor 76
Ebert, Roger 217–218
Ecker, Kit 31, 80, 104–105, 110, 112, 205, 219;
and *Thirteen Days* movie premiere 214–215
Ecker, Michael and Richard 112
Ecker, Capt William B.: accepted for regular
commission 31; alerted to prepare for low-level
reconnaissance over Cuba 61; and AMCJ-2 136;
assigned to Pentagon in OPNAV 110, 219; and

award of medals and commendations 203, 204, 205–207, 212; awarded DFC 203, 204; basic training 25–26; combat duty in Pacific 26–31; and Cuban defenses 179; death of 219; and disestablishment of VFP-62 242–243; enlists in US Navy 24–25; first carrier landing 25; first combat mission 27–29; first interest in flying 23–24; first Operation *Blue Moon* mission 97–101, 102–103, 109–110, 128; and Homestead AFB news conference 210, 211–212; interference from Washington 156; joins and takes command of VFP-62 31, 36–37; joins VF-10 26, 27; June 1963 photo mission 237; and Kennedy's speech 85; last words to VFP-62 212; later career 110, 219; maintenance crew 160–161; and Marines' involvement in *Blue Moon* 133, 134; marries Kit 31; mission planning 90, 91; on Okinawa 29–30; Operation *Blue Moon* orders received 78–79; ordered to VF-74 after end of war 31; receives commission in US Naval Reserve 25; and role of FAPL 209; and routine mission schedule 157–159; sends Tad Riley to Washington 76–77; at Stanford University 31; and *Thirteen Days* movie 213–214, 215, 216; trained in jet fighter photographic reconnaissance 31; and USAF public relations 209–211; visit to Cuba for 2002 conference 218–219; visit to Little White House 205–206; wait before being cleared for first mission over Cuba 81–82
Edminston, Cdr Bud 61, 110–111
Edminston, Carolyn 110–111
Eisenhower, President Dwight D. 38, 39, 40, 41, 60, 110, 124, 144, 227–228, 232; and Bay of Pigs invasion 42–43, 48
Eisenhower administration 39, 41, 42
ejecting from an aircraft 180–181
electronic countermeasures (ECM) 172, 173
Engler, Aviation Electronic Technician 2nd Class Greg 243
English, Capt Bert 111
Enterprise, USS 26, 80, 180, 183, 185, 186
Escalante, USS 31
Espinoza, Cholene 144–145
Essex, USS 30
ExComm *see* National Security Council: Executive Committee
Eyeball to Eyeball: The Inside Story of the Cuban Missile Crisis 69–71, 96–97, 117, 121

Fairchild CAX-12 70mm cameras 37
Feeks, Capt Edmond M. 177, 207
Fidel: A Critical Portrait 51–52
Fiery Peace in a Cold War, A 110
Fiske, USS 80
Flake, Chief Aviation Structural Mechanic Richard 159, 160
flares, photographic 184, 186
Foreign Intelligence Advisory Board 230
Forrestal, USS 83–84, 183, 184
Fowler, Mrs 112
Franklin D. Roosevelt, USS 173, 242
Fulbright, Senator William J. 233, 239
Gault, Chief Petty Officer Barney 209
Gillcrist, RAdm Paul T. 215–216

Gilpatric, Roswell 64
Glenn, Maj John A. 80–81, 169, 170
Gray, Maj Gen David W. 46
Gray, Capt Will 182
Green, Lt Norm 242
Greenwood, Bruce 213
Grumman: F6F Hellcat 25; F8F-2P Bearcat 34, 35; F9F-6P Cougar 34, 35; F9F-8P Cougar 35; TBF Avenger 26
Guanajay, Cuba 72, 128, 147
Guantanamo Naval Base (GITMO), Cuba 133, 134, 186; Bachelor Officers' Quarters 185; defenses 186; evacuation of dependents 82–83; night photo missions over 183, 184–187
Guevara, Che 41

Haggerty, Lt "Red" 76
Hallcom, Lt(jg) Terry V. 207
Havana conferences: 1992 201; 2002 109–110, 146, 218–219, 225, 241
Hawkins, USS 80
"hawks" 64–65, 75
Hayden, LCpl Jack 135–137
Hays, Lt(jg) Wes 28
Hero for Our Times, A 48
Hersh, Seymour M. 233
Hewitt Jr, Lt(jg) John James 97, 204
Heyser, Maj Richard 62, 113, 145
Hocutt, Chief Photo Petty Officer William T. 54, 58, 69, 89–91, 121–122
Hollister, Lt(jg) Holly 28
Hudson, Capt John I. 207, 134, 210, 211, 212
Hurricane "Connie" 34
Hyades, USS 82, 83

Ilyushin Il-28 "Beagle" 51, 58, 73, 81, 164, 190, 192, 199, 200, 223
image motion compensation (IMC) 35–36, 117
In Retrospect 152
Independence, USS 43–44, 45, 80, 183, 186
intelligence, human (HUMINT) 38, 230
intelligence failures 229–232
Internal Revenue Service 200–201
Intrepid, USS 27, 28, 30, 31
Iraqi weapons of mass destruction 130
Isaev, Sergey 53, 194–195

Jacksonville Journal 23–26, 27, 28–31
Johnson, Capt Len 181–182
Johnson, President Lyndon B. 65, 161, 167–168, 240
Joint Chiefs of Staff (JCS) 43, 47, 57, 64, 84, 94, 189, 193, 196, 197, 216, 224, 226; Crisis mounts 151, 154, 155, 161, 164; Ecker briefs after first mission 107, 108–109, 111; strike plan 152–153
Jusko, PI Don 158

kamikaze attacks 26, 27, 28, 30
Kansas City, Mo. 24
Kauflin, Frank 112
Kauflin, Lt Cdr James A. "Jim" 93, 97, 204, 205
Keating, Senator Kenneth 54, 58, 84, 161, 235
Kelt, Cdr William Newby 72, 172, 177, 179–180, 181, 197, 207

Kennedy, President John F.: and 48-hour deadline
145–146; addresses US and world about Cuban
Missile Crisis 82, 83, 84, 85, 123; advised of
presence of MRBM sites in Cuba 63, 64;
anti-Castro stance 42, 47, 50, 60; appearance 206;
apprehensive after agreement 189; approves June
1963 photo mission 237, 238; assassinated 239, 240;
and Bay of Pigs invasion 42, 43, 46, 47, 48, 226–227,
228, 233; and Cuban SAM report 57, 58; discusses
air strike against missile sites 65–66; early advocate
of diplomacy to resolve crises 234; and emergency
steps in event of nuclear attack 143; and evaluation
of missile threat 74, 75; gains control over CIA 56;
and Gen LeMay 226; gives credit to low-level
reconnaissance aircraft for their role 200; insistence
on maintaining control of information on offensive
weapons 231; and Jupiter missiles 84; Khrushchev
accepts his offer 165–166, 167; Khrushchev assures
no SAMs or offensive weapons in Cuba 57;
Khrushchev offer following his proposals 162–164,
165, 223; Khrushchev's view of 227–228; lifts
"quarantine" on Cuban shipping 199; loses patience
at ExComm meeting 151–152; meetings with
congressional leaders 233; mid-term elections 196,
197; and MiG-21 incident 195–196; and naval
"quarantine" (blockade) of Cuba 82, 85, 105,
119–121, 199; and night reconnaissance 184;
nuclear war averted 224, 225–226, 227; and photo
intelligence after agreement 192–193, 196, 197, 199;
popularity 235; portrayed in Thirteen Days movie
213; and possible attack and invasion of Cuba 189,
190; presents VFP-62 with Navy Unit
Commendation 206, 208, 212; proposal to
Khrushchev 161–162; proposals from Khrushchev
148–151, 154, 155; public support for 48–49;
reluctance to go to war 152, 153; resists requests
for low-level photo missions 235–236; respected
by Khrushchev 239–240; restriction on distribution
of intelligence 88, 89; and shooting down of U-2
154–155; and Stevenson UN speech 127; strength
of character 227, 228; suspends Blue Moon missions
223; telephone conversation with Macmillan 146;
and use of low-flying jets for intimidation 144;
use of photo intelligence 228–229
Kennedy, Robert 50, 57, 119, 151, 154, 189, 213, 226;
and agreement with USSR 164, 167; and beginning
of Crisis 64, 65, 66–67; favors action against Cuba
75; meeting with Dobrynin 233; and negotiations
to release Bay of Pigs prisoners 78; and Operation
Mongoose 72; and President's proposal to Khrushchev
161–162; and shooting down of U-2 155
Kennedy administration 42, 144, 211, 235
Kent, Sherman 123, 124
Key West, Fl. 135–136; Holiday Inn 118, 119; Little
White House 205–206; see also United States Navy:
NAS Boca Chica, Key West, Fl.
Khrushchev, Chairman Nikita: agrees to Kennedy's
demand 223; assesses Kennedy as weakened and
indecisive 50; assures Kennedy no SAMs or
offensive weapons in Cuba 57; and Chinese
relations 144; death of 241; downfall 240; and
installation of nuclear missiles in Cuba 51, 52–53,
62, 221; Kennedy's offer accepted by 165–166, 167;
Kennedy's proposal to 161–162; offer following

Kennedy's proposals 162–164, 165; proposals to
Kennedy 148–151, 154, 155; reaction to Kennedy's
speech 85; respect for Kennedy 239–240; rise of
221; satisfied with Cuban Missile Crisis result 240;
seizes opportunity to expand communism in west
and seals relationship with Cuba 51; style of
leadership 48; and U-2 incident 40; and US
blockade 121; US visit 40; view of Eisenhower
and Kennedy 227–228
Khrushchev Remembers 121, 144, 239–240
Knott, Capt Ron 101–102, 171–172, 174–175, 198
Koch, Cdr Robert "Bob/Daddy Photo" 37–38, 61,
75–76, 77, 90, 93, 106, 107, 157, 183, 204, 205
Kortge, Lt Cdr Bernard W. "Bill" 76, 89–94, 122, 146
Kremlin 38, 52, 58–59, 85, 175, 221, 240
Kuznetsov, Ambassador Vasily V. 163, 195, 196

Lake Michigan 25–26
Larkins, Lt Cdr Burt 237
Lawford, Christopher 215, 218
Lechuga, Dr Carlos 238
Lee, RAdm Bobby 45
Legacy of Ashes 55
LeMay, Gen Curtis 77, 109, 117, 145, 161, 164, 207,
210, 211, 224, 226
Lemnitzer, Gen Lyman 56, 57
Life magazine 210–211
Lockheed
    Constellation 204–205
    F-104 Starfighter 118
    P-2 Neptune 54, 174
    P-3 Orion 174
    TV-2 34
    U-2 38, 42–43, 55, 57, 124, 222; flights over Cuba
    55, 56, 57, 58, 59, 60, 61, 71, 72, 73–74, 87, 88, 89,
    92, 113, 119, 121–122, 127, 128, 144, 145, 153,
    154, 221–223, 235; flying the aircraft 144–145;
    incidents 55, 148, 166, 224, 230; shot down over
    Cuba 154, 155–156, 224; shot down over Soviet
    Union 39–41, 55, 177, 232, 234
Love, Col Edgar A. 134, 136, 137–138, 207
Lovett, Robert 64
Lundahl, Arthur C. 38, 64, 66, 69, 70, 72, 73, 74, 142,
143, 237

McCloy, John 64, 65, 195–196, 232
McCone, John 56, 59, 64, 200, 231, 235, 236, 239
McDonnell: F2H-2P Banshee 34, 35; F-101A Voodoo
116; RF-101 Voodoo 56–57, 179; RF-101C 116,
117, 120, 210, 223
McDonnell Douglas: A-4 Skyhawk 180; F-4 Phantom
II 171, 175; F-4E 175
McDonnell F-101 Voodoo 116, 117–118
McElroy, RAdm Rhomad 78–79
Macmillan, Harold 124, 146
McNamara, Robert S. 48, 50, 56, 59, 64, 72, 113, 139,
141, 142, 147–148, 155; and agreement with USSR
164; decides to continue surveillance despite defenses
153; denial of low-level photography 230; grounds
all U-2 flights 166; at Havana Conference, 2002
218, 241; later details learnt of Crisis 201; and night
reconnaissance 141, 142, 184; proposes major air
strike then invasion of Cuba 151, 152; and removal
of missiles 190, 196; and USIB assessment 236

INDEX

Malinovsky, R. 59
Mangrum, Maj Gen Richard C. 207
Mariel, Cuba 99
Martin, Bruce 171
Martin, Ralph G. 48
Martin PBM Mariner ("Dumbo") 28, 29
May, Ernest R. 213
medals 203–204; DFCs awarded 203–204, 207,
 209–210, 212
Merck 200
Miami, Fl. 201
Miami Herald 219
Miklovis, Capt Adam 83
Mikoyan: MiG-15 88, 178; MiG-15UTI 53; MiG-17
 88, 174–175, 178; MiG-19 88, 178; MiG-21 51, 81,
 138, 164, 178, 193–195, 235; MiG-21F-13 53
Mikoyan, Anastas I. 190, 221, 223
Miller, Lt(jg) James 176
"missile gap" 39, 42, 52
missiles
 AIM-9 Sidewinder air-to-air 176
 FKR cruise 186
 intermediate range ballistic (IRBM) 128, 192; SS-5
  "Skean" 72, 74
 Jupiter medium-range 84, 150, 151, 152, 153, 162,
  164, 227
 Luna ("FROG") surface-to-surface cruise 58, 59,
  77–78, 143, 154
 medium-range ballistic (MRBMs) 67, 72–73, 127,
  128, 192, 193; discovery of sites in Cuba 62, 64,
  66–67; SS-3 67; SS-4 "Sandal" 67, 74, 138, 143,
  147
 nuclear payloads 74, 201
 SA-2 "Guideline" surface-to-air 39, 78, 81, 145,
  178, 241
Montgomery, Personnelman 3rd Class George 82–83
Morinas, Claudio 55
Moscow after news of Kennedy's speech received 85
Moscow conference (1989) 201
Moscow Radio 85, 149, 164

National Photographic Interpretation Center *see* CIA
National Security Council (NSC) 63
 Executive Committee (ExComm) 63, 64, 65–66,
  72, 74, 75, 120, 123, 143, 144, 162, 166, 189, 192,
  228; meetings 119, 139–140, 141–142, 145–146,
  147–148, 150–152, 153, 154–155, 190, 196
 "Special Group (Augmented)" 50, 72
Naval Aircraft Factory N3N 25
navigation equipment, Hayrake 30
navigation in early 1960s 87–88
Neustadt, Richard E. 189, 233
New York Times 196, 197
Nitze, Paul 64, 234
Nixon, Vice President Richard M. 42
Norstad, Gen Lauris 151
North American: AJ-2 Savage 169; SNJ 25; SNV 25
nuclear bombs, US 83–84; hydrogen bomb test,
 Johnston Island 139
nuclear war, avoidance of 224–226, 227
nuclear warheads in Cuba 74, 201

O'Bierne, VAdm Frank 207
O'Donnell, Kenny 213, 216

Ogles, Lt(jg) H. Cecil 76, 183–184
O'Grady, Lt Col Joseph 210–211
Okinawa campaign 27–29
Omaha, Neb. 23–24
One Minute to Midnight 49, 115, 140–141, 142–143,
 153, 229
Operation *Blue Moon see also* Cuban Missile Crisis
 afterburner use 103–104, 141, 144
 canceled on day-to-day basis 199–200
 Cdr Ecker briefs JCS after first mission 107–113
 ECM missions by Marines 133, 134
 June 1963 mission 199
 Marines involvement 133–138
 missions flown 223
 multiple low-level surveillance strikes planned
  139–140
 photo missions after agreement 190, 192, 193–195,
  196, 197–198, 199, 221, 223, 228, 235, 237–238
 preparations for 61
 squadron liaison officer assigned 76–77
 VFP-62 reconnaissance missions 128, 144, 156, 177,
  179–180; bird strike 179–180; distribution of
  photos to intelligence agencies 121–122; mission
  planning 89–94, 146, 156–157; missions to
  monitor removal of missiles 164–165, 193–195,
  197–198, 237; night photo missions 183–184;
  orders issued 78–79; Remedios IRBM site
  mission 140–141, 142–143; routine mission
  schedule 157–159; selected for first mission 69–
  70, 71; ten sorties on October 25: 122
 VFP-62's execution of mission 87–106; afterburner
  use 103–104; first mission 97–101, 102–104,
  105, 107, 109–110; instruction to launch aircraft
  received 94; mission planning 89–94; navigation
  to target 87–88; preparations 95, 97; public
  response 112; restriction on distribution of
  intelligence 88, 89; tactics for first mission 96–97
Operation *Mongoose* 50, 80, 217, 234; Special Group
 50, 72
OPLAN 312-62 60, 66; OPLAN 314-62 60–61;
 OPLAN 316-62 61, 66
Organization of American States (OAS) 105, 165
Oriskany, USS 170
Ortiz, Dr Rene Vallejo 239

Pacific operations, World War II 26–31
Pages of History of the 32nd Guards Air Fighter Regiment
 53, 194–195
Pakhomov, Lt Col Nikolay 53, 179
Parker, Lt(jg) Joe 90, 91, 92, 93, 94
Pentagon 39, 42, 43, 45, 57, 75, 77, 154, 161, 219;
 briefing by Cdr Ecker, Oct. 23, 1962 107, 108–113;
 Joint Reconnaissance Center (JRC) 110, 111;
 National Reconnaissance Office (NRO) 61, 110
Perovsky, Lt Col 194
Pfizer 200
Philippine Air Force 215–216
Philippines, shooting of *Thirteen Days* movie in 215–216
photographic interpreters (PIs) 191, 229; NPIC 62, 66,
 67, 68–69, 73, 142–143; skill of 196–197; USAF 117
photographic reconnaissance
 camera settings 100
 on communists 38–39
 Cuban 40–41; Bay of Pigs 43–46; sea imports 54

interpretation of images 68–69, 73
low-level 99–100
night, using flares 141–142, 148, 183, 184–187
RF-8A 35–36, 37–38, 68, 81–82, 99–100
skills required for 181–182
U-2 spyplane 38, 39, 124; over Cuba 55, 56, 57, 58, 59, 60, 61, 71, 72, 73–74, 87, 88, 89, 92, 113, 119, 121–122, 127, 128, 144–145, 153, 154, 221–223, 235
World War II and early post-war 33–35
Playa Giron, Cuba (*Blue Beach*) 43, 46
Ponce, Reyes 117
Powell, Colin 130
Powers, Frank "Francis" Gary 39–41, 55, 57, 78, 124
Project Bullet 80–81, 169–170
Pulley, Lt Cdr Jerry 205, 209

radar, "Fan Song" guidance and "Spoon Rest" early-warning searching 39
Rasenberger, Jim 46
Remedios, Cuba 140–141, 142–143, 147, 193, 237
Republic F-84F Thunderstreak 169
Ricketts, Adm 167
Riley, Lt Cdr Tad T. 131, 140, 141, 159; awarded DFC 204; and ECM experiment 173; first *Blue Moon* mission 87–88, 97, 103–104; flying the RF-8A 172; and mission planning 156–157, 164–165; Pentagon visit 76–77; and Soviet fighter threat 178; and USAF participation 120; verifying removal of missiles 193–195, 197
Robert Kennedy and His Times 64, 65, 232
Roemer, Cdr Bob 158
Rostow, Walt 142
Rusk, Dean 60, 73–74, 105, 148, 152, 166, 190, 217

Sable, USS 25–26
Sagua La Grande, Cuba 147, 193
Saltonstall, Senator 105
San Antonio AFB, Cuba 167
San Cristobal, Cuba 72–73, 78, 98, 100–101, 127, 128, 143, 147, 218–219
San Julian, Cuba 73, 192
Santa Clara AFB, Cuba 179, 197
Saratoga, USS 176
Schlesinger Jr, Arthur M. 64, 65, 167–168, 218, 225, 232, 234
Schrader, Aviation Electrician's Mate 2nd Class Frank 44–45
Scott, Lt Thomas B. 170
security classification, *Talent* 88, 89, 94, 121–122
Sein, Capt Larry "Deacon" 171
Self, David 213
Senate Foreign Relations Committee 235
September 11, 2001, terrorist attacks 231
Sharkov, Maj Victor 53
Sheehan, Neil 110
Sherman, Adm Fred 30
Shoup, Gen David M. 64, 141, 206–207
Sierra del Rosario Mountains, Cuba 64
Skidmore, Capt Howard 26, 27, 111–112, 113
Smith, Capt Phillip "P.J." 49
Smithsonian Institution, Air and Space Museum 214
sonic booms 170
Sorensen, Theodore "Ted" 64, 110, 154, 218, 225

Soviet Air Force: encounter with photo mission aircraft 193–196; move to Cuba 53–62
Soviet Union: Cuba's continuing relationship with 241; forces in Cuba 201; Kennedy's speech received in 85; relations with China 143–144; response to Kennedy's speech 125; response to VFP-62's photos 126, 129
spying on communists 38–41
Stalin, Joseph 52, 221
Stanford University, Cal. 31
State Department 152
Steakley, Col Doug 108, 110, 154, 237
Stevenson, Ambassador Adlai E. 64, 66, 101, 111, 113, 142, 144, 152, 195–196, 238–239; showdown at the UN, Oct. 25, 1962 125, 126–127, 128, 129, 130
Supersonic Cowboys 101–102, 174–175, 198
Sweeney, Gen Walter 117
Szulc, Tad 51–52, 155, 191–192, 241

TASS 149
Taylor, Gen Maxwell D. 64, 65, 75, 109, 184, 197, 206–207, 227; Crisis mounts 141–142, 153, 154, 155, 161
Taylor, Lt(jg) William L. "Bill" 197, 207
Thant, U 142, 144, 163, 165, 166, 189, 190–191
Thirteen Days 66–67, 155, 164, 189, 213, 226, 233; movie 112–113, 213–218, 226
Thompson, Ambassador Llewellyn 64
Thompson Trophy 170
thunderstorms, dangers of 101–102
TIME magazine 211
Tinsley, Capt Dick 134
Truman, President Harry S. 205
Turkey, Jupiter missile sites 84, 150, 151, 152, 153, 162, 164, 227

U Thant *see* Thant, U
Udvar-Hazy National Air and Space Museum, Dulles airport, Va. 242
United Nations 142, 163, 164, 165, 166, 191, 199, 238–239; Security Council 101, 111, 113, 125–130
United States Air Force: Air Defense Command 103; Andrews AFB, Washington, D.C. 76, 77, 106, 107–108, 112; Cuban Missile Crisis participation 115–116, 117–119, 120; DFCs awarded to reconnaissance pilots 209–210; Homestead AFB, Fl. 49, 210, 211; MacDill AFB, Fl. 210; photographic interpreters (PIs) 117; public relations management 209, 210–211; Strategic Air Command (SAC) 60, 61–62, 117, 139, 144; Tactical Air Command 89; Tactical Reconnaissance Squadron, 29th 210; Tactical Reconnaissance Wing, 363rd 116, 117–119, 210, 223; U-2 flights over Cuba 61, 71, 72, 73–74, 87, 88, 89, 92, 113, 119, 121–122, 127, 128, 129, 144, 145, 153, 154, 221–223, 235
United States Intelligence Board (USIB) 56–57, 236
United States Marine Corps
at Guantanamo Naval Base 186–187
involvement in Operation *Blue Moon* 133–138
VMCJ-2 129, 133, 134–137; *Playboy* Bunny logo 134, 136, 137
United States mid-term elections 196, 197

INDEX

United States Navy
  advantage of using, for reconnaissance 70–71
  AIRLANT 159
  Atlantic Fleet 134, 242; submarines 85
  bonds between officers and enlisted crew 96
  Bureau of Aeronautics Certificate of Merit 170
  Carrier Air Group (CAG) 10: 27, 31
  chief petty officers 209
  CVG-7 45, 183
  Destroyer Squadron 16: 85
  Fleet Air Processing Laboratory (FAPL) 76, 105, 106, 208–212
  Fleet Aircraft Service Squadron (FASRON) 3: 33
  Guantanamo Naval Base see Guantanamo Naval Base (GITMO), Cuba
  low-level reconnaissance ability assessed 75, 76
  "mustang" officer rank 94
  NAS Boca Chica, Key West, Fl. 78–79, 85, 90, 94, 118, 131, 135, 136–137, 157, 173, 206–207
  NAS Cecil Field, Fl. 36, 37, 49, 72, 76, 79, 102, 134–135, 207, 242–243
  NAS Corpus Christi, Tx. 25
  NAS Jacksonville, Fl. 34, 44, 93, 102, 103, 105, 111, 131, 157, 204–205; Fleet Air Processing Laboratory (FAPL) 76, 105, 106, 208–212
  NAS Los Alamitos, Cal. 170
  NAS Oceana, Va. 31
  NAS Penasacola, Fl. 31
  NAS Vero Beach, Fl. 25
  Naval Photo Intelligence Center (NAVPIC) 112, 113
  photographic reconnaissance, World War II and early post-war 33–35
  photographic squadron types 158
  plane captain responsibilities 160
  public relations management 209, 210, 211–212
  "quarantine" (blockade) of Cuba 82, 85, 105, 119–121, 223–224
  sailors, teenaged enlisted 96
  Sixth Fleet 84
  VAP-62 157–158
  VBF-10 "Grim Reapers" 27–30
  VC-61 34
  VC-62 (later VFP-62) 26, 33–34
  VF-10 "Grim Reapers" 26–27, 30
  VF-32 "Swordsmen" 175–176
  VF-62 "Boomerangs" 101, 173–175
  VF-74 31
  VFP-62 "Fightin' Photo/Eyes of the Fleet" (formerly VC-62) 31, 33, 35, 36, 38, 158; after Cuban Missile Crisis 242; Cdr Ecker joins and takes command 36–37; complement and mission 36; Det(achment) 41: 43–44, 45–46; Det 42: 173, 242; Det 62: 183; Det 65: 180, 183, 185, 186–187; disestablished 242–243; early Cuban missions 49–50; financial considerations 159; and Kennedy's speech 85; Key West ("Rotten Cotton Ball" – RCB/"Keating's Kids") Det 160–161; last Cuban photo mission 237; low–level reconnaissance ability assessed 75, 76; maintenance standards 159–160; mission symbols on jets 158–159; Navy Unit Commendation awarded 206–208, 212; Operation Blue Moon missions 156, 177 see also Operation Blue Moon: VFP-62 reconnaissance

missions and VFP-62's execution of mission; pilots awarded DFC 203, 204, 207; praise from admirals 207–208; prepares for reconnaissance flights 71, 80; ten sorties on October 25: 122
  VFP-63 "Eyes of the Fleet" 33, 242
  VU-4 106
United States' reputation plummets after Bay of Pigs invasion 47
Upshur, USS 82, 83
Utz Curtis A. 70, 79–80

Vietnam War (1955–75) 175, 181–182, 185, 187, 240, 242
Vought
  F4U-1D Corsair 27
  F4U-4P Corsair 34, 35
  F4U-5P Corsair 34, 35
  F-8 Crusader: carrier launches 171; flying the aircraft 102, 171–172, 182; love and fear surrounding 171–172; sleek design 177–178; wins Collier Trophy 170
  F-8B 101, 173–175
  F-8D 175
  F-8H 215–216
  F8U Crusader 35, 37
  F8U-1 169
  RF-8A (formerly F8U-1P) Crusader 35, 37, 56–57, 113, 115, 133, 134, 159, 169; accessing 95; Bay of Pigs reconnaissance 44–46; BuNo 144608 (coast-to-coast speed record-breaking) 80–81, 169–170; BuNo 145604 72; BuNo 145607 237; BuNo 145645 242; BuNo 146894 180; cameras 37–38, 70, 71, 96–97, 99–100, 113, 117, 183–184, 208, 222; ECM pod 172; engine, Pratt & Whitney J57 turbojet 95, 96, 169; flying the aircraft 172, 182; high-speed carrier flyby 177–178; photographic reconnaissance equipment 35–36, 37, 68, 81–82; starting 95–96
  RF-8G 172–173, 242; BuNo 144624 242; BuNo 146860 242
  "Thousand Miles-Per-Hour Club" 171
  XF8U-1 170

Wallace, Aviation Mechanic 3rd Class Pete 180
Walling, Ken 118–119, 175–176
Warrensburg, Central Missouri State Teachers' College 25
Washington Post 104, 130
Weiner, Tim 55
Wheeler, Gen Earle G. 161, 164, 206–207
White House 43, 45, 46, 50, 62, 78, 94, 167, 175; "Situation Room" 63
Wilhelmy, Lt Christopher Bruce 97, 98, 99, 100, 102–103, 109–110, 128, 204
William R. Rush, USS 80
Williams, Jack 23–24
Winslow, Cdr George 36–37, 49
Wolle, Chief Photographer's Mate Frank 37–38, 81–82
Wolverine, USS 25–26
World War II 23–31, 33; Pacific operations 26–31

Zabicki, Aviation Mechanic Vinnie 159–160
Zakharov, M. 59
Zorin, Ambassador Valerian 101, 125, 126, 129, 142

287

LIKED BLUE MOON OVER CUBA?
THEN YOU WILL ENJOY THESE...

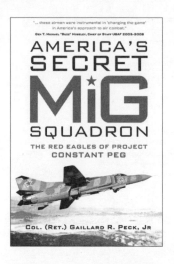

RED EAGLES: AMERICA'S SECRET MIGS

During the height of the Cold War, the USAF operated a secret squadron dedicated to exposing American fighter pilots to enemy technology and tactics. Operating in restricted airspace above the little-known Tonopah Nuclear Test Range in the northwest corner of the Nellis Air Force Base in Nevada, these Red Eagles were the mainstay of the top secret CONSTANT PEG program.

In this revised second edition, author Steve Davies provides 30,000 words of new material, including interviews with intelligence analysts that reveal details about the behind-the-scenes workings of the American intelligence agencies that helped secure the MiGs. There are also new Red Eagles pilot and maintainer interviews, a detailed backstory about the programs that led up to the creation of the Red Eagles, and a more comprehensive timeline of events. Finally, this new edition draws on information gained through the recent declassification of several other MiG exploitation programs.

£18.99
US $ 25.95
CAN $30.00

AMERICA'S SECRET MIG SQUADRON: THE RED EAGLES OF PROJECT CONSTANT PEG

As a Vietnam veteran and Phantom F-4 pilot, Colonel Gail Peck (call-sign "EVIL") had been disappointed with the level of training offered to US fighter pilots. He was determined to ensure that they were unbeatable in the air, particularly against their Cold War adversaries flying the already legendary MiG fighter jets. Working with the support of General Hoyt S. Vandenberg, Jr, and under conditions of the utmost secrecy, the CONSTANT PEG program was launched with Peck as the original "Red Eagle." This fascinating history was first revealed in Steve Davies' acclaimed *Red Eagles: America's Secret MiGs*, but this book is the insider's perspective, complete with never-before-published anecdotes and photographs, revealing how Peck battled bureaucracy and skepticism to ultimately establish the premier fighter pilot training center.

£20.00
US $25.95
CAN $30.00

ALSO AVAILABLE AS AN EBOOK